on my visit
4/22/05
Valencia, CA

Also by George F. Kennan

American Diplomacy, 1900—1950

Realities of American Foreign Policy

Soviet-American Relations 1917—1920
Vol. I: Russia Leaves the War
Vol. II: The Decision to Intervene

Russia, the Atom, and the West

Soviet Foreign Policy, 1917—1941

Russia and the West Under Lenin and Stalin

On Dealing with the Communist World

Memoirs 1925—1950

From Prague After Munich: Diplomatic Papers 1938—1940

Democracy and the Student Left

The Marquis de Custine and His "Russia in 1839"

The Cloud of Danger: Current Realities of American
Foreign Policy

Decline of Bismarck's European Order

The Nuclear Delusion: Soviet-American
Relations in the Atomic Age

The Fateful Alliance: France, Russia,
and the Coming of the First World War

Sketches from a Life

MEMOIRS 1950-1963

GEORGE F. KENNAN

MEMOIRS 1950-1963

PANTHEON BOOKS
NEW YORK

The author wishes to thank *Foreign Affairs* for permission to quote sections of his article "America and the Russian Future," which appeared in April 1951.

Library of Congress Cataloging in Publication Data

Kennan, George Frost, 1904–
Memoirs.

Reprint. Originally published: 1st ed. Boston:
Little, Brown, 1967–1972.
Includes indexes.
Contents: [1] 1925–1950—[2] 1950–1963.
1. Kennan, George Frost, 1904–   . 2. United
States—Foreign relations—Soviet Union.   3. Soviet Union
—Foreign relations—United States.   4. Ambassadors—
United States—Biography.   5. Historians—United States
—Biography.   I. Title.
[E748.K374A3   1983]   327.2'092'4 [B]   83–4200
ISBN 0–394–71624–8 (v. 1)
ISBN 0–394–71626–4 (v. 2)

Preface

THE purpose of this book, like that of the companion volume to which it is the successor,* is to describe the evolution of a philosophy of public affairs in general, and foreign affairs in particular.

In the period covered by the earlier volume, the narrative was based, of necessity, on the experiences of the Foreign Service career which had constituted my only professional life over the quarter of a century with which it dealt. The present volume is conceived to include the remaining periods of governmental service: the tours of duty as ambassador in Moscow (1952) and in Yugoslavia (1961–1963), and the circumstances of my retirement from the career service in 1953. I have chosen to carry it no further than 1963, lest what began as memoirs should end as something quite different. Since, however, in the years 1950 to 1963 both the stimuli to thoughts about public problems and the expression of those thoughts had their locus largely in my new life as a scholar and a publicist, I have incorporated some of the experiences of that life as well, wherever they seemed to be of significance for the central theme.

I have made no attempt to summarize the outlook to which these various experiences led. To do that would be to depart entirely from the character of memoirs and to undertake a treatise on the

* *Memoirs: 1925–1950.* Boston: Atlantic–Little, Brown, 1967.

philosophy of politics, as I see it today; for it would be quite impossible to separate entirely the views held in 1963 from the outlooks and prejudices of the present day. Some of this philosophy
will, I trust, shine through the accounts of episodes now long past;
and the various elements of it may — this, at least, is my hope —
gain in vividness and force by being presented in the context of the
experiences from which they were derived or to which they were
related.

G. K.

Princeton, December 1971

Contents

MEMOIRS 1950-1963

1

Transition

THE reader who had sufficient patience to pursue to its final pages the first volume of these memoirs may recall that in the spring of the year 1950, while serving as Counselor of the Department of State, I became increasingly worried over the growing evidence of difference in outlook between myself and my colleagues there, including the Secretary of State; I realized that many of the points at issue were ones that deserved deeper and more systematic thought on my own part than an active Foreign Service life had permitted them to be given; and I therefore requested, and was granted, a long "leave of absence without pay," to be spent in Princeton, at the Institute for Advanced Study, to which Robert Oppenheimer had kindly invited me. The reader may also recall that this change in status was delayed, over the summer of 1950, by the outbreak of hostilities in Korea. Whether because the initial crisis of policy provoked by that development was now considered to be overcome (if so, this view was decidedly in error) or whether I had by this time contrived to disagree with my colleagues over Korea as extensively as over everything else, I cannot recall; in September 1950, in any case, whatever lingering usefulness I might have had in the face of the situation in Korea was considered to be sufficiently exhausted, and I was released from duty in the department and permitted to move to Princeton. There I remained, officially still on the government's books as a Foreign Service Officer, Class I, but not on active duty, until, at the direction of President Truman, I went to Moscow as ambassador in the spring of 1952.

The family, resembling many another academic family in its peregrinations from one campus to another, arrived in Princeton on September 10, 1950, in a station wagon, with the baby's crib installed in the back. The baby was son Christopher, born the previous year in Washington. Other passengers included myself and my wife; the two older daughters Grace and Joan, of whom the first was about to go on to Radcliffe for her freshman year; and a Russian *émigré* lady, Zhenya, who at that time lived with us and did what she could to ease the problems of the household.

The Institute for Advanced Study assigned to us, temporarily, an apartment in a small wooden building on the edge of its extensive fields, then even more open and rural than they are today. The installation was simple. By evening everything was unpacked; the playpen was erected in the middle of the living room; the baby stood in it, leaning his head idyllically on his outstretched arm (belying, in this peaceful pose, I may say, the more frantic tendencies of later years). Outside, on the meadows, the late-summer mists were rising, and there was the soothing, dreamlike drone of the crickets.

It seemed, at that moment, as though I had found both peace and freedom. For just twenty-four years my time, my movements, my decisions, had been at the beck and call of the Department of State. Now, with this burden removed, the hours and days of liberty seemed to stretch forward abundantly into a future too remote to be considered finite. There would now, it seemed, be time for everything. There was no luxury of curiosity that could not now be indulged.

The euphoria lasted through the next day. I went over to the University and wandered, intoxicated with the illusion of freedom,

along its paths among the familiar buildings: a man of leisure, at
last. The mind, I fancied, could now go where its footsteps led it.
Entering the University bookstore, I selected from its ample
shelves, with regal arbitrariness, a volume of Calvin's *Institutes*,
which I had never previously read, purchased it, took it outside,
seated myself on a bench, and read in it with pleasure and profit.

Needless to say, things could not long remain that way. The time
available was of course not infinite. Within a matter of hours,
rather than days, the strains of reality began to demolish the illusion.

These strains were of two kinds. The first was spiritual.

I would not say that awareness of one's own imperfections was
any greater in the halls of academe than it had been in the government office, but there was more time — there were more odd moments of solitude — in which to indulge it. The private diaries now
began to contain more in the way of self-reproaches, complaints of
the vanity of current preoccupations, protests about the aimlessness
of one's existence, yearnings for a greater unity and seriousness of
purpose. The very expansion of freedom of choice, the absence of
the governmental discipline as an excuse for evading personal
decisions, compelled a greater measure of this sort of introspection.

It did no good, of course. The coveted unity and seriousness of
purpose were never found. Such positive contributions as I was able
to make had previously been forthcoming in response to governmental demands. Now they flowed, insofar as they flowed at all,
only from commitments frivolously and thoughtlessly accepted, reflecting no system, no singleness of focus, nothing, in many instances, but lack of overriding purpose and an inability to say "no."
The life of such a person as myself inevitably had a liberal quota of
personal failures, some small, some large, and many moments of discouragement and remorse — but all of this was borne by a temperament too superficial, too unserious, too much the prisoner of
moods, too vulnerable to enthusiasms, too buoyant under the stress
of external stimuli, to remain for long depressed or reflective. It was

a life controlled not by any deliberate will but by the requirements of what one had inadvertently let oneself in for.

The second kind of strain that arose to assail the illusion of total freedom and leisure was the problem of the organization of one's life — and particularly its arrangement in such a way as to leave time and space for prolonged concentration. This, it might well be argued, was precisely what the Institute for Advanced Study was there for. But it was not the Institute, God bless it, that gave rise to my problem. It was the society in which it was imbedded, the flabbiness of my own will, and the extent of my unpreparedness for the experience of being a semi-public figure.

American society is both competitive and herdlike. It is herdlike even in the objects for which it competes. It seems to be impossible for anyone in America — for anyone, at least, whose interests engage those of the mass media — to be only moderately in demand. The problem, for anyone who would like to make a modest contribution to thinking on major public questions, is similar to the classic problem of the eligible female: either no one wants her or a thousand people immediately do. To have one's name not known at all is to confront a barrier that can be broken through only with much effort and luck. To become known, on the other hand, too widely — to become known, in particular, as having something to offer that a great many people want — is to step out onto the slippery path that leads to fragmentation of effort, hyperactivity and — eventually — sterility. To get one's name on American lists is almost certainly to be lost.

This was my position in the initial period after leaving government. I was reputed to possess something — an expertise on Russia, based on personal experience, and an ability to talk interestingly and not too controversially on problems of international affairs generally — which was much in demand. To several hundred universities, schools, clubs, discussion forums, and what not, all now struggling to recover from the bewilderments and emotional exaggerations of the wartime period and to orient themselves with relation to a new state of affairs in our relations with the Soviet Union for which nothing in American experience and very little in our governmental statements had prepared them, this seemed the answer to a prayer. The mass media, aware that the so-called "X-article," published in *Foreign Affairs* in 1947, had gone the rounds, had attracted much attention, and had made money for more than a few people, crowded in with their various offers and importunities. Individuals, too, appeared in numbers, demanding personal interviews: people who wanted jobs, people who wanted me to read their manuscripts, people who wanted to say they had talked with me, people who would have liked me to do anything under the sun other than what I had come to Princeton to be doing.

These and similar pressures were to continue unabated, indeed at times in greatly increased intensity, over most of the ensuing twenty years. I never learned to cope with them very well. Ninety percent of the appeals I learned, with time, to decline; but the total number often ran to several hundreds per annum, and the mere declining of the ninety percent was a major burden on one's time. And then there was the problem of the other ten percent: the undeclinables. They were often ones that came from friends, or relatives, or one's children, or one's children's schools, or very important people, or the executive branch of the government, or congressional committees, or foreign governments; or — like the honorary-degree-plus-commencement-speech approach — they involved honors embarrassing to refuse. Most difficult to cope with were the obviously very worthy ones: ones that came from people for whom one's heart bled, people who needed and deserved help, people pursuing causes about which one felt deeply. And finally, there were the really flattering ones: the ones that did, of course, tickle the ego but also gave one to realize that by accepting them one would be enhancing the power of one's own voice and with it one's possibilities for usefulness.

I was under no illusion that this was my problem alone. I recall reading, many years ago, a most perceptive article by Stephen Spender, the English poet, in which he pointed out that the American writer (and by this he had in mind the writer in the field of belles-lettres — the poet, the novelist, the short-story writer) faced two great and terrible dangers: the one — failure, the other — success; because in America failure was not easily forgiven, whereas success brought down upon the head of him who achieved it so appalling a flood of publicity and commercial pressures that he had only two choices: to emigrate and live abroad or never again to write anything worthwhile at all. My own experience now taught me that it was not in the field of belles-lettres alone that this dilemma could present itself.

I never found the satisfactory answer; and never, as I say, even after years of experience, did I cope very well with the resulting strains. But for the initial impact of these pressures, in particular, I was completely unprepared. The illusion that the time at my disposal had no limits betrayed me, in those initial years outside government, into the assumption that some way or other there would now be time for everything. Pleased with all the attention, I cheerfully accepted proposals right and left, with the result that I soon came into danger of losing all control over my own life. I reminded myself, many times, of the victim in the game played at the Christmas party, in the Bolshoi Theater's *mise en scène* of the *Nutcracker* ballet, where the children form a large circle and the old blindfolded dancing master is pushed, spinning and staggering, from one side of the circle to the other, evincing new bewilderment and helplessness at each push, sent off on one dizzy spin before he can regain his equilibrium from the last one. Within a short space of time I had become, so recollection tells me, an alumni trustee of Princeton University, a consultant to the Ford Foundation (which at that time meant periodic trips to Pasadena), a cofounder and president of an organization set up in New York to assist refugees from Soviet power, and a participant, together with Arthur Schlesinger, McGeorge Bundy, Don Price and other agreeable friends, in a study group at the Woodrow Wilson Foundation in New York. In addition to this I had agreed, with staggering frivolity, to give individual lectures at several places and entire lecture series at two places (Northwestern University and the University of Chicago). I had also undertaken to write a second "X-article" for *Foreign Affairs*. Finally, I set out (and eventually gathered around me a group of younger scholars to assist me in the process) to make a study of the domestic background of American foreign policy: of what was happening to the physical resources of our continent, of what sort of society we were becoming, of what demands we would have to place on our world environment in the coming decades. Among the dictates of these various involvements, hitting me at different times and from different sides, I tumbled back and forth like the blindfolded dancing master, equally helpless, equally ridiculous.

There was one other sort of strain to which people were often subjected when they came from more active pursuits to the Institute for Advanced Study. It was the sense of panic and helplessness that could affect you when you were suddenly confronted with a total freedom of authorship. Robert Oppenheimer warned me of it when I called on him, on arrival. "Never forget," he admonished me, "that there is nothing harder in life than to have nothing before you but the blank page and nothing to do but your best."

He could, in my case, have saved his words. This panic never assailed me. The reasons therefor did me no credit. I never found it difficult, as some people do, to make beginnings. An irrepressible intellectual brashness, a feeling that it didn't really matter much just where or how you began, and a love for a certain florid showmanship in prose, made it always easy to find the initial passages. What came later was harder, and sometimes vitiated one's purple beginnings. But then, one could always rewrite.

There was another bit of advice Oppenheimer gave me that I would have done better to heed. Instead of trying to write anything at all, he suggested, I might just settle down for those first few months and read widely and unprogrammatically, to give a broader intellectual and cultural foundation to what was, after all, an intense but narrow educational experience. No sounder advice was ever given me. I did not accept it, of course. I was full of schemes for tackling this and that in the way of concrete projects for study and writing. But I could not have followed this advice anyway unless I had had the fixity of purpose to decline all the external involvements and to regard my presence at the Institute as a total renunciation of every immediate participation, even intellectual, in the public life of my own time.

I would not like to give the impression that scholarship went totally neglected, either in those early postgovernmental years or later. As will be seen below, I did manage to do enough historical research, even in the hectic initial months, to produce a work that continues, twenty years later, to be used in dozens of college courses across the country. Two or three years later, after one further tour of duty in Moscow, I plunged more seriously into history. Setting out to compose what I envisaged as a small historical monograph of perhaps eighty to a hundred pages on the course of Soviet-American relations from 1917 to the present, I found the source materials just for the 1917–1918 period so abundant, so intriguing, and so little explored, that I ended some four years later as the author of two fat volumes, totaling some sixteen hundred pages, on just the first nine months (November 1917 to July 1918) of the relationship in question. After that, the lighthearted acceptance of various invitations to write or lecture on the history of Soviet foreign relations drove me to further major efforts of research and authorship. These undertakings, supplemented by various articles, individual lectures, courses, and reviews, on these and related subjects, were enough to bind me for the rest of my days to a life never remote, for any appreciable length of time, from archives and libraries.

Nor could I complain of any lack of satisfaction in this work. To eke the living past out of the hieroglyphics of the dead page — to feel the personalities of a bygone age come to life, achieve plausibility, and respond to the revivifying touch of one's own attention and imagination — to know oneself to be involved in the discovering of new and significant historical truth: all this, surely, if one has the taste for it, is one of the truly great creative experiences of which men are capable.

But it is lonely work. The economic or social historian may be able, at times, to work in partnership with other people. The student of political or cultural history is normally condemned by the nature of his discipline to work in loneliness. Particularly is this true if he feels it necessary (and he usually does) to clothe what he has to say in literary form, in the interests of its communicability. I cannot say that I derived no companionship at all from those dim figures, the historical characters with whom I concerned myself in the course of my researches. They became part of my life, and I see them now in retrospect as though I had known them in the flesh. But they were never able to see me, or to react to my interest. I wandered through their lifeless world like a solitary visitor through a wax museum, observing their costumes, their figures, the frozen expressions on their faces. Sometimes words and phrases, preserved for posterity by the written page, stood out from their lips like the little balloons of utterance that emerge from the characters of a comic strip. Sometimes actions, depicted in the historical record, could be re-created in imagination. But it was a one-sided relationship. My concern for them was not matched by any reciprocal concern on their part for me. For that interaction with others that man, as a social being, requires, I had to look elsewhere. And yet, this involvement in the past carried with it challenge, excitement, and satisfaction. It had, as occupations go, a certain purity and innocence about it. It proceeded at the cost of no one. Yet it tapped the highest resources of mind and imagination; and in this sense it sufficed — or would have sufficed had I been able to devote my entire, undivided strength to it — to make a life's work, if not a life itself.

I could not, finally, complain of any lack of appreciation for my effort. *Russia Leaves the War*, the first of the two volumes on Soviet-American relations, received just about every prize it could get, including the National Book Award, the Pulitzer Prize, and the Benjamin Franklin Award for the year's best work of history as literature. The 1957 Reith Lectures, delivered live in London over the Home Service of the BBC in the course of several successive Sunday evenings, attracted consistently wider listening audiences, I was told, than any in the history of that series to that time, excepting only the initial lecture by the late Bertrand Russell, in 1948. The lectures, similarly, that later went to make up the volumes *Realities of American Foreign Policy* and *Russia and the West under Lenin and Stalin* drew record student audiences at Princeton and Harvard, and something very close to that at Oxford.

All this was naturally gratifying; and had I been able to combine a consistent and unbroken application to historical scholarship during the academic year with some contact with nature and the sea on weekends and vacations, I would have felt my capacities for the enjoyment of life as well fulfilled as they were capable of being. Unfortunately, this was not possible. It was the outside pressures — the contemporary ones, the demands for contributions immediately related to the current scene — that continued to make this impossible.

Why did I not resist all these pressures? Why did I yield to even a fraction of them? I have touched on some of the reasons. But back of them all was the unwillingness to reconcile myself to the suggestion that I had no further role to play in the events of my time.

It was evident to me, as to every thinking person, that my world, and that of my children, was in serious danger. Was there then nothing I could do about it? I had had many years of experience in government. I was convinced, rightly or wrongly, that had my views on Russia been heeded during the wartime period, a number of our problems and embarrassments of the postwar period might have been alleviated. I felt that the contribution of the Policy Planning Staff to the solution of some of these problems, during the days of my incumbency as its director, had been a positive one. I was still only forty-six years old. It was difficult for me to believe that I had nothing further to offer. The extent to which my voice was sought after, and listened to when used, seemed to me to constitute in itself an obligation. It was an asset that might or might not be deserved, but it existed. Not everyone had it; and, once in possession of it, one had no right to waste it. To these reflections was added, finally, the influence of friends. A lasting impression was left, in particular, when the English historian Veronica Wedgwood — a woman for whose scholarly experience and general good sense I had the greatest respect — admonished me not to make the mistake of permitting a preoccupation with history to cut me off from any and every involvement in the affairs of my own time.

So I struggled along, over those postgovernmental years, maneuvering between the past and the present, giving myself entirely to neither: a semi-historian and a semi-commentator, at times the writer and teacher of history, at times the advisor to governments or the participant in the discussion of public problems and crises, uncomfortable to the point of desperation under the tensions and conflicts engendered by this double life, yet unable to give up either aspect of it, and becoming only belatedly aware (it was the latest of my long-suffering secretaries, Janet Smith, who drew my attention to it) that the two seemingly conflicting attractions were actually interrelated and interdependent — that part of my strength as a diplomatic historian came from the fact that I had been responsibly involved with contemporary problems of diplomacy, whereas whatever value I had as a commentator on contemporary affairs was derived, in part at least, from the belief on the part of the public that I knew something about history.

This is surely the place to say something about the Institute for Advanced Study, which was the seat of most of this activity. Except for two further episodic tours of Foreign Service duty (in Moscow and in Belgrade) and several terms spent in Oxford some years later, this institution was destined to be my professional home and center of activity from 1950 down to the present day. From 1950 to 1956 I was there, like most of the scholars who use the Institute's facilities, in the quality of a temporary visitor. Since 1956 I have been a member of its permanent faculty.

The Institute for Advanced Study is unique, among American institutions of higher learning, for its absence of students and teaching, for the general distinction of its visiting scholars and faculty, and for its single-minded devotion to the highest standards of scholarship. It is almost exclusively a place for individual research: quiet, ascetic, devoid of distracting activities. There are no laboratory facilities. Until recently, higher mathematics, natural science (primarily theoretical physics) and history were the three disciplines cultivated; more recently, a new program has been added, in fields related to the social sciences.

The quality of the work performed at the Institute is assured by the care taken in the selections for membership. Once invited and received, the visiting scholar has complete freedom to pursue his work as he wishes. If he wastes his time, which seldom happens, it is to itself — for the unsoundness of its choice — not to him, that the reproaches of the faculty are directed. Nothing prevents faculty members or visiting scholars from getting together, if they are so moved, for lectures, discussions, and seminars; the Institute gladly extends, in this case, the necessary facilities. But it takes no initiative in organizing such activities. It is concerned, as Robert Oppenheimer once put it to me, "to deprive these people of any excuse for not doing whatever it was that they came here to do."

I can find no adequate words in which to acknowledge the debt I owe to this establishment. The Institute took me, already a middle-aged man devoid of academic credentials, substantially on faith, gambling on the existence of scholarly capacities that remained to be demonstrated. Not only did it give me, then, the possibility to develop these capacities, such as they were, but it provided the examples, and in a gentle way the discipline, without which they could never have been developed.

I stood to gain, and did gain, a great deal over the course of the years from contacts with the many visiting scholars. But the deepest and most lasting enrichment came, quite naturally, from the enduring association with some of the truly great members of the Institute's permanent faculty. Of the living ones I shall not attempt to speak, although there are several who would deserve inclusion under this heading. But there are others, now no longer with us, whom I cannot fail to mention.

It was, I suppose, the rigorous and versatile military-diplomatic historian Edward Mead Earle who more than anyone except Oppenheimer himself was responsible for bringing me to the Institute. It was under his tactful but vigorous guidance that I did my first work there. He died in June 1954, and my debt to him was one that I never had opportunity to acknowledge to him personally.

In scholarship, as in the family, it is primarily by example, not precept, that people influence one another. There could have been no more wonderful example for a person in the early stages of scholarly development than Erwin Panofsky. One of the greatest art historians of all time, "Pan" combined immense erudition with a rich, warm, engaging humor, endless curiosity and love of subject, and a generosity in communication that was the mark of the born teacher. The impression left on me, as on so many other people, was indelible.

Panofsky was only one of several priceless gifts from Adolf Hitler to American scholarship in general and to the Institute for Advanced Study in particular. Another was the great mediaevalist Ernst Kantorowicz — "Eka," as he was always known to friends and colleagues. A bachelor, an aesthete, and a man of ineffable Old World charm, Eka, cozily installed in his little home on Alexander Street, was an essential feature of the Princeton of the 1950s, as I first knew it; and his passing left a gap that could never be filled.

Let me give an example of what the interest of such a person as Eka could, and did, mean to a younger scholar. When I finished the draft of *Russia Leaves the War*, I asked him if he would care to look it over. It dealt, after all, with the period of World War I, of which he had vivid memories, he having at that time served in the German army; and we had sometimes talked of the problems and events of that day. It was my first major effort, and I was not quite sure what it was, actually, that I had produced. He took the typescript home and read, at least, great parts of it. Then he asked me to dinner, alone, at his home. Being not only a gourmet but also an accomplished cook, he prepared with his own hands a marvelous meal for the two of us, served it with the best of wines, and then, seating me in the living room over coffee and brandy, took out the typescript and said: "Now, my friend, we will talk about what you have done," whereupon he proceeded to subject the piece, not from the factual standpoint (for he did not pretend to be familiar with the subject matter) but from the standpoint of technique and taste in historical writing, to the most searching, useful, and unforgettable criticism. This, I thought, was the mark not just of a great scholar but of a great gentleman.

Another faculty colleague from whose company I profited over most of the years of my residence at the Institute was the former British Foreign Office historian, Oxford professor and Fellow of All Souls, Sir Llewellyn Woodward. English as it was possible to be, tweedy and whimsical, given to long solitary stalking walks around the ample fields and environs of the Institute, Woodward was not an easy man to get to know. On top of the normal English shyness he had the gruffness, the critical skepticism, and the chariness with praise characteristic of the fine workman in any field; for a fine workman — severe, painstaking, exacting in the demands he placed on himself — was precisely what, as a historian, he was. But this scholarly rigor, so essential to the fashioning of the fine volumes of British diplomatic documents published under his coeditorship, concealed, as though by another expression of native diffidence, a philosopher, an aesthete, a first-rate, greatly unappreciated writer in the field of belles-lettres, and a very perceptive commentator on the affairs of his own time.

After the death of his sweet and charming wife, to whom my own wife and I were much attached, Woodward was a broken man. His grief was unassuageable. He stopped coming to Princeton, because — he told me — the two of them had been so happy there, and the associations were too numerous and too harrowing to endure.

Woodward was never a demonstrative man. Considering my background and all my peripheral involvements, he must initially have viewed my scholarly potentialities, I am sure, with the liveliest skepticism. My views on World War I, too, were far from his own; and this was a subject about which he had deep feelings, having himself served as an artillery officer on the Western Front at that time. But he gradually came to recognize, I think, the earnestness of my admiration for him as well as my readiness to learn from him where I could; and in his lonely final years our relations developed into ones of friendship and even a form of affection.

Also at the Institute during the first years of my residence there was, of course, Albert Einstein. He was aware of my identity and my presence. We sometimes exchanged friendly notes. But we never met. It is hard for me to explain why. I knew nothing and understood nothing of his scientific concerns. I had nothing to see him about, and I was only too well aware of the pressures constantly put upon him by casual visitors, well-wishers, would-be exploiters, and curiosity-seekers of all sorts. I had no desire to add to this burden, and I concluded that the best way of manifesting my respect for him would be to leave him alone. I am not sure, in retrospect, that this was right. But there was much to be said for it. He was old and presumably tired. He was not likely to learn much about Russia, and I was certain to learn nothing about physics or mathematics, from a courtesy visit.

I must mention, finally, the remarkable and unforgettable man who was not only a member of the Institute's faculty but, for the first sixteen years of my own association with the establishment, its director and the man to whom, more than anyone else, I owed my affiliation with it: Robert Oppenheimer.

Could there, I wonder, be anyone harder to describe than he? In some ways very young, in others very old; part scientist, part poet; sometimes proud, sometimes humble; in some ways formidably competent in practical matters, in other ways woefully helpless: he was a bundle of marvelous contradictions. Of his greatness there can, in my opinion, be no question. His mind was one of wholly exceptional power, subtlety, and speed of reaction. He was one of the few people who could combine in one intellectual and aesthetic personality vast scientific knowledge, impressive erudition in the humanities, and an active, sophisticated interest in the international-political affairs of his own time.

He was often described as arrogant, and criticized for it. Perhaps, perhaps — though the evidences of it seemed often to me to reflect primarily the influences of people around him rather than the natural impulses of his own personality. The shattering quickness and critical power of his own mind made him, no doubt, impatient of the ponderous, the obvious, and the platitudinous, in the discourse of others. But underneath this edgy impatience there lay one of the most sentimental of natures, an enormous thirst for friendship and affection, and a touching belief — such as I never observed in anyone else — in what he thought should be the fraternity of advanced scholarship. He would have agreed with Bukharin, I think, that intellectual friendship was the deepest and finest form of friendship among men; and his attitude towards those whose intellectual qualities he most admired — Niels Bohr, for example — was one of deep, humble devotion and solicitude. The greatest tragedy of his life, I often suspect, was not the ordeal to which he was subjected over the question of his loyalty, though this — God knows — was bad enough, but the fact that the members of the faculty of the Institute were often not able to bring to each other, as a concomitant of the respect they entertained for each other's scholarly attainments, the sort of affection, and almost reverence, which he himself thought these qualities ought naturally to command. His fondest dream had been, I think, one of a certain rich and harmonious fellowship of the mind. He had hoped to create this at the Institute for Advanced Study; and it did come into being, to a certain extent, within the individual disciplines. But very little of it could be created from discipline to discipline; and the fact that this was so — the fact that mathematicians and historians continued to seek their own tables in the cafeteria, and that he himself remained so largely alone in his ability to bridge in a single inner world these wholly disparate workings of the human intellect — this was for him, I am sure, a source of profound bewilderment and disappointment.

For the charges brought against him and the harassments to which he was subject in the early 1950s in connection with the question of his loyalty, I can find no patience whatsoever. The actions on his part which served as their pretext were peccadillos — foolish actions, as he himself soon recognized, but not ones involving the passage of any information to any foreign government and not ones that could have served to justify any suspicion of disloyalty. They were known to the United States government years before that government entrusted him with the chairmanship of the Scientific Advisory Committee; and for the revival and the formal levying of these charges against him in the 1950s, I can conceive of no motive other than personal vindictiveness and shameless, heartless political expediency. The United States government, if it is to realize America's possibilities as a great power, will have to learn that even our country is not so rich in talent that it can afford to proceed thus brutally and recklessly with that which it has.

I remember Oppenheimer primarily by certain episodes of our acquaintance.

I remember him, first of all, as he was when I saw him for the first time. It was in the fall of 1946. He had come to the National War College to lecture. He shuffled diffidently and almost apologetically out to the podium: a frail, stooped figure in a heavy brown tweed suit with trousers that were baggy and too long, big feet that turned outward, and a small head and face that caused him, at times, to look strangely like a young student. He then proceeded to speak for nearly an hour, without the use of notes — but to speak with such startling lucidity and such scrupulous subtlety and precision of expression that when he had finished, no one dared ask a question — everyone was sure that somehow or other he had answered every possible point. I say "somehow or other," because, curiously enough, no one could remember exactly what he had said: The fascination exerted by his personality, the virtuosity of the performance, and the extreme subtlety of expression had actually interfered with the receptivity of the audience to the substance of what he was saying. This was a phenomenon that was to dog him throughout his life whenever it fell to him to address any other than a scientifically specialized audience.

I recall, again, the scene at his house one rainy Sunday morning when I asked him (it was during the ordeal of the public hearings on his fitness to continue as chairman of the Scientific Advisory Committee) why he remained in this country at all in the face of such harassment. He was at home, I pointed out, in other parts of the world: he had taken his doctorate in Holland; he had many friends in the European academic world; there was not a university anywhere across the globe that would not welcome him with open arms.

He stood there a moment, tears streaming down his face. Then he stammered, with a corniness of which he was as well aware as I was but the very helplessness of which increased the forces of the statement: "Dammit, I happen to love this country."

It was true. For all his discouragements with his own people, for all the misunderstandings he met with on the part of his own government and sections of the American public, Oppenheimer was, and always remained, a profoundly American figure.

I remember him, finally, as he was on November 22, 1963, when the two of us, standing in his office at the Institute, both shattered by the early incomplete reports of the assassination, received over the radio the confirmation of Jack Kennedy's death. He said nothing, nor did I — there was no need. But I saw — and shared — the quick, terrible stab of anguish and disheartenment that came over his eyes. Neither of us knew Jack Kennedy intimately, but we were both aware that it was more than just that one life that had been obliterated: that the world we cared about had been grievously diminished, together with our own ability to be in any way useful to it. For Oppenheimer, with his great imaginative insight, it was a dreadful blow; and I wonder if I am wrong when I ascribe to that moment, as I instinctively tend to do, the beginning of his own death.

I mention all of these deceased colleagues not just because they taught me a great deal but because their generosity towards myself was such that I can never today do less than I am capable of doing, as a writer and a scholar, without feeling myself guilty of a sort of betrayal of the confidence they placed in me — a betrayal even shabbier and more painful to the conscience now that they are dead than it would have been had they been still alive.

This, I suppose, is the way people help each other — perhaps the only way they can ultimately help each other — in the lonely, rarefied life of the mind. It constitutes the reason why those who are conscious of having been well and generously taught have an obligation, at some time and in some way, to teach.

2

Korea

THERE was one involvement of those hectic first months out of government that was not of my doing: it was, in fact, a carry-over from recent responsibilities in government. This was the problem of Korea.

I had approved from the start our decision to resist by force of arms the incursion by the North Koreans into South Korea that began on June 25, 1950. But I had done so on the assumption and understanding that our action was only for a limited purpose: namely, the restoration of the *status quo ante* on the Korean peninsula, and that our forces would not, even if military successes permitted, advance beyond the former demarcation line along the 38th parallel. I saw in the North Korean attack adequate reason for us to undertake military operations for this limited purpose; I did not see in it justification for involving ourselves in another world war. Even in the event that a major war might develop, contrary to our wishes, out of this limited one, it was not at all clear to me that the Korean peninsula would be the place on which we would choose to fight it. I was greatly concerned, therefore, to assure that a decision to resist North Korean aggression in South Korea should not be permitted to grow imperceptibly into something more than it was meant to be.

I made it clear as early as July 1950, in the internal discussions of our government, that I was opposed to any advance beyond the 38th parallel. That this view did not fail to register was evident from the fact that Mr. John Foster Dulles cited it (most improperly, from the standpoint of governmental security) to a journalist as evidence of a dangerous waywardness of opinion on my part. I continued to press this view down to the time of my departure from Washington in September. On August 8, for example, I wrote, in a memorandum for my superiors in the department:

As Bohlen emphasized when he was here, when the tide of battle begins to change, the Kremlin will not wait for us to reach the 38th parallel before taking action. When we begin to have military successes, that will be the time to watch out. Anything may then happen — entry of Soviet forces, entry of Chinese Communist forces, new strike for UN settlement, or all three together.

Two weeks later, just before leaving the department, I reiterated this view in an off-the-record press conference with a number of Washington journalists. Asked about Russian reactions in the case of a North Korean defeat, I gave it as my belief

that the Russians will not be inclined to sit by if our forces or United Nations forces . . . of any sort push the North Koreans beyond the 38th parallel again. . . . They may . . . reoccupy North Korea, or they might introduce other forces which would be nominally Chinese Communist forces . . . (goodness knows who would be really controlling them). . . . Obviously, they are not going to leave the field free for us to sweep up the peninsula and place ourselves forty or fifty miles from Vladivostok.

My anxieties on this whole subject were heightened by the difficulty we in the State Department experienced in getting any satisfactory explanations from the Pentagon about our bombings of the port of Rashin on the eastern coast of North Korea. This had caused me to doubt that General MacArthur was under any very effective control by anybody in Washington, or that anyone really knew precisely what he was doing. It seemed to me that official

Washington had in effect, for domestic-political reasons, consigned the fortunes of our country and of world peace to an agency, namely General MacArthur's headquarters, over which it had no effective authority. "By permitting General MacArthur," I wrote on August 21 to Secretary Acheson (to whom it would scarcely have been a revelation),

to retain the wide and relatively uncontrolled latitude he has enjoyed in determining our policy in the north Asian and western Pacific areas, we are tolerating a state of affairs in which we do not really have full control over the statements that are being made — and the actions taken — in our name.

It will be understood, against this background, that it was with something more than a lack of confidence or enthusiasm that I watched, after removal to Princeton in early September, the further course of the Korean War: the crossing of the parallel by our forces in the first days of October; the growing evidences in October and November of preparations for Chinese intervention; the arrival of American forces at the Manchurian border on November 21; General MacArthur's inauguration on November 24 of a "win the war" offensive; the sudden entry of the Chinese in force the following day; and finally — on November 26–28 — the overwhelming of American units along the Yalu by superior Chinese forces, and the beginning of the American retreat. Living away from Washington, I naturally did not know that my misgivings about an advance towards the Manchurian border had now come to be shared by a number of highly placed people in Washington, and to some extent even by the Joint Chiefs of Staff themselves; nor did I know that General MacArthur had twice given assurances, once personally to the President at Wake Island and again in reply to a direct query from Washington in the first days of November, that a Russian or Chinese intervention was nothing to be feared.* I was

* Harry S. Truman, *Memoirs*, Volume II, *Years of Trial and Hope, 1946–1952*, chap. 24. Garden City: Doubleday, 1956.

also unaware that the Chinese Communists had told the Indian ambassador in Peking, Mr. K. M. Panikkar, on October 3, 1950, that China would enter the war if American forces advanced beyond the parallel, and that the United States government had knowledge of this.* Had I known these things, I would have been even more disturbed. But what was in the press was enough to cause my heart to sink.

The final days of November, in particular, were dark ones. The papers were full of the disaster that had befallen us. On December 1, I received a long-distance call from Charles E. Bohlen, then serving as minister at our embassy in Paris. He was greatly disturbed, he said, not just over the news from Korea, but, precisely in conjunction with it, over the impression he had gained that there was at that moment no one among the senior advisors of our government present in Washington who had any great experience in Russian affairs or any deep knowledge of Soviet policy and psychology. "I am calling to implore you," he said, "to go down to Washington and insist on seeing General Marshall, who I know has high regard for your views, and also the Secretary of State, and to try to impress upon them the real considerations which undoubtedly underlie the Russian and Chinese reactions and on which you and I have been consistently in agreement."

In response to this question I offered to the department — through the intermediation of friends in Washington — whatever help I could give. Word came back the following day that my presence would be welcome, and the result was that at ten on Sunday morning, December 3, I reported once more to the office of the Secretary of State.

Alarming news had just come in that morning from MacArthur. He now saw no chances for further success, and even — over the long run — little chance for effective defense "unless ground rein-

---

* Dean Acheson, *Present at the Creation: My Years in the State Department*, p. 452. New York: Norton, 1969.

forcements of the greatest magnitude are promptly supplied." *
Washington had no such forces available, had no desire to involve
itself in a major war, and could not have carried out any escalation
of the conflict on this scale without incurring a complete break with
its UN allies. The situation was therefore dark in the extreme.

The Secretary himself was absent at the time of my arrival, con-
ferring with the military leaders and with the President on the situation in the light of MacArthur's telegram. I first sat in on the military briefings for the Under Secretary of State, Mr. James Webb,
and then talked with the latter personally. The picture that
emerged from these discussions was confused but alarming. Mr.
Webb, my diary records, was

obviously in a state of considerable agitation. He said that the military
leaders felt that a complete withdrawal from Korea was the only alternative to the loss of what was practically our entire ground establishment. They thought that we had perhaps 36 hours for a decision as to
an orderly withdrawal. If that decision was not made, the result might
be complete disaster and effective loss of the entire force. He said discussions were in progress concerning the attitude we should adopt in
the United Nations and in the conversations with Attlee [the British
premier], who was expected to arrive the following morning. No course
would be decided on until we had talked with the British. One of the
variants that would be discussed with the British would be a direct approach to the Russians with a view to bringing about a cease-fire in
Korea. What they wanted from me, he said, was a view as to the prospects of negotiation with the Russians on this problem at this time.

The Secretary, returning to his office after lunch, confirmed this
assignment. What was wanted from me was an opinion as to the
prospects for direct negotiations with the Russians, as a possible escape from our military embarrassment. I accordingly withdrew and
set about, with the help of John Paton Davies and the late G. Frederick Reinhardt (also an old Moscow hand, later to serve long and

* Truman, *Memoirs,* vol. II, p. 392.

with distinction as our ambassador in Rome) to write such an opinion.

What we produced, in that memorandum of December 3, 1950,
were four pages, single-spaced, of the bleakest and most uncomfort-
ing prose that the department's files can ever have accommodated.
We could do no other.

There were, it was clear, only two conceivable frameworks in
which diplomatic discussions could be conducted with the Russians
about the Korean situation: either we talked about it as an isolated
problem, declining to bring it into connection with the broader
problems of the Far East as a region; or we took it up as part of the
whole range of Far Eastern problems, including such delicate ones
as the question of a Japanese peace treaty and our policy towards
Communist China.

For this last, plainly, we were wholly unprepared. This was at
the height of the McCarthyist hysteria. The China lobby, in particular, was in full cry. There were violent differences in Congress
over Far Eastern policy. No attempt could be made to give any
final definition to that policy, and especially to discuss it with the
Russians, without blowing the domestic political situation sky-high.
So delicate was the situation that we could not even discuss it intelligently with our allies.

But the alternative — an attempt to discuss the Korean situation
with the Russians as an isolated problem, without relation to the
many wider questions it obviously affected — was still worse. "Any
approach to the Russians," we wrote,

. . . simply asking for an immediate cease-fire in Korea and not connected with any political agreements about the future of Korea or other
Far Eastern problems would probably be taken by the Kremlin leaders
as a bid for peace by us on whatever terms we can get.

They would regard this as confirmation that we were faced with the
alternative of capitulation, on the one hand, or complete rout and military disaster on the other. In such a situation their main concern would

be to see that the maximum advantage, in terms of damage to our prestige and to non-Communist unity, should be extracted from our plight. This being the case, they would see no reason to spare us any of the humiliation of military disaster. They would not be interested in promoting a cease-fire unless it were on terms at least as damaging to our prestige as a continuation of military operations might be expected to be. . . .

The present moment is probably the poorest one we have known at any time in the history of our relations with the Soviet Union for negotiations with its leaders. . . . The prerequisite to any satisfactory negotiation about the local situation in Korea is the demonstration that we have the capability to stabilize the front somewhere in the peninsula and to engage a large number of Communist forces for a long time. If we are unable to do this, I see not the faintest reason why the Russians should wish to aid us in our predicament. . . . Any approach we make to them without some solid cards in our hand, in the form of some means of pressure on them to arrive at an agreement in their own interest, may simply be exploited by them for purposes of spotlighting our weakness and improving their own position in the eyes of other peoples. . . .

The prerequisite to any successful negotiation on political subjects would be a posture of unity, confidence and collected strength on our side.

When I took this paper into Secretary Acheson's office it was already seven o'clock in the evening. He, for whom in those times there were no weekends or days of leisure, was obviously tired, and was just leaving for home. I did not have the heart to prolong his exhausting Sunday with so wretchedly unhelpful a paper, and forbore to hand it to him until the following morning. He, however, kindly asked me to come home and have family supper with Mrs. Acheson and himself, and this I gratefully did.*

---

* These pages, and all other references in this book to the late Dean Acheson, were written before his death. I regret that they could not have been subjected, as I supposed they would be when writing them, to the test of his inimitable, critical reaction. I can only give them as written and ask the reader to bear in mind that Mr. Acheson's memory might well have been different from mine, as his views were certain to have been.

I have no memory and no record of what, specifically, was discussed that evening. I remember, in addition to Mrs. Acheson's great charm, only the Secretary's characteristic spirit and wit, which no crisis and no weariness seemed ever to extinguish; and I recall a feeling of sympathy and solicitude for him which not even the public disagreements of later years were able to dim. Here he was: a gentleman, the soul of honor, attempting to serve the interests of the country against the background of a Washington seething with anger, confusion and misunderstanding, bearing the greatest possible burden of responsibility for a dreadful situation he had not created, yet having daily to endure the most vicious and unjust of personal attacks from the very men — the congressional claque and other admirers of General MacArthur — who, by their insistence on this adventurous and ill-advised march to the Yalu, had created it. I had often disagreed with him — our minds had never really worked the same way; but never for a moment could I deny him my admiration for the manner in which he bore this ordeal. And I was aware that this particular evening — with our Korean forces in full retreat, with many of our military leaders in near-panic, and with the British Prime Minister arriving tomorrow to demand an accounting from us in the name of our UN allies — must have been for him one of the blackest moments of a career not poor in trials and discouragements.

I tried, as I recall it, to spare him further talk about the problem of decision to which his day had been devoted; but we must, I think, have spoken about the obvious erraticism in General MacArthur's judgments and conduct and the jittery reactions and wild counsels that were now popping up all over Washington, particularly in military and congressional circles. I took my leave that night, in any case, depressed at the thought that my host was sure to find himself surrounded, the following day, by people who seemingly had no idea how to take a defeat with dignity and good grace.

In the early morning, therefore, in the hope of strengthening his hand as he faced the trials of the coming day, I sat down and wrote him a longhand note of the following tenor (he himself included it in his *Present at the Creation*, but I reproduce it here again, because it is part of the story):

There is one thing I should like to say in continuation of our discussion of yesterday evening.

In international, as in private, life what counts most is not really what happens to someone but how he bears what happens to him. For this reason almost everything depends from here on out on the manner in which we Americans bear what is unquestionably a major failure and disaster to our national fortunes. If we accept it with candor, with dignity, with a resolve to absorb its lessons and to make it good by redoubled and determined effort — starting all over again, if necessary, along the pattern of Pearl Harbor — we need lose neither our self-confidence nor our allies nor our power for bargaining, eventually, with the Russians. But if we try to conceal from our own people or from our allies the full measure of our misfortune, or permit ourselves to seek relief in any reactions of bluster or petulance or hysteria, we can easily find this crisis resolving itself into an irreparable deterioration of our world position — and of our confidence in ourselves.

This I handed to him, when we met in the morning, together with the official paper Davies and Reinhardt and I had written the day before. Both documents were then discussed at the Secretary's regular morning meeting with his chief advisors. There was no dissent to the tenor of the official paper. It was generally accepted that no useful purpose could be served by any attempt to negotiate with the Russians about Korea, as an isolated problem, at that moment.*

But there still remained the question of military policy. I was unable to conceive that a total and abrupt military withdrawal from

---

* Mr. Acheson said to the British Prime Minister, Mr. Attlee, the following day, that the moment seemed to him to be "the worst one for negotiation with the Russians since 1917." The Russians, he added, "saw themselves holding the cards and would concede nothing" (Acheson, *Present at the Creation*, p. 482).

the peninsula was the only answer; and Dean Rusk,* among others, shared this opinion. He, my notes record,

introduced the question as to whether we were really obliged to abandon Korea altogether and whether it might not be a good thing for us
to attempt to hold some sort of a beachhead, particularly in the light of
what I had said about negotiations with the Russians. I took occasion to
reinforce the point he had raised. I was afraid, I said, that perhaps our
military leaders were not sufficiently aware how similar our position had
become to that occupied by the British for a long period in the past and
how necessary it was for us, on occasion, to hold stubbornly, on the
basis of sheer political instinct, to positions which by military logic
might appear to be useless. One could never know about these things. I
recalled the battles in North Africa during the recent war and the
drastic and repeated changes in military fortune which carried the front
hundreds of miles back and forth along the North African littoral. Had
the British not stubbornly clung to a position just short of Cairo, in the
face of discouraging odds, they would never have won their final victory. If we could prove, I said, that we could hold some sort of line or
beachhead in central or southern Korea, which would pin down a large
number of enemy forces, I was not sure that the prospect of continuing
such a contest in the face of air attacks on their lines of communications
would prove attractive to the enemy.

I cannot recall that there was any disagreement with this view at
the morning meeting. Our problem, obviously, was not there, in
the State Department; it was on the other side of the river. Rusk,
Matthews† and I therefore left directly from this meeting, at the
Secretary's request, and drove over to the Pentagon to see General
George Marshall, who had just recently taken over as Secretary of
Defense. Here we found, as we were sure we would, a calm, wise
and steady ally. The General expressed, my notes record,

his complete agreement with us in principle. It was impossible, he said,
to determine at the present moment whether any line or beachhead

---

* Dean Rusk, future Secretary of State, was then Assistant Secretary of State for
Far Eastern Affairs.
† H. Freeman Matthews, then Deputy Under Secretary of State.

could be held. What was essential was the security of the Command, which must not be jeopardized. We had first to see whether the forces on the east coast could be evacuated, and in what condition and with what equipment. Then we had to determine what was the situation in the Seoul-Inchon area. At present the situation was obscured by the fog of battle, and we had no adequate information.

Referring to the point of principle we had raised, the General recalled his experiences in the past in the case of Bataan and Corregidor, and cited this as an example of the virtue of hanging on doggedly for reasons of prestige and morale.

Before we completed our talk with General Marshall, we were joined by Mr. Robert A. Lovett, then serving as Deputy Secretary of Defense, who had just come from Capitol Hill, where he had been briefing the members of the House Armed Services Committee and discussing the situation with them. The prevailing feeling there, he reported, was that our entire entry into Korea had been a mistake and that we ought to pull out as rapidly as possible. I received this news with consternation; but the General took it in his stride. This sort of fluctuation in congressional opinion was not, he said, a new thing. The present mood might not last for very long.*

By midday, the matter was settled. On returning to the Department of State, we lunched with Secretary Acheson. He had just been talking with President Truman. The President's decision was, as always in the great crises, clear, firm and unhesitating. He had no patience, Mr. Acheson told us, with the suggestions that we abandon Korea. We would stay and fight as long as possible.

The British Prime Minister, Mr. Clement Attlee, arrived that afternoon; and the discussions between him and our governmental leaders began the following morning. With relation to these discussions my own advice was not needed. I was in agreement with the

---

* This summary of General Marshall's reaction, while almost identical with that which appeared in Mr. Acheson's memoirs (*Present at the Creation*, p. 477), comes from my own personal notes, written at the time.

President and the Secretary, I believe, in feeling that the British should be satisfied with our assurance that we proposed neither to abandon South Korea nor to push the conflict there to the point of a new world war, and that there was no necessity for going beyond that and attempting to reconcile our respective views at that time on the thorny subject of China. And so, indeed, the matter was allowed to rest. After remaining in Washington, therefore, only long enough for an effort (apparently successful) to stop some of the department's senior UN enthusiasts from attempting to drive through another UN resolution, this time condemning the Chinese Communists as aggressors (an undertaking that would have forced the issue of our differences with the British and others over China), I took my leave and returned to Princeton. The greatest danger — that of a panicky abandonment of the entire effort in Korea — had, through the stoutness of the President and the good sense of his secretaries for State and Defense, been momentarily overcome. But the general situation was such that it was with a sense of near despair that I boarded the train for Princeton that afternoon. Washington, it seemed, was in the greatest and most disgraceful disarray. "You were right," I wrote to Bohlen, that day,

in your anguished conviction about the need for another outlook in Washington. But it is much too late today to do anything but pick up the pieces. We are the victims mainly of an absolutely unbelievable and stupendous military blunder; but even this could not have placed us in dilemmas as bitter as those that are rending us today if the basis of our political policy in the past weeks and months had been a realistic, rather than a legalistic, one. You may blame me for not having done more to correct this situation; but remember that there is a real ceiling on the usefulness of any one of us, and that is the point at which he becomes so importunate with his views that they cease to be listened to with any respect at all. My absence in recent weeks has prevented me from passing into that area, but I am sure that I would have ended up there had I continued in the department in my former capacity. I would end up there very soon right now if I continued to drift around too long in the capacity you once magnificently described as that of a "floating kidney."

The stabilization of a front along the middle of the peninsula proved, of course, to be an entirely feasible undertaking. The Chinese, by the time they arrived at that point, began to feel the length of their supply lines; and a reasonable balance of forces was soon restored. With this, the groundwork was laid for the sort of negotiations for an armistice which I had opposed in the unfavorable situation of December 1950. A political basis was now also provided for these negotiations, not only by the readiness of our government to recognize at long last that it was unwise for us to attempt to liberate all of North Korea by force of arms, but also by President Truman's courage in relieving General MacArthur of his command and thus bringing our policy in Korea for the first time under Washington's control. The question now posed itself, however, in the late spring of 1951: How could we, without inviting or risking humiliating rebuffs, ascertain whether the Russians were disposed to go along with such negotiations and to give them their support? A public initiative on our part that produced only an insulting North Korean rebuff could be much worse than no initiative at all.

On May 6, 1951, Mr. Stewart Alsop, writing in the *New York Herald Tribune* on the consequences of an advance beyond the parallel, compared favorably my own known views on the dangers of such an advance with certain public statements recently made by General MacArthur. General MacArthur had said, according to Mr. Alsop: "I do not believe that anything that happens in Korea, or Asia for that matter, would affect the basic decision [of the Kremlin] whether to intervene openly in the Korean War." This was, of course, directly contrary to my own view that the Russians were extremely sensitive to the security of their own border in the Far East and of the Manchurian border as well, and would certainly react militarily before permitting us to establish ourselves militarily in that region.

"Kennan believes," Alsop then added, "that a real political victory in Korea may soon be possible, if we do not again make the fatal mistake of demanding 'unconditional surrender.' If not, war may come anyway. But Kennan is reported to believe that before edging into a world war by the back door, we should make a final effort, by the secret processes of diplomacy, to reach at least some temporary settlement with the real masters of the situation, the men in the Kremlin."

This report was not inaccurate nor, apparently, was it without effect. Twelve days later, I was called to Washington and was asked whether I would make an effort to get into touch privately with the Soviet representative on the United Nations Security Council, Mr. Jacob Malik, with a view to explaining to him our government's position and inclinations and learning something, if possible, about the position and inclinations of his own. I was to make it clear that our discussions would be purely informal and exploratory, that neither government would consider itself committed by their results, and that nothing would be made known publicly of either the fact of our meeting or the tenor of our discussions. I was, perhaps, fitted for this task in a way that most others would not have been, insofar as, knowing the Russian language, I was able to speak with Mr. Malik tête-à-tête, without the presence of interpreters, which avoided the necessity of numerous protocols and simplified problems of security.

Dean Acheson described well and accurately in his memoirs the background of these talks, as well as the degree of success that they may be said to have had.* They took place on June 1 and June 5, 1951. They were successful insofar as they provided the background, unknown to the public at the time, for Malik's statement on June 23, made on a UN radio program, to the effect that

* *Present at the Creation*, pp. 532–533.

the Soviet government believed the Korean conflict could be settled; that the first step would be discussions among the belligerents (of whom the Soviet government, formally, was not one); and that there was a possibility for the success of such a step "if both sides really wished to stop the fighting."

Stimulated by this Soviet initiative, formal talks were, as everyone knows, soon inaugurated. They were long, wearisome, and — from the American and United Nations standpoint — exasperating almost beyond belief. It must have been hard for the American negotiators, at times, to believe that their Korean opposite numbers were animated by any motive other than to drive them from the negotiating table and reopen hostilities. There was, as Mr. Acheson observed, a possibility that things might have gone better had we, for our part, been content to talk in terms of a line of division lying once again along the 38th parallel, instead of one somewhat to the north of it. But here again, for better or for worse, military considerations were allowed to prevail over political ones. Whether for this reason or for others, the talks were sticky and often, from our standpoint, infuriating. Some of our negotiators, had they known of my part in making them possible, would have cursed me for the effort, and I could scarcely have blamed them.

The fact is, however, that the talks did take place. Fighting, for the most part, stopped. Eventually, a new line was established — more favorable, actually, to the South Koreans than the one that had existed before the Korean War began. And while the subsequent maintenance of this line was never for anyone on the non-Communist side a pleasant or easy task, the heavy and largely useless bloodshed that marked the unhappy years 1950–1951 has not yet, mercifully, been renewed.

My own role in all this was, as has been seen, relatively minor. What it amounted to was simply that it fell to me, after unsuccessfully opposing the advance of MacArthur's forces beyond the 38th parallel in 1950, to take a small but not negligible part in steadying down the military when this folly had produced its predictable consequences, and then, once the results of this reverse had been absorbed and the situation stabilized, to take a similar part in easing the transition from open hostilities to a tense and uneasy, but generally workable, armistice. This armistice has endured, with painful strains and stresses, to the present day. It seems to me to have been, despite all the attendant difficulties, preferable to the alternative with which we were then confronted: to press on with hostilities on the Korean peninsula in the pursuit of military and political objectives which, to the extent their realization was approached, would almost certainly have brought the Russians in against us and would probably have assured the outbreak, then and there, of World War III.

If this tale has its morals, they are two. The first is merely the further emphasizing of a lesson that flows from all the other literature surrounding this particular episode in our national history; namely, the terrible danger of letting national policy be determined by military considerations alone. Had the military been given their head (and this goes for the entire combination of MacArthur and the Joint Chiefs of Staff in Washington) — had they not been restrained by the wise discipline exercised, in the face of unprecedentedly savage political opposition, by President Truman, Secretary of State Acheson, and General Marshall — disaster would almost certainly have ensued.

The second moral, illustrated in this case only by Mr. Acheson's memoirs and my own, is the great and sometimes crucial value — so seldom heeded, so difficult perhaps to heed, in American statesmanship — of wholly secret, informal and exploratory contacts even between political and military adversaries, as adjuncts to the overt and formal processes of international diplomacy.

3

The Far East

BEFORE one leaves the subject of the Korean War there is one more aspect of it that deserves mention, particularly because it serves to illustrate the connection between that conflict and the wider problems of American policy in the Far East, as they presented themselves at that time. It is a question not of what happened, or what we should have been doing, during the course of the hostilities in Korea, but rather of the motives and calculations which may have led the Soviet leaders to sanction and support the North Korean attack in the first place.

In the first volume of these memoirs, I included among the various considerations that might have impelled Stalin to authorize this action "our recent decision to proceed at once with the negotiation of a separate peace treaty settlement with Japan, to which the Russians would not be a party, and to accompany that settlement with the indefinite retention of American garrisons and military facilities on Japanese soil." *

In evaluating this statement, it is necessary to recall that in urging, as I had done in 1948 (see pages 393–394 of the first volume of these memoirs), "that no decision be made at that time regarding the possible stationing of American forces in Japan in the period following conclusion of a treaty of peace," I was acting on the

---

* *Memoirs, 1925–1950*, p. 498. Boston: Atlantic–Little, Brown, 1967.

hope "that we would eventually be able to arrive at some general understanding with the Russians, relating to the security of the northwestern Pacific area, which would make this unnecessary." Once internal conditions in Japan had been stabilized, and once the country had been provided with forces adequate to protect against subversion and assure internal security, we might be able to afford, it seemed to me, "to offer to the Russians in effect the withdrawal of our armed forces from the Japanese archipelago (about Okinawa I was not so sure) in return for some settlement that would give us assurance against the communization of all Korea." * With this in mind, I had hoped that we would not press the question of a Japanese peace settlement, and particularly a separate one that would involve the indefinite retention of American bases there, before exploring with the Russians the possibilities for some arrangement to which they could give their assent.

These, as I say, were the hopes I had entertained in 1948, when General Marshall was at the State Department. It would be misleading to say that Dean Acheson, when he became Secretary of State, disagreed with them: he had, I am sure, never heard of them, and I very much doubt that any of the gentlemen in the department's Far Eastern Division was moved to bring them to his attention. I expressed, in the earlier volume of memoirs, my doubt that thoughts so unusual as these ever entered the mind of anyone in the department but myself in those busy months of 1949 and 1950 when the Korean War was in the making;† and to this, Dean (with a twinkle, I am sure, in his eye) cordially assented when he wrote his own reminiscences.‡

It was, then, in consultation with his advisors from the Far Eastern Division and with the British, certainly not with me, that Mr. Acheson came to the conclusion in the autumn of 1949 that it was

---

* *Ibid.*, p. 394.
† *Ibid.*, p. 395.
‡ Dean Acheson, *Present at the Creation: My Years in the State Department*, pp. 429–430. New York: Norton, 1969.

both desirable and urgent to press for the early conclusion of a treaty of peace with Japan regardless of the objections of the Russians and, if necessary, without their consent and participation. The fact that it took nearly a year to bring the Joint Chiefs of Staff to the acceptance of this undertaking changes nothing in the fact that it was the desire and policy of the State Department, in the last months of 1949 and the first months of 1950, to move in this direction.

Dean Acheson took me severely to task in his memoirs (pp. 429–430) for those of my views that I have just described, and particularly for the suggestion that our decision "to proceed with a peace treaty designed to win Japan as an ally" might have had anything to do with the Soviet disposition to unleash their North Korean protégés. The final decision to proceed to such a treaty was not taken in Washington, he pointed out, until three months after the outbreak of hostilities in Korea. How, in these circumstances, could the Russians have anticipated it? And why, he further asked, should anyone have supposed that Soviet policy could be influenced by such "unilateral concessions" as I, implicitly, had advocated?

Each of these points calls out, it seems to me, for an answer. I regret that these answers could not have been given while Dean Acheson was alive, so that they could have had to meet the test of his sharp, skeptical eye and his telling pen. I must give them, nevertheless, asking the reader to bear in mind that this was a test to which they could not be submitted.

I find it hard to accept the suggestion that the Russians should have waited for the final denouement of the State Department's differences with the Pentagon over the timing of our renewed approach for a Japanese peace treaty before drawing their own conclusions as to what was cooking in Washington. I would submit that *by the middle of February 1950*, at the latest (I stress here the element of time), it was clear to all responsible people in Moscow (1) that the treaty for which the State Department was angling was to be a separate one (unless the Russians wished to adhere to something they had never approved and to which they had not been invited to adhere); (2) that this treaty was to mark, or be accompanied by, an arrangement that would turn Japan into a permanent military ally of the United States; (3) that the arrangement would provide for the continued use of the Japanese archipelago by the American armed forces for an indefinite period to come; and (4) that the remaining differences of opinion within the official American establishment in this matter were ones that might at best delay, but would not prevent, the ultimate realization of such a program. The Japanese press was replete in the first months of 1950, as the columns of just the *Nippon Times* will show, with stories that made all this evident. And in his own speech before the National Press Club (January 12, 1950), Mr. Acheson had said that

the defeat and the disarmament of Japan has placed upon the United States the necessity of assuming the military defense of Japan *so long as that is required,* both in the interest of our security and in the interests of the security of the entire Pacific area, and, in all honor, in the interest of Japanese security. . . . I can assure you that there is no intention of any sort of abandoning or weakening the defenses of Japan and that *whatever arrangements are to be made either through permanent settlement or otherwise, that defense must and shall be maintained* *

This language left nothing to be desired in clarity; and there is no reason to doubt that the Russians got the message. "Translated into concrete terms," *Pravda* asserted on January 24, 1950, these words of Mr. Acheson meant "that the American imperialists have settled down in Japan and have no desire to leave it."

A day or so after this *Pravda* statement, the American Joint Chiefs of Staff set out in a body on a tour of American military installations and bases in Japan. That this visit stood in connection with the intention to place many of these facilities on a permanent basis was widely noted in the press, and not ignored in Moscow. In

---

* Italics added by GFK.

Stalin's day, foreign news stories did not appear in the Soviet press unless there was a specific purpose to be served thereby. It was not by accident, therefore, that the Soviet papers carried, on February 4, a Tokyo story on the visit of the Joint Chiefs, specifically citing, as an example of the significance of that visit, the statement of Admiral Decker, commander of the Yokosuka base, to the effect that the US Navy would require that base permanently.

In mid-February 1950, *U.S. News & World Report* carried a two-page spread on the subject of American bases in Japan. The American Chiefs of Staff, it was said here at the outset, had "just left Tokyo with plans for permanent U.S. bases in Japan. At least three air bases, a naval base and an Army headquarters are wanted." The bases in question were then described in detail, and their location was illustrated on a large map which, incidentally, showed South Korea (understandably, in the light of statements made repeatedly by American governmental leaders, of whom Mr. Acheson happened to be one) as lying outside the American defense perimeter. The Yoshida government, it was further stated, was "prepared to cede bases to the U.S. in exchange for a permanent American-Japanese military agreement." In this, to be sure, Yoshida would be faced with heavy internal opposition; but, it was pointed out, the question of "what to expect in Japan" was one that depended, after all, "on decisions made in Washington, not in Tokyo." *

Once again, the Russians were not slow to get the point. The appearance of this article coincided closely in time with the conclusion in Moscow, on February 14, of the Sino-Soviet treaty: the first basic and formal agreement between Soviet Russia and the new revolutionary China, and the fruit of Mao's two-month negotiating sojourn in the Soviet Union. There is good reason to believe that the wording of Article I of that treaty, binding the parties to take measures "for the purpose of *preventing* aggressive action on the

* *U.S. News & World Report,* February 17, 1950, pp. 26–27.

part of Japan *or any other State which should unite with Japan, directly or indirectly, in acts of aggression,*" * was drawn up precisely with a view to the prospect that the status of the United States with relation to Japan was soon to change from that of an occupying power to that of an ally. However that may be, when *Pravda*, two days later, laid down the official Soviet line of interpretation of the Sino-Soviet treaty in a major front-page editorial, it printed significantly in its news columns for the same day a detailed report on the *U.S. News & World Report* story just mentioned, and it included in the editorial comment on the treaty a passage for which the news item was clearly intended to serve as the illustrative basis. Reiterating the charge that the United States was turning Japan into a platform for its own military purposes, the editorial went on to say: "Precisely with this in mind, ruling circles in the USA are delaying the conclusion of a peace treaty with Japan while they search for means of concluding with Japan a separate treaty of such a nature as to give them the possibility of continuing the occupation for an indefinite period and keeping their armed forces there for a longer time." † The very fact of the inclusion of this reference in an editorial of so solemn and important a tenor is adequate proof, for anyone familiar with the practices of the Soviet press, that the question of a Japanese peace treaty was not without relation to the provisions of the Sino-Soviet treaty under discussion. And we may be sure, in turn, that the provisions of that treaty were not without their relevance to the behavior of both of the contracting parties in their policies towards Korea during the decisive months that ensued.

In the weeks that intervened between the conclusion of the Sino-Soviet pact and the outbreak of war in Korea, the Soviet reader was

---

* Italics added by GFK. Note that the word used was "preventing," not "repelling." This should not be lost sight of in judging the motivation of the North Korean attack.

† In talking about the US government's "delaying" conclusion of a treaty, the paper meant, of course, delaying the conclusion, in the Council of Foreign Ministers where the Soviet government was insisting that negotiation of a peace treaty ought to take place, of a general treaty, to which the Soviet government would be a party.

not allowed to forget that the United States was moving towards a military alliance with Japan. On March 19, commenting on Mr. Acheson's reference to the Japanese peace treaty question in his recent Berkeley speech (March 16), and particularly on his charge that it was the Soviet Union that was blocking progress toward such a treaty, *Pravda* pointed out that "it would not be difficult for Mr. Acheson, presumably, to recall his recent statement to the effect that independently of whether there would or would not be signed a treaty of peace with Japan, the USA would not leave Japan in any case."

How it can be suggested, in the light of such statements, that the Russians had to wait until September 1950 to become aware that the United States government was going to make Japan a permanent feature of its own military deployment, is indeed difficult to understand.

It would also be hard for me to agree that what I had in mind, in suggesting the exploration with the Russians of the possibilities of agreement with them on the security problems of the northwestern Pacific region, could properly be defined as "unilateral concessions." I put my views on this point to Mr. Acheson in a memorandum (he referred to it in his book*) of August 21, 1950, three weeks before the President was finally brought to approve the peace settlement that was ultimately concluded. "Our best bet," I wrote,

would be to establish real diplomatic contact with the Russians (this means contact along the lines of the Malik-Jessup talks of last year) aiming at the achievement of something like the following state of affairs: we would consent to the neutralization and demilitarization of Japan (except for strong internal police forces) whereas the Russians would agree to a termination of the Korean war involving withdrawal of the North Korean forces and of our forces and a period of effective United Nations control over Korea for at least a year or two, the UN

* *Present at the Creation*, pp. 445–446.

utilizing for this purpose the nationals and forces only of other Asian countries.

It will be seen that what was being demanded of the Russians under this concept, as a *quid pro quo* for our own consent to Japan's neutralization and demilitarization, was nothing less than the realization of our maximum objectives in the Korean War. That this might have been regarded as an insufficient *quid pro quo*, I could understand; but that it could be viewed as of such total insignificance that any concessions made by us to achieve it could be properly classifiable as "unilateral," * is difficult for me to accept.

Taken as isolated phenomena, these differences of opinion would have little importance today, and would scarcely deserve mention in this account. But they were indicative of matters far more important than the views of any two individuals; and this, I believe, will readily be seen if one proceeds to an examination of the larger issues of American Far Eastern policy with which they were connected.

My own appreciations about the history of American policy in the Far East were actually to be considerably deepened after I left government by the reading done for the lectures at Chicago, and particularly by study of the admirable work of the late president of Yale University, Professor A. Whitney Griswold: *The Far Eastern Policy of the United States.* But even before leaving government, I had given a bit of attention to the history of international relationships in the Manchurian-Korean region and had formed certain views that were destined to be refined, but not essentially changed, in future years.

In the nineteenth century, down to the 1880s, the international position, and indeed the very integrity, of Korea had rested on a very fine and delicate balance of power between the Chinese and the Japanese, which found its expression in both the effective neutralization and isolation of the country. It was an American, Com-

---

* See above, p. 41.

mander Robert W. Schufeldt, who, with the complacent tolerance, if not the blessing, of the United States government, took a major part in shattering this fragile equilibrium by forcing the "opening up" (as the phrase went) of the country to American trade. In doing so, he opened it up in no smaller measure to foreign political penetration and intrigue. Such was the delicacy of the arrangement he helped to destroy that the total number of Chinese officials in Korea, in the period before his action, was exactly one, and of Japanese — none at all. Within a few years after his exploit, the country, being now a political vacuum, aroused both the ambitions and the anxieties of surrounding powers, and became overrun with foreign political agents of one sort or another. Of these, initially, the most numerous were the Japanese. But by the end of the century, the Russians had also emerged as a strong power in the Far East, the Chinese-Eastern Railway was being built across Manchuria to Vladivostok, and Russians now edged out the Chinese in the role of prime competitors to the Japanese for control of Korea.

For some decades to come, this Russian-Japanese struggle would continue, marked by a progressive weakening of the Russian position. This was a consequence of the unfavorable outcome of the Russo-Japanese War, the effects of World War I, and the Russian Revolution. By the 1930s, Japan was supreme and the Russians were in effect expelled as competitors. But as a consequence of China's weakness, the alternative to Japanese power in this region was never — down to World War II — Chinese power, it was Russian power. American statesmen refused to see this. They were legalists; and China was legally the proprietor of Manchuria, even if her power there was a fiction. They were sentimentalists; and China, pictured as poor, noble, grateful for American patronage and admiring of American virtues, was their darling. For forty years, therefore, they exerted themselves to dig the Japanese out of their positions on the mainland, stubbornly convinced that the absence of the Japanese would mean the installation of the Chinese as masters of the situation, believing that this would facilitate an expansion of American opportunities for economic penetration and trade, never consenting to recognize that to get the Japanese out was to let the Russians in.

In the years prior to the Second World War, these efforts related primarily to Japanese positions in Manchuria and China proper. The martial fervor of the war in the Pacific, however — that strange weakness of understanding that causes Americans, once at war, to idealize their associates, to make inhuman demons of their opponents, and to become wholly oblivious to the long-term requirements of any balance of power — impelled us to exploit our victory as a means of removing the Japanese from Korea as well, thus leaving that unfortunate country, insofar as we would not protect it ourselves, at the mercy of the Russians and — within three or four years — of the Russians and Communist Chinese together. Having self-righteously expelled the Japanese from their positions in Korea, we now found ourselves, in the postwar period, faced with the necessity of shouldering the burden they had long borne of containing rival mainland power — once Russian, now Russian and Chinese-Communist combined — on that peninsula.

It was ironic and revealing, I often reflected, that the line which I wished us to try to hold — the 38th parallel — was precisely the line that had been proposed to the Russians by the Japanese special representative at the coronation of the last Tsar, Nicholas II, in 1896, as a demarcation of the Russian and Japanese spheres of influence on the peninsula. Challenged in a military way by Communist puppets in 1950, we had accepted, and borne, the burden of keeping South Korea out of Communist hands. As the Korean War progressed, it became evident that we would be successful, if precariously and uncomfortably so, in holding some line across the center of the peninsula, for at least the time being. But what of the future? Could we, and should we, remain there forever? I did not think so. It was, for us, an unnatural effort, and one that — as the events of 1950 had shown — was not without danger. What, then, could we do?

The first nostalgic thought, of course, was to reintroduce the Japanese. But this was now no longer possible. Japan was demilitarized. The Japanese had been asked, and required, by no one more insistently than by ourselves, to repent of all their previous positions of domination over other peoples. The feeling against them in Korea was so violent as to make their return, even in the role of an ally, unthinkable. And the Korean people deserved, if it could possibly be arranged for them, control over their own affairs.

The ideal, of course, would have been some sort of neutralization of the territory, both political and military. A complete political neutralization, however, was unlikely. For this the Korean Communists were too strong and too well organized as a political faction. They could be driven out of North Korea only by the device General MacArthur, against the warnings of Bohlen and myself, had attempted: i.e., conquest and occupation of the entire country, right up to the Yalu, by American forces. But this, as had now been demonstrated, was bound to affect the vital interests of both Russians and Chinese and bring them both in as military opponents.

One was left, therefore, with the possibility of a military neutralization — a state of affairs, that is, in which political forces might be left to find their own level, even if this had to be by armed strife, but all outside parties, ourselves included, would agree not to occupy portions of the territory or to make use of any of it for their own military purposes. If this could be achieved, even the existence of a Communist regime within the country might not — as the Yugoslav example had shown — be wholly disastrous.

But this, obviously, was something that stood a chance of being considered by the Russians only in the event that we ourselves were not to remain in occupation of Japan. It was idle to expect the Russians not to make whatever military use they could of Korea if we insisted on retaining Japan indefinitely as an extension of our own military deployment. Any understanding on the military neutralization of Korea would have to include a similar neutralization of Japan.

Was this unthinkable? It was, ostensibly, what *had been* American policy. It was what General MacArthur had always previously asked for. It was not necessary for us, he had told me in 1948, to have bases in Japan, provided we could be sure that the Japanese islands would continue to be demilitarized and not armed against us. And if so: well, was there not the possibility of a deal here — at least between ourselves and the Russians? That they were sincere, if misguidedly and unnecessarily so, in regarding the presence of our forces in Japan as a threat to themselves, could not be doubted. Surely they would be willing to pay *some* price to assure our military departure from those islands. Should we not at least explore with them, then, the question as to whether the price they were willing to pay was large enough to include, or to consist of, the agreed demilitarization of Korea as well as Japan?

Dean Acheson would have said, surely: How could you trust the Russians? Their "breaches of inter-allied agreements" had already, as he has observed in his book, begun. How could you be sure that they would not someday come storming back and suddenly reoccupy Korea, and perhaps Japan as well?

These questions, raising as they did issues of a most fundamental nature, were ones destined soon to throw me into conflict not just with Mr. Acheson but with the entire United States government and most of the NATO governments as well, and not just over Pacific problems but even more importantly, over European ones. This is not the place to undertake an exhaustive discussion of these issues. But I might just say this much by way of explanation as to why these counterarguments never commended themselves to me. The reasons were three:

(1) For the Russians, and for Stalin in particular, there were agreements and agreements, just as there were negotiations and ne-

gotiations. Highly specific agreements, relating to military dispositions and control over territory, were more likely to be respected by them than vague subscriptions to high moral principles. Agreements founded in an obvious and concrete Soviet interest of a political and military nature were more likely to be respected than ones based on an appeal to international legal norms or to the decisions of multilateral international bodies. Agreements negotiated quietly and privately, representing realistic political understandings rather than public contractual obligations, were more apt to be respected by Moscow, so long as the other party also respected them, than were agreements arrived at in negotiations conducted in the public eye (the Russians called these *demonstrativnye* negotiations) where the aim was, or appeared to be, to put the other party in a bad light before world public opinion.

(2) I saw no evidence at that time, and have seen none since, of any Soviet desire to assume the burdens of occupation over any extensive territories beyond those that came under their occupation or control as part of the outcome of World War II. Particularly was this true in the Far East. Sanction of the use of puppet forces was another thing, particularly if and when their operation could take place within the framework of a *civil* rather than an *international*, conflict. The Russians, after all, were careful to keep their own forces out of the Korean War. This was not by accident. One could not understand Soviet policy there or anywhere else unless one was ready to recognize and to respect the distinction, as they saw it, between the armed forces of the Soviet Union itself and those of other Communist countries, and the distinction between the use of *Soviet* forces in an *international* conflict and of *puppet* forces in a *civil* conflict. I had never supposed, or claimed, that the Soviet leaders would be reluctant to permit or encourage the latter, if they thought their political interests could be thereby advanced; and what they did in Korea was not, in principle, surprising to me. But this was precisely what was *not* involved in the specter of a

sudden Soviet armed attack on Japan. The likelihood of anything of that sort seemed to me then, and has seemed to me ever since, to be very small indeed.

(3) The sanction against any Soviet military return to Korea could and should have consisted in the possibility of our replying to such a move by the immediate return of our own forces to Japan. Was this militarily impossible? I think not, unless we wished to re- gard it as so. I had pleaded as early as 1947 for "the maintenance of small, compact, alert forces, capable of delivering at short notice effective blows on limited theaters of operation far from our own shores." * It might someday be necessary, I had pointed out, "on very short notice to seize and hold other . . . outlying island bases or peninsular bases on other continents, if only for the purpose of denying them to others during the period required for further mili- tary preparations." †

The American military very much disliked this idea. They ab- horred the concept of limited warfare and were addicted to doing things only in the most massive, ponderous and unwieldy manner. Had we followed this suggestion, however, we would have been far better situated than we actually were to meet the challenge in Ko- rea when it came; and such a force would have had its uses, simi- larly, as a guaranty of the inviolability of any agreement on the demilitarization and neutralization of Japan.

Another reason why I was opposed to the indefinite retention of our bases and forces in Japan was the strain I thought it would eventually impose on American-Japanese relations. I have repeat- edly expressed the distaste with which I viewed large American mil- itary establishments in other countries. This distaste was no doubt exaggerated, but the anxiety over the long-term effects of maintain- ing such establishments abroad was not wholly unfounded. I ex- pressed this anxiety again, in 1950, in connection with the problem

* *Memoirs, 1925–1950*, pp. 311–312.
† I reiterated this recommendation in my memorandum of August 21, 1950, to the Secretary of State.

of the future of Japan. We could not indefinitely, I wrote in the memorandum of August 21,

continue successfully to keep Japan resistant to Soviet pressures by us-ing our own strength as the main instrument in this effort. The only adequate "main instrument" for this, *in the long run,** will be the en-lightened self-interest of the Japanese people, as translated into action by a Japanese government. If we insist on keeping troops in Japan, their presence there will inevitably be a bone of political contention, and the Communists will vigorously make capital of it.

As I look at this statement in the light of what has happened over the intervening twenty-one years, I see that it was exaggerated. We have, just barely, contrived to squeeze through, in the sense of keeping American forces there and preserving the military alliance with Japan without wholly or decisively disrupting the equilibrium of Japanese political life. But the strain has been great. Our military presence has played a major part in polarizing opinion in Japan, and particularly in alienating Japanese youth in the most serious way from moderate and democratic political institutions. One has only to think of the repeated fearful street disorders, and the forced can-cellation of the Eisenhower visit, to realize what a strain this has placed on Japanese democracy during this early trial period of its existence. What the consequences will be of this alienation of the youth, in the further development of Japanese political life, is diffi-cult to say; they could scarcely be good ones.

I have dwelt at length on Korea and Japan. This was the complex of problems that was, in those years of the Korean War, most prominently on my own mind, at any rate, and was the cause of most of the agony of official decision. But views held on Korea and Japan were of course only part of a wider pattern of views on American relations with the Far East generally, and a word is due

---

* Italics added later by GFK.

about the subjects, even then hotly debated, of China and Southeast Asia.

The triumph of the Chinese Communists on the mainland of China was then only two to three years old, and we were still struggling with the problems of policy this development posed for us and the international community. I have described in the first volume of these memoirs the reasons why, though devoid of enthusiasm for the entry of the Chinese Communists into the United Nations, I thought it unwise on the part of our government to oppose their admission. I also shared with my friend John Paton Davies the feeling that it was a great mistake on our part to permit the Chiang regime to establish itself on Formosa. My views were summed up in a memorandum which I drafted (and never used) in September 1951, attempting to define my differences with the Department of State over matters of policy. "As for China," I wrote,

I have no use for either of the two regimes, one of which [that of Chiang] has intrigued in this country in a manner scarcely less disgraceful to it than to ourselves, while the other has committed itself to a program of hostility to us as savage and arrogant as anything we have ever faced. The tie to the Chiang regime I hold to be both fateful and discreditable, and feel it should be severed at once, at the cost, if need be, of a real domestic-political showdown. After that, the less we Americans have to do with China the better. We need neither covet the favor, nor fear the enmity, of any Chinese regime. China is *not* the great power of the Orient; and we Americans have certain subjective weaknesses that make us ill-equipped to deal with the Chinese. . . . I could never see any justification for returning Formosa to China in the first place, nor, once China had been plunged into civil war, any further obligation on our part to do so; and I recommended in 1949 that we reassert the authority of SCAP (i.e., MacArthur's headquarters) over the island and hold it until more satisfactory arrangements could be made.

These views rested on certain impressions about China which need, perhaps, elucidation.

I did not, in the first place, see China as a great and strong power.

Her industrial strength was minimal compared with that of any of the real great powers. Her military strength was formidable only in the immediate vicinity of her own frontiers: she had no amphibious capability. Her ability to accumulate capital was small. Her problem of overpopulation was appalling. Her vast numbers were a source of weakness, not of strength. Time and again I pleaded with my colleagues to believe that, faced with the choice of having as an ally and associate either Japan or China, the Soviet leaders would instantly have chosen Japan: the only place in the Orient where modern weaponry of the most sophisticated sort could be produced in massive quantities, and the only country that had great quantities of industrially trained and highly educated manpower.

Secondly, I looked for no good to come of any closer relationship between the United States and China, even if the existing political antagonism could be overcome. This was why I had no more enthusiasm for the development of our relations with Chiang than I did in the case of the Chinese Communists.

This view reflected no disrespect for the Chinese. On the contrary, I regarded them, and still do, as probably the most intelligent, man for man, of the world's peoples. What inclined me to this outlook was what I had been able to learn of Chinese nationalism and the Chinese tradition of statesmanship from reading in the history of China's international relations.

Three things seemed to me to be reasonably clear. One was that the Chinese were, as a people, intensely xenophobic and arrogant. Their attitude towards the foreigner and his world, based as it was on the concept of China as the "Middle Kingdom" and the view of the foreigner as a barbarian, was essentially offensive to other peoples and did not provide a basis for satisfactory international relations, other than ones of the most distant sort.

Secondly, it was clear that the Chinese, despite the highly civilized nature of their normal outward behavior, were capable of great ruthlessness when they considered themselves to be crossed.

Admirable as were many of their qualities — their industriousness, their business honesty, their practical astuteness, and their political acumen — they seemed to me to be lacking in two attributes of the Western-Christian mentality: the capacity for pity and the sense of sin. I was quite prepared to concede that both of these qualities represented weaknesses rather than sources of strength in the Western character. The Chinese, presumably, were all the more formidable for the lack of them. This was a reason to hold them in a healthy, if wary, respect. It was not a reason to idealize them or to look for any sort of intimacy with them.

Thirdly (and this is in a sense a return to the question of the Chinese view of the outside world) I observed, or thought I did, that while the Chinese were often ready to make practical arrangements of an unwritten nature, and usually ones that could be reversed at will if this suited their purposes, they were never prepared to yield on matters of principle. They would occasionally consent, under pressure, to let you do certain things in practice, but only provided they were permitted to insist that you had no real right to do them at all. They, accordingly, were always theoretically in the right, and you in the wrong. This, too, seemed to me a form of arrogance that augured badly for really good relations with any outside power.

Finally, I was dismayed to note both the skill and the success with which the Chinese had, over the decades, succeeded in corrupting a large proportion of the Americans who had anything to do with them — and particularly those who had resided for longer periods in China. I do not mean to imply that this corruption was always, or even usually, financial. It was far more insidious than that. The Chinese were infinitely adept at turning foreign visitors and residents, even foreign diplomats, into hostages and then, with a superb combination of delicacy and ruthlessness, extracting the maximum in the way of blackmail for giving them the privilege either of leaving the country or remaining there, whichever it was

that they most wished to do. In their exploitation of the situation of
the American missionaries and merchants of the prerevolutionary
period, not to mention the success of the Chiang regime in building
up a violent political claque in this country, the Chinese had made
fools of us all — a thousand times. We, in our sentimentalities, our
bumbling goodwill, our thirst for trade or converts, our political
naïveté, and the ease with which we could be both flattered and
misled by the obsequiousness of talented servants who hated our
guts behind their serving-screens, were simply not up to them.
Reading the history of our relations with China in the last century
and in the first half of this one, I found myself welcoming the Chinese Revolution for the effect it had in bringing about the expulsion
of Western foreigners from China. For the first time in more than a
century, I thought to myself with satisfaction, the Chinese now had
no American hostages. They could now neither make fools of us
through the corruption, nor put pressure on us by the mistreatment, of Americans who had rashly placed themselves in their
power.

For this reason, opposed as I was to obstructing Communist
China's entrance into the United Nations if others wanted it there, I
never favored the conclusion of formal bilateral diplomatic relations
between the United States and China. I could never see the assurance
that American diplomats would be treated in Peking with the respect necessary to make their missions successful. I saw nothing to
be gained by putting people into the power of the Chinese leaders if
we had no assurance that they would not be humiliated and made
sport of for the gratification of the insatiable Chinese thirst for
"face" and prestige. To understand these thoughts one has only to
imagine what would have happened during the so-called Cultural
Revolution — at the time, that is, when the British chargé
d'affaires was being made to stand up in the midst of a screaming
street mob and have his head yanked down by the hair in a forced
gesture of obeisance before the little red book of Comrade Mao —

what would have happened in such a time to an American representative in Peking, had there been one. Yet at no time did I have any desire to see us "ignore" the existence of Communist China. I was well aware that there would be times and occasions when we would have to deal with its leaders. Warsaw, in later years, would strike me as an admirable place for doing just that.

I recognized that the admission of Communist China to the United Nations would create a problem for the Chinese regime on Formosa. I favored the use of our fleet to protect that island (not the regime) from attack by the mainland Chinese. But I never favored our adherence to the view that the Chiang regime was the rightful government of China. My position, even in those early days, was that we should express our readiness to abide by the results of a properly conducted plebiscite offering to the people of the island a choice between submission to the regime on the mainland, return to Japan, or independence — provided only that we could be assured that the island would remain demilitarized, that it would not be armed as a platform for amphibious power in the Pacific, and that, whatever solution was arrived at, those who were opposed to it would be granted an amnesty and an opportunity to emigrate if they so wished. This, in essence, has been my position ever since.

There remains the question of Southeast Asia. This, too, was on our minds, even in 1950 and 1951, though primarily in connection with the question as to the amount of support, if any, that we should give to the French, who were then fighting much the same sort of fight, and against much the same adversary that we, in the years following 1964, found ourselves fighting.

Here, at least, I agreed wholly and unreservedly with Walter Lippmann. We had, I felt, no business trying to play a role in the affairs of the mainland of Southeast Asia. The same went for the French. They had no prospects. They had better get out.

"In Indo-China," I complained to the Secretary of State in the memo of August 21, 1950,

we are getting ourselves into the position of guaranteeing the French in an undertaking which neither they nor we, nor both of us together, can win. . . . We should let Schuman [Robert Schuman, French Foreign Minister] know . . . that the closer view we have had of the problems of this area, in the course of our efforts of the past few months to support the French position there, has convinced us that that position is basically hopeless. We should say that we will do everything in our power to avoid embarrassing the French in their problems and to support them in any reasonable course they would like to adopt looking to its liquidation; but that we cannot honestly agree with them that there is any real hope of their remaining successfully in Indo-China, and we feel that rather than have their weakness demonstrated by a continued costly and unsuccessful effort to assert their will by force of arms, it would be preferable to permit the turbulent political currents of that country to find their own level, unimpeded by foreign troops or pressures, even at the probable cost of an eventual deal between Viet-Nam and Viet-Minh, and the spreading over the whole country of Viet-Minh authority, possibly in a somewhat modified form. We might suggest that the most promising line of withdrawal, from the standpoint of their prestige, would be to make the problem one of some Asian regional responsibility, in which the French exodus could be conveniently obscured.

This judgment with regard to the folly of a possible intervention in Vietnam rested, incidentally, not just on the specific aspects of that situation as we faced it in 1950, but on considerations of principle, as well. In a lecture delivered earlier that year (May 5) in Milwaukee, I had said — this time with reference to the pleas for American intervention in China:

I wonder how many of you realize what that really means. I can conceive of no more ghastly and fateful mistake, and nothing more calculated to confuse the issues in this world today than for us to go into another great country and try to uphold by force of our own blood and treasures a regime which had clearly lost the confidence of its own people. Nothing could have pleased our enemies more. . . . Had our Government been carried away by these pressures, . . . I am confident that today the whole struggle against world communism in both Europe and Asia would have been hopelessly fouled up and compromised.

Little did I realize, in penning these passages, that I was defining, fifteen years before the event, my own position with relation to the Vietnam War.

4

Re-encounter with America

IN the midst of such preoccupations with places and problems on the other side of the globe, I was enjoying, in these initial months and years of release from government, the unaccustomed experience of life and travel in parts of the United States other than the District of Columbia. Except for a Wisconsin boyhood, the undergraduate years at Princeton, and the daily peregrinations between home and office in Washington, I had seen little of this country at any time, and had been absent from it over most of the past quarter of a century. The impressions, therefore, were vivid; and impinging, as they did, on the characteristic longing of the expatriate to find something with which he could identify himself, they struck deep. But I find it difficult to generalize about them or to compress them into any analytical system. Dates, scenes and events become chronologically indistinct and swim in memory. The thoughts and reflections then aroused tended in the ensuing years to flow, like tributaries of a river, into that broad stream of curiosity, wonderment and concern about the state of one's own country that has dominated the consciousness of every thoughtful American in recent years; and I find it impossible, except where some record of the moment has survived, to distinguish between what I then thought and what I think today.

I can do no more, therefore, than to recall certain disconnected episodes that remain in memory with special vividness — either because of their novelty or because some record of them has survived, and leave it to the reader to distill from them, if he can, an idea of what it was like to rediscover bits and pieces of one's own country in circumstances of this nature.

Before mentioning these episodes, I should, I suppose, say something about the places where, after the retirement from government, we lived. During the years of official service the family had inhabited only a succession of temporary quarters, sometimes provided by the government, sometimes rented by ourselves. Now, for the first time, it fell to us to live in places that we owned; and these places came to play, like long-term friends, an enduring role in our lives. There were two of them: a house in Princeton and a farm in Pennsylvania, and since both still exist and continue to play a part in our lives, I must speak of them in the present tense.

The Princeton house is a sturdy, spacious turn-of-the-century structure standing, amid ample grounds, on one of those shady, sycamore-lined streets, once quiet and still beautiful, that are peculiar to Princeton. Battered and neglected when we bought it, this house has responded gratefully to the attentions of the years, and has afforded us a comfortable, reliable and pleasant shelter. Having evidently experienced, over the seventy years of its existence, only the normal vicissitudes of family life, it is devoid of ghosts and sinister corners. To us, personally, it is friendly and receptive in a relaxed way, but slightly detached, like a hostess to a casual guest — as though it did not expect us to stay forever.

The place in Pennsylvania is a large, rich river-valley farm in what was, when we first came there, unspoiled farming country, a hundred and fifty miles from Princeton, west of the Susquehanna. It forms, almost to the mile, a part of the western border of the magnificent Pennsylvania Dutch farming country that stretches, to the east of it, nearly to Philadelphia. Just west of it begin the foot-hills of the Appalachians, orchard country, not so fertile as that which lies to the east, and no longer populated by Germans — these latter knew too well where the good land lay. Standing on the higher rises of our fields, on a fine summer day, one can see in the distance the shadowy outlines of the mountains: the northern outrunners of the Blue Ridge, reaching up from Virginia and Maryland.

The place was, and still precariously remains, a proper farm. To reach it, you take a turn south off a secondary hard road and drive straight on for nearly a mile along a gravel lane, between tilled fields, but with hills and patches of woods in the distance. Finally, there is a little stone bridge beyond which the road turns left and runs, now lined with willows on one side and sycamores of my own planting on the other, for a hundred yards or so along the side of a small stream, dry in summer. Then it turns right again and pro-ceeds, up a slight rise between two houses, to a large circle, rimmed with farm buildings. The house on the right is a standard two-story wooden farmhouse of twentieth-century vintage. There the farmer and his family live. The structure on the left is something quite different: a three-story edifice, studded with balconies and sleeping porches, looking, particularly from that angle, like nothing more than a summer hotel.

It is indeed a house like none other, not exactly ugly, but large for that region with its eighteen rooms and eighty-odd windows, and enigmatically, engagingly, almost apologetically, absurd. Once, long ago in the dusk of a winter evening, a local inhabitant, who had given me a lift on the road, kindly undertook to drive me all the way home. Startled to see this structure suddenly looming up in the shadows, he practically stopped the car in his astonishment and, be-ing unaware of where we were, turned to me in wonderment and said: "Now tell me, who in the name of hell would want a house like that?"

Well, we did, and still do. Turning its backside to the circle where everyone arrives, decorated with portico and columns on the side where nobody normally ever goes in and out, entered customarily by a wholly unembellished side door which leads — for no reason at all — directly into the dining room, the house is indeed an absurdity. Yet imbedded in all these incongruities is still the corpus of a hundred-and-sixty-year-old farmhouse; and its interior, once one gets there, is of a coziness, a harmony, and a natural sociability that is the mark of a real, well-worn, intimate home. Never, I think, has any of us, arriving there from anyplace else, entered the house without pleasure. And never, even on the grayest, darkest, sloppiest days of winter, have I had occasion to say to myself, while there: "Oh, what a dreary place."

Across the circle from the house lies the great barn, built in the traditional Pennsylvania Dutch style, a hundred and ten feet by forty, with the usual overhang (the "foreshot," to the natives) covering a brick walk along the southern side, by the barnyard. In the dim recesses of the ground floor of this building, divided into a number of aisles and stalls, there resides — in amicable harmony for the most part — a dense population of animal and wild life: cows, steers, young stock, the bull (referred to by the farmer's family, in a marvelous bit of country understatement, as "cross"), cats, kittens, mice and rats, often a dog or two, sometimes a horse or pony (the place once harbored sixteen mules), and occasionally a huge, parturiating sow, not to mention the barn swallows that swoop in and out when the doors of the milking stable are left open. The barn envelops all these beings in its strong and sheltering arms; and the deep cushion of fresh straw that covers all its floors accommodates agreeably and without offensiveness, by the very power of its bacterial balance, the manifold functions and products of their daily lives. Above all this is, of course, what is called the "barn floor": a vast, lofty chamber, entered by the banked driveway. Here, too, it is dark; but when your eyes get used to the dim light you see that stacks of baled straw and hay reach mountainously upward, to the roof; and in the spaces between them slivers of sunlight, striking down from cracks in the wall or the roof, give to the dusty air the quality of the interior of a cathedral. There is the pungent, life-giving smell of hay and manure; and it is cozy and reassuring to hear the rustling and stomping and munching of the cattle, in their pens below.

Around this cluster of buildings stretch, of course, the fields, heavy in summer with their crops of grain and grass, wet, fallow, often partly snow-covered, in the winter months. On summer nights there is a thick pageant of fireflies over the meadow, the steady, soothing and faintly mysterious ringing of the crickets, a croaking of bullfrogs from the nearby pond and stream, and occasionally the harsh cry of a startled pheasant. In winter, when snow is in the air, crows — thousands and thousands of them — move in seemingly endless procession from northeast to southwest, their flapping figures silhouetted against leaden skies.

These, then, were the points of departure and return for many journeys to other places in the country; and it was from these journeys that the most vivid impressions were gained.

In the late winter of 1950 I made a journey to Latin America. It was an official journey; but departure from government was imminent; inwardly, I already had a foot out of Washington. I began the journey by traveling from Washington to Mexico City by train. (A few of us, in those days, still did that sort of thing.) I have notes of that leg of the journey, written at the time. Let the reader picture the author of these notes, if he will, as a middle-aged man, a bit weary from three hectic years in the Washington bureaucracy, somewhat *dépaysé* and sensitive to the impressions of his native land as only such a person can be, longing for familiarity and reassurance, gulping down every drop of it, in fact, as a thirst-struck wanderer in the desert might gulp down water suddenly encountered, but wincing, as though struck by a blow, under every small discouragement.

Saturday, February 18, 1950

The train pulled out of the Union Station into the early darkness of the February evening, carrying a traveler who felt slightly silly to be embarking, at his age, on so long and spectacular a voyage — to be abandoning the solemn legitimacy of the routine of the department — to be leaving his family for so long — to be imagining that he could see anything or learn anything in the course of such a tour which others had not seen or learned before him.

A couple of hours later, the train was passing through York, Pennsylvania. The traveler's farm home, he reflected, was only sixteen miles away, off there to the west, across the winter darkness. It would be quiet there, now. Annie and Merle would have finished the evening chores, and had supper. It being Saturday evening they would probably have gone to town. No lights would be on about the place. The night would be cold, for the sky was clear. No domestic animals would be out. Even the cats would have crept into the barn for comfort. Only the old drake would be standing, motionless, on the concrete water trough in the barnyard, his white silhouette gleaming ghostlike in the darkness, a tragic, statuesque figure, contemptuous of the cold, of the men who neglected him, of the other birds and beasts who basked in the warmth of human favor — contemptuous even of the possibility for happiness in general, human or animal. He would be standing there through the hours of darkness; and the crisp silence of winter night would be about the place; and there would be only the crunching and stomping of animals in the barn behind him, the rustling of some wild thing down in the meadow, the drone of a distant truck, and perhaps the sudden and thunderous rumbling occasioned by my neighbor B's car, as it rattled — homebound — over the loose planks of the little bridge in the valley below.

Well, the train was moving on, now — increasing with every minute the distance between us, soon destined to become so great. Might God help us all, I thought. . . .

Sunday, February 19

I woke up early, raised the curtain in the berth, and looked out. We were crossing a river. It was just the beginning of a Sabbath dawn. The half-light reflected itself in the oily scum of the water, left in kindly obscurity a desolation of factories and cinder-yards and railroad tracks along the shore, but caught and held, in its baleful gleam, the cold mute slabs of skyscrapers overhead. It was the business district of some industrial city: what city I did not know, nor did it matter.

And it occurred to me that for cities there is something sinister and pitiless about the dawn. The farm, secure in its humility and its submission, can take it. It can even welcome it, joyously, like the return of an old friend. But the city, still sleeping, cowers restlessly under it, particularly under the Sabbath dawn. In this chill, calm light, the city is helpless and, in a sense, naked. Its dreams are disturbed, its pretense, its ugliness, its impermanence exposed, its failure documented, its verdict written. The darkness, with its neon signs, its eroticism, and its intoxication, was protective and forgiving — tolerant of dreams and of delusions. The dawn is judgment: merciless and impassive.

. . . . .

The train was moving through the approaches to St. Louis, just east of the Mississippi: a grim waste of crisscrossing railroads, embankments, viaducts, junk lots, storage lots, piles of refuse, and the most abject specimens of human habitation.

A tall and youthful individual, nattily dressed, with a thin neck, big ears, and an obvious freedom from inhibition, calmly inspected the labels on my suitcases and launched on an interrogation beginning: "Say, are you the fellow who . . . ?" To that beginning, he tacked on a series of confused associations, too close to reality to be wholly denied, too far from it to be flatly admitted. Having finally extracted from me enough to satisfy his surmises, he started in with questions about foreign affairs — China in particular.

I took refuge in counter-questions, and discovered that he was a politician: a member of the Missouri State Legislature. He had just been to Washington for the Jefferson-Jackson Day dinner. He was a veteran, and had been encouraged by friends to enter politics when he returned from war service. I tried to get at his views and interests, but failed to find that he stood for anything in particular except himself, or that he held any particular convictions about how life ought to be lived, as distinct from the way it is lived now, in the State of Missouri. One had the impression of a certain bewildered complacency, and of a restless, vacuous curiosity about people who got their names in the papers.

I tried to find out what he knew about regional planning. He *had* heard of the Missouri Valley Authority project, as a political issue; but when I asked him where the Missouri entered the Mississippi, he was stumped, and thought, in fact, that it was the Missouri we were about to cross. With difficulty, I explained to him why it would not be possible for us to cross the Missouri before we had crossed the Mississippi, and he thought he understood.

In the Fred Harvey restaurant of the St. Louis station there were nostalgic murals of old river scenes. Canned music (*The Rustic Wedding*) mingled with the clatter of dishes, the shrill cries of waitresses, and the murmur of a cross-section of that rich stream of oral exchange which embellishes and characterizes the life of the Midwest: "Yessir, the President of our company is only forty-four. . . . We got five o' the best girls in the business. . . . They put him in the hub-nut division, an' he warn't there more'n a month before the others went to the old man and said if he stayed there they'd all quit. . . . I'm goin' to eat kinda light, today. . . . Eleanor'll run for President, sure as you know. . . . The Hub Ice Fuel Company is a big company; you move at a fast pace over there. . . . First time I ever seen a woman walkin' along towin' a cat; the cat ain't used to it, don't know what to make of it. . . . Now what on earth d'ya suppose he's goin' to do with that nightgown? . . ."

Outside the station, a pale winter sunshine — Sunday afternoon sunshine — fell on the blank fronts of the station-district joints: Pop's Pool Hall; Hotel Rooms $1.50 and up; Danny's Tavern; Pressing and Cleaning While-U-Wait; Julio's Place.

I caught a bus in the direction of the river. Infected by the customs of the nation's capital, it also sported canned music (*Rose Marie*).

The last two or three blocks had to be covered on foot. There were solid rows of saloons and rooming houses, and seedy-looking men slouching in front of the windows of the closed stores, leaning against the walls, in the sunshine, waiting. (What are they waiting for? What are they looking for? What is it they expect will happen in this died-out street in downtown St. Louis on a Sunday afternoon in winter? That a girl will pass? or that there will be a fight? or that some drunken bum will get arrested? Could be, could be . . .)

Here was the Court House — mid-XIX Century style: heavy stone, tall blank windows. In it, the placard said, the Dred Scott case was tried. Beyond the Court House — parking lots, and the great cobbled incline toward the river. The lower part of it, near the water, was covered with mud which looked dry but was really slimy; and there was an occasional stick of driftwood.

On this particular afternoon, the riverbank was inhabited by six stray dogs, a bum who sat on a piece of driftwood and held one of the dogs in his lap, two small colored children with a bag of popcorn, and a stranger from Washington who sat on another piece of driftwood and sketched a cluster of four abandoned craft tied up by the shore: to wit, one scow with gasoline drums, one dredge, one dirty motorboat, and one genuine old showboat, still in use but slightly self-conscious. The colored children hovered over my shoulder, chattering pleasantly and dropping popcorn down my neck as they watched the progress of the drawing. The faint sunshine slanted in upon us, across the rooftops. Railroad trains clattered along both sides of the river and across the high bridge upstream. A gull came ashore to dabble in the slime between the cobblestones. And the river moved lazily past: a great slab of dirty-gray water, gleaming here and there in the sunshine, curling and eddying and whispering quietly to itself as it went along.

I walked back through the old business district: a district of narrow, dark streets, of sooty, fortress-like bank buildings, and hotels which once were elegant. (The trouble with American cities is that they have grown and changed too fast. The new is there before the old is gone. What in one era is functional and elegant and fashionable survives into the following era as grotesque decay. These cities have never had time to clean up after themselves. They have never had time to bury their dead. They are strewn with indecent skeletons, in the form of the blighted areas, the abandoned mansions of the Gay Nineties, the old railroad and water-front vicinities, the "houses by the railroad tracks.")

On the train from St. Louis to Texas the lounge car had canned music (*Ave Maria*) emerging from somewhere in the roof. We used to say: "The customer is always right." But what of the man, today, who doesn't like *The Rustic Wedding* or *Rose Marie* or *Ave Maria*, or who has heard them too often, or who doesn't like music at all through loudspeakers, or who doesn't like music? I raised this question in my mind, as I fled back to the sleeping car; and the wheels of the train, which used to clatter in so friendly and reassuring a way on the railroad voyages of my boyhood, seemed to be clicking off the words: "That-to-you; that-to-you; that-to-you."

Monday, February 20

On the sleeping car from San Antonio to Mexico City, I was seated across from a gentleman from Indiana, with spouse. Feeling deeply disloyal to my own Midwestern origin, I found that I could take no pleasure in any of my neighbor's characteristics. Neither the penetrating voice which boomed relentlessly through the cars in the service of an unquenchable loquaciousness, nor the toothpick which never left his mouth except at mealtimes (I'm sure he slept with it), nor his breezy curiosity about the rest of us ("What-cha carryin' that ink around fur?"), nor the incessant talk with fellow Indianians about things back home ("Yeah, I remember him; he used to run the bank at New Cambridge; and his uncle had a real estate business over at Red City"), nor the elaborate jokes with said fellow countrymen about marriage ("Now I'll tell you what you want to do: you and your wife git in that there berth with your clothes on, and then when she kicks you out, you ain't in such a fix, he, he, he.") — none of these characteristics excited my local pride. Why, I found myself muttering, did he come to Mexico if all he wanted to talk about was Indiana? And why, in general, do people have to act like caricatures of their own kind?

About one year after this visit to Latin America it fell to me to deliver a series of lectures in Chicago. It was, as I recall it, at just the time of General Douglas MacArthur's recall and dismissal — an event which fell with special traumatic effect on the Chicago of that day, with its congenital isolationism, its anti-Europeanism, and its strong immersion in the anti-Communist hysteria of the time. All of this heightened, for me, the poignancy of the experience.

To explain how I came to give these lectures, I have to return for a moment to the ideological problems of American foreign policy.

I had been struck, in my work as head of the Planning Staff, by the chaos that prevailed in official Washington circles when it came to such things as concept and principle in the formulation of foreign policy. No two people had the same idea of what it was that we were trying to achieve, and such assumptions as the various individuals entertained on the subject tended to be superficial, emotionally colored, and inspired by a desire to sound impressive to other American ears rather than by any serious attention to the long-term needs of our own country and the world community. In such casual reading on American diplomatic history as I had had occasion to do while in government, I had been struck by the contrast between the lucid and realistic thinking of early American statesmen of the Federalist period and the cloudy bombast of their successors of later decades. I wanted now to leaf through the annals of American diplomacy and to try to ascertain on what concepts of national interest and national obligation, as related to foreign affairs, the various American statesmen had operated.

Pursuing this quest at Princeton, I was surprised to discover how much of our stock equipment, in the way of the rationale and rhetoric of foreign policy, was what we had inherited from the statesmen of the period from the Civil War to World War II, and how much of this equipment was utopian in its expectations, legalistic in its concept of methodology, moralistic in the demands it seemed to place on others, and self-righteous in the degree of high-mindedness and rectitude it imputed to ourselves. I set out, then, to spell all this out in a series of essays addressed to the various undertakings and initiatives in which these tendencies had manifested themselves: notably, the inordinate preoccupation with arbitration treaties, the efforts towards world disarmament, the attempt to outlaw war by the simple verbiage of the Kellogg Pact, and illusions about the possibilities of achieving a peaceful world through international organization and multilateral diplomacy, as illustrated in the hopes addressed to the League of Nations and the United Nations. I endeavored to show how successive statesmen had sought, in these ostensibly idealistic and pretentious undertakings, a concealment for our failure to have a genuine foreign policy addressed to the real problems of international relations in a changing world — how all these vainglorious and pretentious assertions of purpose, in other words, had served as unconscious pretexts for the failure, in fact the inability, to deal with the real substance of international affairs.

Rough drafts of these essays were completed during the year and a half that I spent in Princeton immediately after leaving government — they repose in my files today in a thick black binder marked, with exaggerated modesty: "Notes for Essays." But many of the ideas evolved in this way did eventually find expression of a sort, as a rule by the acceptance of lecture engagements for which one had to find, at the last moment, something to say. It was in this way that I was launched on the prolonged, and to this day unfinished, polemic about the role of morality in foreign policy.

Before leaving government, and in fact nearly a year in advance of the event, I had been asked by the University of Chicago to deliver, in the spring of 1951, the series of lectures given annually there under the sponsorship of the Charles B. Walgreen Foundation. It was the first time I had been thus approached with such a suggestion, and knowing that by the spring of 1951 I would be on leave of absence from government, I lightheartedly accepted and put the matter, for many months, quite out of my mind.

When the time approached for the journey to Chicago and I was compelled to reflect on what I should talk about, I decided I would base the lectures on the subject of my incompleted essays about American diplomacy and discuss a few episodes in the annals of our diplomatic history that would illustrate some of the conclusions at which I had arrived. I therefore sat down and batted out some thoughts on the Spanish-American War, as an example of superficiality in concept as well as of the power of chauvinistic rhetoric and war hysteria; on the Open Door episode, as an example of the gap between public understanding of our statesmanship and the reality of its achievements; and on our Far Eastern policy of the first half of the present century generally, as an example of the application of legalistic and moralistic concepts in the judgment of other peoples' affairs; I also set down some preliminary notes on American diplomacy in the First World War, as an example of the lack of consistent principles and objectives in foreign policy, and of the extraordinary effect that wartime emotionalism could have on our concepts of purpose. This last I showed to my colleague at the Institute, the late Ed Earle. He was a bit shaken, I suspect, both by the boldness of the approach and by the far-reaching implications of the conclusions — all of it coming, or intended to come, from the lips of one not greatly erudite in the subject matter; and the result was that he did me a great favor by bringing together a small group of highly qualified diplomatic historians, including Arthur Link and Richard Leopold, to take the draft under critical scrutiny. This they did, gently but unsparingly; and while none of them, I am sure, would have agreed entirely with the final conclusions, they made of the lecture a much better one than it would otherwise have been.

Armed, then, with three lectures and notes for a fourth (the remaining ones of the intended six I thought I could work up on the spot), I departed for Chicago, little suspecting how deeply, and for how many years to come, I was about to commit myself.

I find in my notes a record of the arrival in Chicago, again by train, on a Sunday afternoon in early April 1951.

The train got in at 1:00 P.M. I had had some discomfort on the train, and had eaten no lunch.

There was a milky sunshine here, but it was still pre-spring, in contrast to the East.

The taxi, battered and dirty, pounding south on the Outer Drive in the broad stream of Sunday afternoon traffic, brought me to a huge hotel on the drive, in the South Side. Viewed more closely from the pedestrian's angle, the hotel was a great brick box, trimmed with some stone casing and metal ornamentation on the ground floor, for elegance' sake. It gave an impression of shaggy, besooted ornateness, springing like a mushroom out of a sea of cinder lots, traffic, filling stations, and long streets of one-floor brick saloons.

Late in the afternoon I went for a walk. I went first over to a point on the lakefront. It was a little park, with lawns, a stone administration house and public toilet, and an embankment braced by tiers of great concrete blocks against the attacks of the lake. At the stone building two soldiers were picking up a couple of sloppy little teen-agers in blue jeans and flowing shirt-tails. The girls, hardly more than thirteen, leaned against the wall, chewed gum, and spewed profanity at their admirers. A boy on the top of the embankment busily hurled fist-sized rocks at another boy below him. Had they hit him, they could have split his skull. I was moved to stop the operation but, recalling the family's embarrassment over any such public interventions on my part, refrained, reminding myself that it is no doubt the privilege of the younger generation to kill each other in public places, particularly in Chicago. . . . On the south side of the point, students were ensconced on the steps of the embankment, sunning themselves and reading. One was reading the *New Yorker*. Above them, on the lawn, a young man and his girl friend were trying to take pictures of each other and she was staggering around, so you couldn't tell whether she was hilarious or just drunk.

I left the lake and went inland. The streets were dirty. Only the saloons and drugstores and the flashiest motorcar sales agencies were open. You met men with no hats, blue overcoats, no ties, hair uncombed, shoestrings dragging. They all looked as though they had hangovers. On a street corner, three older men stood silent and motionless, staring up a side street. I looked, too, but could not see what they were staring at.

Having had no lunch, I went into a drugstore, thinking I ought to get something to eat. The soda fountain counter was wet and dirty. There was no one serving. A man was pushing litter off the floor with a wide push-broom. I waited until his little heap of paper cups, cellophane wrappers and cigarette butts had passed under my feet. Then I gave up and went back to the hotel. On the way, I thought of the things I had seen, and of the *Chicago Tribune* I had been reading in my room. It had had, among other things, an article on communism at Harvard. I remembered that my grandfather and my mother had come from this town. I heard some boys on bicycles screaming at each other across the street, and I realized that even the language was unfamiliar to me.

So I shuffled back to the hotel, in the depression born of hunger plus an overpowering sense of lack of confidence in my surroundings; and a small inward voice said, gleefully and melodramatically: "You have despaired of yourself; now despair of your country!"

I feel apologetic in reproducing these depressing images of first encounters with my native Middle West. They were, I must point out, impressions only of the façade of its life — the external shell which the stranger sees. They were balanced, of course, by more positive ones, particularly when things were viewed from within and not from without. As will be seen presently, the Chicago lectures themselves afforded me no grounds for feeling myself repelled — at least not by the youth of that time. The very despair of these reactions to the impact of Midwestern life was a reflection of the fact that I knew myself to be back in the only part of the world to which I truly belonged — a part of the world which, in memory, I loved as one can love only the place in which one grew up. I believed then deeply in the Middle West, and still do — in its essential decency, its moral earnestness, its latent emotional freshness. I viewed it, and view it now, as the heart of the moral strength of the United States. This was precisely why I was so sensitive to its imperfections. Increasingly, under the impressions of this and other visits in midcentury, I came to see this native region as a great slatternly mother, sterile when left to herself, yet immensely fruitful and creative when touched by anything outside herself. But was this not, I often asked myself, the character and function of all these regions, everywhere across the world, that would respond to the French meaning of the term "province"? How much of artistic creativity had to be laid, after all, in all times and places, to the superimposition of the excitement of the jaded metropolis onto the bored receptivity of the "province"?

The lectures at the University of Chicago began in a large, square room, a sort of student lounge, lacking, as I recall it, even a proper dais. Respectable even at the start, attendance grew most unexpectedly. With the third lecture, students were already sitting in droves on the floor and in the aisles and spilling out into the corridors. The proceedings were then moved, unavoidably, to a large auditorium capable of holding many hundreds of people. This largely ruined the oral effectiveness of the lectures. In the smaller room, I had been able to talk to the students directly and personally, almost as though we were in conversation. In the auditorium I was separated from them by a great distance and could make myself apparent to them only as a remote silhouette and a canned, electrified voice. Attendance, however, held up; and I was surprised, delighted, and yet in a sense sobered, by the success of the undertaking. For the first time in my life, I experienced the excitement and satisfaction of teaching and could understand why, for many people, this could be reward enough to make a life.

Seriously unprepared — because I had taken the whole thing far too casually — I managed by frantic effort to keep up with the writing and editing of the lectures until it came to the very last one. This, as of the dawn of the day of delivery, I had not yet written at all. The publishers (the University of Chicago Press), discovering this and fearful lest I get out of town without delivering a text, now claimed their own. Ignominiously, in the course of the morning, I was summoned to the offices of the Press and there, in a great office room clattering with a dozen typewriters, and with my letter of acceptance lying reproachfully before me, I was put to work to produce some sort of publishable document.

Only one who has faced many lecture audiences knows, I suspect, that peculiar sense of tension and desperation that can overcome the unprepared lecturer as the hour for the lecture inexorably draws nearer and his mind is whipped by the realization that within so and so many minutes he must get up there and say *something*, but does not yet know what he wants to say. So deeply has this state of panic seared my consciousness that I continue even now, when lecturing is a matter of the past, to relive it as a recurrent nightmare. Never did I experience it more keenly than on that morning in Chicago. But I should have been even more shaken had I known that certain of the prose I was producing amid the cacophony of this unusual setting would continue to pursue me, and compel me to live with it, through decades to come. For the little volume that emerged from this exercise, appearing in the autumn of 1951 under the title of *American Diplomacy 1900–1950,* was destined, as it happened, to have a sale more enduring than anything I was ever to write. Over the course of at least twenty years into the future, edition after edition of it, in hardcover and paperback, would come off the presses. Royalties, never overwhelming but seldom unsubstantial, would continue year by year to roll in, to the gratification, but almost to the embarrassment, of the startled author. Most of this may be attributed, I suppose, to the fact that the volume, precisely because of the casualness with which it was conceived, met the needs of several thousand teachers of American history, anxious to find for their students some easy collateral reading on foreign policy in the present century. It was, in any case, the real beginning of an academic career.

At some point, in the years in question, I had what was for me the unusual experience of being asked to run for public office, and nearly doing so. One night in late winter (I had, as it happened, just returned from Washington), the doorbell rang at the Princeton house. It was a young farmer and his wife from our section of Pennsylvania. They had driven all the one hundred and fifty miles, on the chance of seeing me, and were planning to return that same evening. They and some of their neighbors, they told me, were unhappy about the candidates who were probably going to be nominated in the primary for election to the federal House of Representatives. Would I consider running?

I had never had anything to do with either political party. I was in fact incapable of recognizing any very significant difference between them. I was obliged to ask him which party they had in mind. It turned out to be the Democrats. It would have made no difference to me had it been the other one.

I was much moved by the spontaneity and sincerity of the approach, and said I would consider it. I phoned, when my guests had left, to a friend who was a prominent attorney in the county seat of Gettysburg, and told him what had happened. He listened with astonishment and said he would call me back. He did so, the same evening. Was I, he asked, seriously interested? Time was short.

Somewhat taken aback, but feeling it practically a civic duty to serve when one was asked in such a way to do so, I said I was interested. "All right," was the response. "Be in my office, here in Gettysburg, at three o'clock on Sunday afternoon."

On Sunday afternoon, I presented myself as requested. Some twenty or thirty gentlemen had assembled — all the Democratic leaders of that congressional district, I was told, except those of the city machine in York, who had their own ideas. I spoke briefly about the origins of the suggestion of my candidacy, and about how I would view my campaign, if nominated. There then ensued, in my presence, with myself sitting silently by, a discussion of my suitability for this venture — a discussion which, for its total and not unfriendly frankness, positively delighted my heart. It ranged all the way from skeptical and strongly negative sentiments ("Why, he ain't even registered as a Democrat." "Yeah, but his wife is.") to enthusiastically positive ones ("Why hell, we could run him for the Senate.")

In the end, the positive voices prevailed, and I was given the blessing of those present to proceed with registration as a candidate. I drove to Harrisburg, for this purpose, a day or so later, with the county chairman, and received from him much good advice, including one admonition which, I thought, had wider application than just to candidates for the House of Representatives. We were driving back to my home after the registration. I was doing the driving, and when stopping dutifully at a stop sign, I said to him something to the effect that since I was now a candidate I supposed I would have to be very careful how I drove. He turned and put his hand on my knee. "Listen," he said, in dead seriousness, "I want to tell you something. If you're a drinkin' man, keep on drinkin'. If you're chasin' women, keep on chasin' women. They're goin' to know it anyway."

Even before registering, I had worried about the costs of campaigning. I read the laws, state and federal, on campaign expenditures, and was somewhat uneasy as a consequence. But I thought that perhaps I could swing it out of my own pocket. On return to Princeton, however, I was horrified to learn that neither of the two organizations which had been financing my life and work in Princeton, the Institute for Advanced Study and the Rockefeller Foundation, was prepared to continue to do so if I remained a candidate for public office. Both were afraid of beng accused of financing political activity, and thus losing their tax exemption. Although both had been advised of my intention before I went out to register, neither had been able to arrive at a final decision until after the registration was completed.

All this was only around the end of March. Even if elected, I would not begin to receive salary as a congressman before the following January. I had almost no income aside from these two institutions. I did have one child in college and another in a private school. It was impossible to see where, in this nine-month interval, the money for this, and for our own lives, not to mention the campaign, would come from. Consultation with knowledgeable people out in the congressional district elicited only the suggestion that in circumstances such as this, one would normally turn to some of the big dairy owners or other local tycoons who happened to be Democrats and solicit their support for the campaign. This I was decidedly disinclined to do. Obviously, acceptance of support from these quarters would deprive my status as an independent of all meaning.

Reluctantly, therefore, and feeling an awful fool for it, I withdrew my candidacy. But the lesson was a severe one. I have since believed that the best solution would be to arrange matters in such a way that a man without independent means could run for office without losing his normal sources of income and without having to dive into his own pocket. But so long as this is not possible, one must be grateful to have men of private means holding public office. They are at least above the temptations of petty corruption, and can exercise whatever office they hold without having to give heed to the problem of how they are going to live when they have completed it. I had often thought, in the years of foreign service, that no one should be in the Foreign Service who was not in a position, financially or otherwise, to tell the government to go to hell if the demands made upon his conscience exceeded the point of no return. Even more must this be true, I now thought, in the field of politics.

Service as a part-time consultant to the Ford Foundation necessitated, in those years, occasional trips to Southern California. I had never been in California before, with the exception of one brief speaking tour in 1946. The first impressions, once again, were vivid and disconcerting.

Pasadena, Nov. 4, 1951

I have today that most rare of luxuries: a day of complete leisure, with no obligations, away from home where not even family or house or neglected grounds can lay claim to attention. I am out here for three days on business and am the guest of a friend whose home, swaddled in gardens, looks down from the hill on the roof-tops and foliage of Pasadena. It is strange, and somewhat enervating, after watching the death of the year in the growing austerity of the east-coast autumn, to sit now in a garden, to listen to the chirping of birds and the tinkling of a fountain, to watch the foliage of the eucalyptus trees stirring in a summer breeze, and to feel the warm sunshine on the back of one's neck.

It is Sunday, and I am apparently being left to my own devices — than which nothing could please me more.

I have learned that whenever pressure is suddenly removed from me, it does not leave me serene and contemplative. On the contrary, the fragments of thought surge back and forth in my mind aimlessly and futilely. There is a feeling of empty agitation, and the attention flits distractedly around the chambers of experience and impression, like a restless person in a house, touching objects here and there for no reason at all. Peace of mind and serenity, like most other human attributes, are apparently matters of habit.

My thoughts are full of this Southern California world I see below me and about me. It is easy to ridicule it, as Aldous Huxley and so many other intellectuals have done — but it is silly, and a form of self-condemnation to do so. These are ordinary human beings: several million of them. The things that brought them here, and hold them here, are deeply human phenomena — as are the stirrings of anxiety that cause them to be so boastful and defensive about it. Being human phenomena, they are part of ourselves; and when we purport to laugh at them, as though we stood fully outside of them, it is we who are the ridiculous ones.

I feel great anxiety for these people, because I do not think they know what they are in for. In its mortal dependence on two liquids — oil and water — which no individual can easily produce by his own energy, even together with family and friends, the life of this area only shares the fragile quality of all life in the great urban concentrations of the motor age. But here the lifelines of supply seem to me particularly tenuous and vital. That is especially true of water, which they now have to bring from hundreds of miles — and will soon have to bring from thousands of miles — away. But equally disturbing, to me, is the utter dependence on the costly uneconomical gadget called the automobile for practically every process of life from birth and education, through shopping, work and recreation, even courtship, to the final function of burial. In this community, where the revolutionary force of motorization has made a clean sweep of all the patterns of living and has overcome all competition, man has acquired a new form of legs. And what disturbs me is not only that these mechanical legs have a deleterious effect on man himself, drugging him into a sort of paralysis of the faculty of reflection and distorting his emotional makeup while they are in use — these things are not too serious, and perhaps there are even ways of combating them. What disturbs me most is his abject dependence on this means of transportation and on the complicated processes that make it possible. It is as though his natural legs had really become shriveled by disuse. One has the feeling that if his artificial ones were taken away from him, he would be crawling miserably and helplessly around, like a crippled insect, no longer capable of conducting the battle for existence, doomed to early starvation, thirst, and extinction.

One must not exaggerate this sort of thing. All modern urban society is artificial in the physical sense: dependent on gadgets, fragile and vulnerable. This is simply the apotheosis. Here the helplessness is greatest, but also the thoughtlessness. And the thoughtlessness is part of the helplessness.

But alongside the feeling of anxiety I have at the sight of these people, there is a questioning as to the effect they are going to have, and the contribution they are going to make, to American society as a whole. Again, this is not conceived in terms of reproach or criticism. There is really a subtle, but profound, difference between people here and what Americans used to be, and still partly are, in other parts of the country. I am at a loss to define this difference, and am sure that I understand it very imperfectly.

Let me try to get at it by overstating it. Here, it is easy to see that when man is given (as he can be given only for relatively brief periods and in exceptional circumstances) freedom both from political restraint and from want, the effect is to render him childlike in many respects: fun-loving, quick to laughter and enthusiasm, unanalytical, unintellectual, outwardly expansive, preoccupied with physical beauty and prowess, given to sudden and unthinking seizures of aggressiveness, driven constantly to protect his status in the group by an eager conformism — yet not unhappy. In this sense, Southern California, together with all that tendency of American life which it typifies, is childhood without the promise of maturity — with the promise only of a continual widening and growing impressiveness of the childhood world. And when the day of reckoning and hardship comes, as I think it must, it will be — as everywhere among children — the cruelest and most ruthless natures who will seek to protect their interests by enslaving the others; and the others, being only children, will be easily enslaved. In this way, values will suddenly prove to have been lost that were forged slowly and laboriously in the more rugged experience of Western political development elsewhere. It is not meant as an offense to the great achievements of the Latin cultural world if I say that there will take place something like a "latinization" of political life. Southern California will become politically, as it already is climatically, a Latin American country. And if any democracy survives it will be, as in Latin

America, a romantic-Garibaldian type of democracy, founded on the interaction of an emotional populace and a stirring, heroic type of popular leader. Where, as in many Latin countries, this sort of political system can operate within the framework of a great ecclesiastical and civil tradition, it is still compatible with a respectable civilization; but what will be the effect where it starts from the wrong end and represents the disintegration of liberty rather than, as in Rome, the raising of a structure of law and custom from the chaos of primeval despotism? Will it not operate to subvert our basic political tradition? And if so, what will then happen to our whole urbanized, industrialized society, so vulnerable to regimentation and centralized control?

These observations about California sound more critical, I am sure, than they were meant to sound. They convey only an inadequate portion of the view of that great state that took shape in my mind in the course of a succession of visits. Not only did I soon realize the danger of generalizing about an area so varied in both its natural and its human composition, but I was always conscious of the impossibility, for any American, of distancing himself from it entirely. California, it soon occurred to me, was only the rest of America, but sooner and more so. To look at it was, for someone from another part of the country, to see his own habitat — but fifteen years later. And if, as it sometimes seemed to me, there lay at the origins of every family resident there someone who was an escapist, in the sense of having shaken off the problems of the place where he was born in the hopes of finding what promised to be an easier life, was this any the less true of the United States as a whole? Was there not a similar escapist at the origins of every white American family, someone who had escaped from the strictures and responsibilities of a European life to seek the greater freedom of a new world? This, surely, was why Americans had never really come to terms, in their national philosophy, with the deeper dilemmas in the predicament of man as a member of a crowded and inescapable political community. California was only an extreme example of this; and none of us, in judging it, had the right to forget the little Californian always present in himself. California was simply America-in-emergence. If not all of it was to my liking, this was because I did not like what America as a whole was becoming. And of this, the American future, California, more than any other part of the country (except perhaps Texas, which I did not know), seemed to me to be the most striking and expressive symbol.

I summed up some of the impressions of this re-encounter with the United States in a letter written, in January 1952, to a man who asked me what I meant when I said that the most important factor in determining the ultimate outcome of the cold war was the quality (the "spiritual distinction," as I had unfortunately described it) of our own civilization. "It seems to me," I wrote,

that our country bristles with imperfections — and some of them very serious ones — of which we are almost universally aware, but lack the resolution and civic vigor to correct. What is at stake here is our duty to ourselves and our own national ideals. When individual citizens no longer find themselves unhappy in our country merely by virtue of their race or color; when our cities no longer reek with graft and corruption; when criminal elements are no longer close to the source of local power in many of our larger urban communities; when we have cleared away slums and filth and blighted areas; when we have taken in hand the question of juvenile delinquency and have found the courage to penalize the parents who are the main culprits in it; when we have revived the meaning of community and citizenship for the urban dweller in general; when we have overcome inflation; when we have had the courage to recognize the educational effect of our mass media as a public responsibility and to find for them the place they should properly have in a healthy and progressive society; when we have taken effective measures to keep our soil from sliding away, our water tables from falling and our forests from deteriorating — when we have taken real measures, in other words, to protect the beauty and healthfulness of the land God gave us to live on and to restore in general a harmonious and stable relationship between the American man and his incomparable natural environment — when we have done such things, then, in my opinion, we shall have achieved spiritual distinction (for without it we would not have found the strength to do these things) and the world will be well aware of that achievement.

Like many other Americans, I never ceased to ponder, in these first years of renewed confrontation with the American scene, the phenomena which the diary notes cited above so depressingly reflect: the obvious deterioration in the quality both of American life itself and of the natural environment in which it had its being, under the impact of a headlong overpopulation, industrialization, commercialization and urbanization of society. And I came up, invariably, before the dilemma which these tendencies presented. Allowed to proceed unchecked, they spelled — it was plain — only failure and disaster. But what of the conceivable correctives? If these were to have any chance of being effective, would they not have to be so drastic, so unusual, so far-reaching in the demands they placed on governmental authority and society, that they would greatly exceed both the intellectual horizons of the American electorate and the existing constitutional and traditional powers of government in the United States? Would they not involve hardships and sacrifices most unlikely to be acceptable to any democratic electorate? Would they not come into the sharpest sort of conflict with commercial interests? Would their implementation not require governmental powers which, as of the middle of the twentieth century, simply did not exist, and which no one as yet — least of all either of the two great political parties — had the faintest intention of creating?

Dilemmas produce agony; and the agony of this one came in the form of the first reluctant and horrifying pangs of doubt as to whether America's problems were really soluble at all by operation of the liberal-democratic and free-enterprise institutions traditional to our country. But if such doubts were justified, to what conclusions did they lead? The traditions, institutions, and assumptions which made it seemingly impossible for us to face up to these evils of the modern age and to tackle them with any prospect of success were ones the Communist countries did not share. Their leaders might not have risen yet to a recognition of these evils as evils — they might still be prisoners of the common fetishes of industrialization, automobilization, bigness, and military strength; but when those leaders did come, as they surely someday would, to these appreciations, then they at least, in contrast to us, would have the political authority and the economic controls necessary to enable them to take the practical consequences of their insights.

What did this mean? Did it mean that they, fundamentally, were right and we — wrong? That modern man in the mass had to be thought of as a lost and blinded child who could be led out of his dangers and bewilderments only by bold, ruthless, self-confident minorities, armed with insights higher than any of which the masses were to be presumed capable — perceiving, or fancying themselves to perceive, interests of the man in the street of which the latter was not, and could not be, himself aware — knowing, or professing to know, more about what was good for people than people knew themselves?

This, obviously, was only the old dilemma of Dostoyevsky's *Grand Inquisitor,* brought home to us in a new form. But it came to us, now, in the age of overpopulation and environmental deterioration, with an urgency and a cruelty such as the people of Dostoyevsky's generation had never known.

It was the Soviet example, rather than the question in itself, that frightened. The possibility that a democratic, free-enterprise system such as ours might have to be fundamentally altered to meet the challenges now looming before us was of course disturbing, because our people had little talent for constitutional reform: vested interests and assumptions would stand in the way, and the path of transition would obviously not be easy. But this was still not a cause for despair. American democracy was not the only way one could live. There had been many other social and political systems in the course of the world's history and not all of them bad or intolerable.

But this was another age. Was there something in the modern air that meant once you had cut loose from the traditional liberal principles of post-Jacksonian American democracy, you could now find no stopping point until you had accepted the whole forbidding baggage of Soviet outlook and practice? Was it necessary, in order to achieve a sufficient concentration of governmental authority to meet the demands of the modern age, to entrust the monopoly of power to a self-appointed minority? And was it then necessary for this minority to insist on its own infallibility, to profess that it had never made a mistake, to lie systematically to the public, to create fictitious enemies where none existed and cite this as a reason for maintaining a virtual state of siege, to silence all contrary opinion, to send such people as Daniel and Sinyavski to prison camps, to suppress the works of a Solzhenitsyn?

I never saw the necessity of accepting this conclusion. But if one did not accept it, one had then to find something else: some middle ground between the permissive excesses of American democracy and the timidities, the hypocrisies and the cruelties of Soviet communism. The problem was to find a method of governing people that would not demean or deceive them, would permit them to express freely their feelings and opinions, and would take decent account of the feelings and opinions thus expressed, and yet would assure a sufficient concentration of governmental authority, sufficient stability in its exercise, and sufficient selectivity in the recruitment of those privileged to exert it, to permit the formulation and implementation of hopeful long-term programs of social and environmental change.

This was of course not our problem alone. In its broader aspects, it was the problem of all modern societies. In other parts of the world people were much more aware of it than we were; and the search for a solution constituted a point at which Western socialists, nationalistic leaders of underdeveloped countries, and dissident Marxian Communists found themselves at least looking in the same direction. It was clear that the solution would have to be a somewhat different one in each country, geared specifically to its habits, geographical peculiarities, and traditions. No country had more urgent need to think about it than did our own. Yet very little thought was given to it by Americans, it seemed to me, in those years of the Fifties (and not even more recently). Liberal opinion, which dominated the universities and much of the press, was preoccupied with the achievement of a greater social justice *within* an existing system rather than with the adjustment of that system to meet the wider needs, environmental and otherwise, of the modern age. "Conservative" opinion was committed to the resistance of these liberal impulses in the name of an outraged patriotism and a compulsive, undiscriminate, anti-Communist fixation. In neither camp did I feel at home. Neither seemed to me to be focusing in the right direction. And the result was the beginning, insofar as American domestic affairs were concerned, of a growing intellectual loneliness on my part and a feeling of inability to contribute usefully to current discussion. Attempts to communicate orally, even with friends, about what was on my mind led to indulgent smiles and kindly observations to the effect that I didn't really know anything about the United States and had better stick to my real métier, which was foreign affairs.

So stick to foreign affairs I did, by and large, when it came to books, articles and other public statements on contemporary problems. But the exercise seemed increasingly, with the years, an empty one; for what use was there, I had to ask, in attempting to protect in its relations to others a society that was clearly failing in its relation to itself? It was under the pressure of this relentless question that I saw my public usefulness decline over the course of the years and tended more and more, so far as my own tastes and desires were concerned, to seek in the interpretation of history a usefulness I could not find in the interpretation of my own time.

5

Russia and the Cold War

OVER all these months of 1950 and 1951 when I was only a Foreign Service officer on long-term leave without pay at Princeton, the focal point of my interest in foreign affairs remained, as it had so long been, Russia; and it was, in the first instance, for expertise about that country and our relations with it that I was looked to by others.

Two years earlier, in 1948, I had had the impression that American opinion, official and otherwise, recovering from the pro-Soviet euphoria of the period around the end of World War II, had been restored to a relatively even keel. True: it was hard to get the Pentagon to desist from seeing in Stalin another Hitler and fighting the last war all over again in its plans for the next one. True: we still had a vigorous right-wing faction which called for war with Russia — usually over China. But by and large, the moderate Marshall Plan approach — an approach aimed at *creating* strength in the West rather than *destroying* strength in Russia — seemed to have prevailed; and I, like those others who went by the name of "Russian experts," felt that our view of the Russian problem — a view that accepted Russian-Communist attitudes and policies as a danger at the political level, but did not see either a likelihood or a necessity of war and did not regard the military plane as the one on which our response ought to be concentrated — seemed to have found general acceptance.

Two years later, all this was rapidly changing. A number of disturbing trends were now detectable, as a result of which I found myself increasingly concerned over the course of American opinion and policy precisely in the area where I was thought to have, and fancied myself to have, the greatest influence.

Some of the anxieties deserve notice before we proceed further with this account.

There was, in the first place, the situation produced by the Korean War. It was my belief at the time that the Soviet reasons for authorizing and supporting the North Korean attack were ones relating strictly to the North Asian region and had no wider connotations. These reasons have been touched on in Chapter 2, above. It seemed impossible, however, to get credence for this view in Washington. I am not sure that even the Secretary of State fully accepted it. The German-Nazi syndrome still dominated people's minds. The attack in Korea, even though Soviet troops were not involved, was viewed as another "Austria" as the first move in a supposed "grand design" of world conquest. And by virtue of this misimpression on our part, more, actually, than by the North Korean attack itself, the peace of the world now seemed to me to be in real, and needless, danger.

This was not because I supposed that the Soviet leaders wanted such a war or would intentionally provoke it. It was because I thought that we ourselves might inadvertently convince them that it could not be avoided. I could not forget that even prior to the Korean War our military — and to some extent our political — planners had adopted for military planning purposes, against my anguished objections, the year 1952 as the probable "peak" of danger which our preparations should be designed to meet. They did not themselves intend to start a war at that time, but they assumed there would be a real danger of the Russians doing so as soon as their current program of military preparations was completed — and for this, 1952, apparently, seemed to them the most likely date. They could not free themselves from the image of Hitler and his timetables. They viewed the Soviet leaders as absorbed with the pursuit of somthing called a "grand design" — a design for the early destruction of American power and for world conquest. In vain I pleaded with people to recognize that this was a chimera: that the Russians were not like that; that they were weaker than we supposed; that they had many internal problems of their own; that they had no "grand design" and did not intend, in particular, to pursue their competition with us by means of a general war. What we were confronted with from the Soviet side was, I insisted, a long-term effort of rivalry and pressure by means short of general war. We should make our plans for steady, consistent effort over a long period of time, and not for any imaginary "peak" of danger. It was, in fact, dangerous for us to think in terms of such a "peak"; for military plans had a way of giving reality to the very contingencies against which they purported to prepare.

These, as I say, were arguments conducted even before the Korean War began. Korea now greatly heightened the danger. One has only to recall the frivolous and dangerous bombing by our air forces of the port of Rashin on the east coast of Korea, so close to the great Russian port of Vladivostok. Now, in late autumn of 1950, the reverses suffered by our forces in North Korea had led to the common allegation from the military side, eagerly seconded by Republican congressional circles, that the President's injunction against bombing objectives in Manchuria meant that our Communist adversaries had a "privileged sanctuary" there, the implication being that if only we had been able to bomb targets on Chinese territory, our defeat along the Yalu would have been avoided. The voices demanding that our air force be permitted to conduct such bombing did not become weaker as the autumn progressed, quite the contrary.* There was never the slightest doubt in my mind, and I fail to see how anyone could have entertained any, that the demand for permission to bomb beyond the Yalu was equivalent to a demand for expansion of the Korean War into a full-fledged war with both the Soviet Union and China. The fact that this demand was being voiced by important figures in our national life, including our commander in Korea, with strong support in Congress and the press, could easily cause the Russians to conclude that there was a real possibility, and even probability, of the outbreak of general war in the near future. If they came to such a conclusion, then, plainly, they might begin to shape their own behavior accordingly, not just in the Korean-Manchurian area but in others as well. This, once more, could easily appear to us as aggressive intent. In this way there could be set in motion, as on the eve of the First World War, a train of events which no one, soon, would be able to halt.

I had voiced these anxieties in my official papers before leaving government. On August 8, 1950, I had advised my superiors that while the Soviet leaders still hoped to avoid general hostilities, they were probably less sanguine about the possibility of doing so than they had been some months back. A week later, after the press revelations about the bombing of Rashin, I was obliged to revise this estimate in a pessimistic direction. That action, I wrote in a memorandum of August 14, could only appear to the Soviet authorities as evidence of a deliberate decision on our part to exploit the hostilities in Korea for the purpose of reducing Soviet strategic capabilities in

---

* Military men have traditionally never been slow to find others to blame for their reverses; but I can think of no claim of this nature more preposterous than the suggestion that our adversary in Korea enjoyed some sort of unfair advantage through our inability to bomb in Manchuria and that had he not enjoyed it, our problems would have been solved. We had, after the stabilization of the front at the middle of the peninsula in late 1950, complete control of the air for nearly two hundred miles beyond our own lines, had the enemy confined to a narrow corridor of operation and communication, and could bomb at will in that area. There was no attack whatsoever against our own rear bases. If anyone enjoyed a privileged sanctuary, it was ourselves.

that area. This being so, we had to be prepared for extreme reactions on their part at any time.

We cannot exclude the possibility that this evidence . . . will . . . affect their estimate of the possibility of avoiding major hostilities, of the likely timing of such hostilities, and of the relative advantages of a Soviet initiation of such hostilities, as opposed to a waiting policy based on the continued hope of avoiding them altogether.

This was of course only a hunch; but it was, as later evidence would show, not wide of the mark. We know today, from documents published in early 1970 in connection with the seventieth birthday of the Italian Communist leader Luigi Longo,* that Stalin, by the end of 1950, had himself come to feel that the situation was one of great gravity and that an early outbreak of hostilities had to be reckoned with as a serious possibility.

The thought of a war with Russia was sickening enough just from the standpoint of the slaughter and destruction it would involve, even if nuclear weapons, as one scarcely dared hope, should not be used. But it was particularly alarming and abhorrent to me because of my acute awareness (both the year at the War College and the later study of diplomatic history had brought this home to me) that in a war of this nature the American side would have no realistic, limited aims. Falling back on the patterns of the past, and seized by wartime emotionalism, we would assuredly attempt once again to achieve the familiar goals of total enemy defeat, total destruction of the enemy's armed forces, his unconditional sur-

---

* These documents, appearing at various times and in various publications, were discussed, and in part reproduced in German translation, in the German magazine *Osteuropa*, No. 10, October 1970. They dealt with the crisis of January 1951 in relations between the leaders of the Soviet and Italian Communist parties, occasioned by Stalin's effort to persuade Togliatti to accept leadership of the Cominform and, for this purpose, to move his residence to the area of Russian-Communist control. In justification of this demand, Stalin cited the extreme seriousness of the international situation and made it clear to the Italian comrades that he considered the danger of general war to be great and imminent.

render, the complete occupation of his territory, the removal of the existing government and its replacement by a regime that would respond to our concepts of "democratization." The concept of limited warfare — of warfare conducted for limited objectives and ending with the achievement of those objectives by compromise with the existing enemy regime — was not only foreign but was deeply repugnant to the American military and political mind. One had already had a clear illustration of this in Korea. (It was to be illustrated again fifteen to twenty years later in Vietnam.) It was perfectly clear that if something were not done to change prevailing thinking on this subject, our people, in the event of war with the Soviet Union, would swing right back into this familiar pattern.

There were two reasons why such a possibility filled me with horror. The first was that this approach had not worked very well even in the two previous world wars. The commitment to total defeat of the enemy, followed by unconditional surrender, had served for us as an excuse for not giving serious thought to political objectives while the war was on. The things said publicly by our leaders on the subject of war aims had tended to be vague, self-righteous, emotional, and — to the extent they had any real content at all — wildly punitive. The result was that we had ended these contests with very little in the way of realistic ideas as to where we wanted to go — what political objectives we wished to pursue with relation to our ex-enemy, once his capitulation had been obtained.

Even more persuasive as evidence of the unreality of such expectations was the fact, of which I was well aware and which I had tried to bring home to my War College students, that in a war between the United States and the Soviet Union, there could be no complete military victory. Neither country was occupiable by the forces of the other. Both were simply too large, too different — linguistically, culturally, and in every other way. Nor was it in the tradition or the psychology of the Soviet leaders to surrender to an adversary who had occupied any sizable portion of their territory. They would retreat, if necessary (actually, it would probably be far from necessary) to the most remote Siberian village; but in whatever territory remained to them they would maintain their power.* Not only this, but in the rest of vast Russia — in the part the US and its allies might conceive themselves to have occupied — the Soviet leaders, ruthless, experienced, and operating on familiar ground, would mount a resistance movement that would make anything known since World War II look tiny. Eventually, therefore, one would have to come to some sort of terms with them, if the war was to end; and these terms would have to be based on a compromise of conflicting interests. But for this, one would have to formulate at some point limited objectives — objectives short, that is, of unconditional surrender. For this, however, if we followed the pattern of earlier wars, we would be wholly unprepared.

Many Americans may have conceived that having occupied a portion of Russian territory, we would install in power there, again on the World War II pattern, a nice pro-American government made up of "democratic elements" among the Russian population; that this regime would be popular with a liberated people to whom the American "message" had got through; and that it would therefore have wide electoral support and would put the Communists in their right political place.

Everything I had learned about Russia taught me that if there was ever a fatuous daydream, it was this. There were no significant "democratic elements" in Russia. Thirty years of Communist terror had seen to that. There had been such elements — a few — before the Revolution; but almost without exception they had died off from natural causes, been killed, or emigrated. Our experience with Soviet defectors had shown us that however such people might hate

---

* For anyone who doubts the reality of this picture of Soviet behavior in the yielding of territory to a hostile force I would recommend the reading of Harrison Salisbury's *Nine Hundred Days,* a magnificent work on the fate of Leningrad and northwestern Russia in the last war.

their Soviet masters, their ideas about democracy were primitive and curious in the extreme, consisting often only of the expectation that they would be permitted and encouraged by us to line their recent political adversaries up against the wall with a ruthlessness no smaller than that to which they professed to be reacting, after which they would continue to rule, with our help, by their own brand of dictatorship. For this, too, there was a precedent, if anyone wished to consult it: the experience of the allied expeditionary forces in Russia with their Russian allies during the various interventions of 1918–1920.

This, then — the total unpreparedness of the mass of our people for any war of this nature — the complete absence of any realistic thinking about the possible objectives of such a contest — was one of the reasons why I viewed with such profound misgivings, in those dark days of the Korean War, the very thought of a war with Russia.

But there was another consideration which gave a special edge to these misgivings. It was the existence in our country of one vocal and not uninfluential element that not only wanted a war with Russia but had a very clear idea of the purposes for which, in its own view, such a war should be fought. I have in mind the escapees and immigrants, mostly recent ones, from the non-Russian portions of the postwar Soviet Union, as well as from some of the Eastern European satellite states. Their idea, to which they were passionately and sometimes ruthlessly attached, was simply that the United States should, for their benefit, fight a war against the Russian people to achieve the final breakup of the traditional Russian state and the establishment of themselves as the regimes of various "liberated" territories.

Prominent among these elements were the Ukrainians, and particularly a number of Galicians and Ruthenians who, having now no other theater of possible political activity, had appropriated to themselves, on the basis of a slender but not wholly fictional linguistic affinity, the Ukrainian name. In many instances, these people had religious as well as political reasons for their hatred of Russia. (For this reason, they also had strong support from the anti-Tito Croats in this country.)

To speak these bitter facts is not to deny that many of these people had been, indeed, victims of shocking persecution at the hands of the Soviet Communists, nor is it to suggest that they failed to include within their number many fine, sincere individuals. But three things must be recognized with relation to them if one is to understand the trend of their influence in American political life. First, the majority of them strongly wanted a Soviet-American war, and were at pains to push our government in that direction. Secondly, this was to be, as they wished it, a war not against the Soviet Union, as such, but against the Russian people, who were to constitute the principal targets of it. Thirdly, it was not, in many instances, American interests that these people had in mind. To their view, our country appeared as an instrument for the achievement of ulterior political aims, not as the prime object of political affection. That they rationalized their interest in the political future of Poland or the Ukraine or the other areas from which they came, and persuaded themselves that this interest was not incompatible with a boisterous American chauvinism, I had no doubt. But I was never persuaded that their motives were related primarily to the interests of this country.

These recent refugees were by no means without political influence in Washington. Connected as they were with the compact voting blocs situated in the big cities, they were able to bring direct influence to bear on individual congressional figures. They appealed successfully at times to religious feeling, and even more importantly, to the prevailing anti-Communist hysteria. An idea of the political power they possessed can be had from the fact that some years later (1959) they were able to recommend to Congress, through their friends there, the text of a resolution — the so-called Captive Nations Resolution — every word of which was written (on his own published admission*) by their spokesman, Dr. Lev E. Dobriansky, then associate professor at Georgetown University, and to get this document solemnly adopted by the Congress as a statement of American policy. This resolution committed the United States, insofar as Congress had the power to do so, to the "liberation" of twenty-two "nations," two of which had never had any real existence, and the name of one of which appears to have been invented in the Nazi propaganda ministry during the recent war.† This, the writing of a congressional statement of policy on Russia and Eastern Europe, was more than I, with many years of official service in that part of the world, could ever have hoped to achieve.

I could think of nothing worse than what these people wanted us to do. To commit ourselves politically and militarily not only against the Soviet regime but also against the strongest and most numerous ethnic element in the traditional Russian land, and to do this on behalf of national extremists among whom there could never conceivably be any unity and who would never be able to maintain themselves, in most instances, against Russian revanchist pressures except by the indefinite reliance on American bayonets: this would have been a folly of such stupendous dimensions that even the later venture in Vietnam now pales to insignificance beside the thought of it. I was not without sympathy for the subject peoples, as they languished under the strictures of Stalinist power; but I was not without sympathy for the Russian people either, who were languishing, after all, under the same yoke. I also had some awareness of the limits of our own power, and I knew that what was being asked and expected of us here far exceeded these limits.

The pressures in question were doubly dangerous because of

* See the *Ukrainian Quarterly*, Vol. XV, No. 3, September 1951, p. 207.
† The two nonexistent nations were something called "Cossackia" and something else called "Udel-Ural."

their close connection with certain outlooks of primarily native American provenance which also seemed to me to contain the seeds of disaster. I have in mind the views of those people (and they included many influential ones) who did not advocate a war with Russia, or even admit to accepting its necessity, but scoffed at the thesis that there might be any gradual mellowing of Soviet power and urged that American policy should be one of purely political attack on the various Communist regimes, aimed at their overthrow by a combination of American propaganda and the action of local anti-Communist groups, the outcome being conceived as the "liberation" of the Soviet peoples generally, including the Russian people. The theory was that this, given proper zeal and persistence on our part, could be accomplished without war. This concept commended itself greatly to certain conservative Republican figures, for it enabled them at one and the same time to deny that they were advocating war and yet to play up to the extreme anti-Communist right wing of American opinion of which they were all, for some reason, in the political sense, mortally afraid, and which none of them was prepared to take on in an open argument. Had talk of this nature come only from the extremists, I might not have viewed it with such alarm; but it had, by this time, made deep inroads on the opinions of people who could not be relegated to that category. Mr. James Burnham's *Containment and Liberation*, a well-written and persuasive book aimed largely against myself and the doctrine of containment, was still a year in the offing, but the atmosphere that it reflected was already palpable on every hand. The Time-Life concern, in particular, leaned strongly in this direction; and a large portion of the daily press followed eagerly in its train.*

---

* An entire issue of *Collier's* magazine was devoted to imagined accounts of our future war with Russia. I can recall glancing with horror, at the time, at the cover of that issue; and I heard from others, with even greater horror, that it contained a suggestion of our celebrating our victory over the Soviet Union by staging *Guys and Dolls* in the Bolshoi Theater in Moscow. I had visions, of course, of a *Collier's*

It was not easy to explain, for one who was himself a strong public critic of Communist power, why he opposed this "liberationist"
thesis. I had three reasons, in particular, for doing so. I thought, for
one thing, that it had small chances for success. We were, as political conspirators, not that good. Beyond that I felt, and often argued
with others, that if one was going to take the responsibility for endeavoring to destroy political regimes in other countries, one ought
to have some realistic idea as to what should be put in their place.
But all this, even in the minds of the leading liberationists, was
wholly un-thought-through. The fact was that we did *not* have in
our pockets any nice democratic regimes to put in the place of
those we were so anxious to overthrow. Some of the individuals
who recommended themselves to us for this role struck me, in fact,
as not likely to be improvements, from the standpoint of humanity
or democratic feeling, on the Communists they would be replacing.

But the main reason why I was leary of the "liberationists" was
that the pursuit of this sort of policy, even if it did not lead to war
(as it probably would have done), would almost certainly be exploited by the Soviet leaders as an excuse, internally, for not agree-
ing to any sort of liberalization or any modification of the intensity
of the cold war. It was bad enough for the Soviet leaders to be
committed, as they had been, particularly in the Lenin period, to
the overthrow of *our* government. For us to be committed to the
overthrow of *theirs* would be to justify all that had ever been said
in Moscow about the evil designs of the capitalist powers against

---

editor conceiving this to be the acme of America's triumph: showing the benighted
Russians what such a great operatic and ballet stage ought really to be used for.

Research succeeded in unearthing from the depths of a warehouse library-
depository a copy of the *Collier's* issue in question, which I confess I had never
previously read — I could not bring myself to do so at the time. To my consternation, it became apparent that the idea of *Guys and Dolls* at the Bolshoi came not
from a *Collier's* editor but from the eminent British playwright and novelist J. B.
Priestley, and the entire issue turned out to have been an attempt to meet my demand that we think ahead and try to picture realistically what a war with Russia
might mean. This issue of the now-defunct magazine, despite the fact that a
number of worthy people contributed to it, was a fantastic gaucherie. I continue
to regard it with embarrassed distaste.

the peoples of the Soviet Union. And since, as I firmly believed, the best discernible possibility for the evolution of Russian society in the direction we desired lay precisely in just such a liberalization and moderation of Soviet power, and since this, in turn, could hardly be expected to take place if the Soviet leaders became convinced that the United States was committed against them come what may and had lost confidence in any outcome other than their overthrow and total destruction, then to permit them to gain that impression might mean, in the end, to forfeit the last and only chance of avoiding a world catastrophe.

These were the trends and the forces which, as it seemed to me, were threatening in those months of 1950 and 1951 not just the soundness of American policy towards Russia but the peace of the world and the entire future of Western civilization. Free, for the first time, to speak out as an individual, I made clear my opposition to them in a whole series of speeches and articles. Of these, the most important, and the one addressed most centrally to the problems just discussed, was an article entitled "America and the Russian Future," which appeared in *Foreign Affairs* in April 1951 and which I myself conceived as a sort of second "X-article" (although this one was signed). Here, I addressed myself to all the problems in question; but the central thrust of the article was on the uselessness and folly of war — not just war with Russia but any war. I urged my readers, among whom I hoped some of the cold war hotheads would be included, to remember

that war — a matter of destruction, brutalization and sacrifice, of separations, domestic disintegration, and the weakening of the deeper fabrics of society — is a process which of itself can achieve no positive aims: that even military victory is only the prerequisite for some further and more positive achievement which it makes possible but by no means assures. We can have the moral courage, this time, to remind ourselves that major international violence is, in terms of the values of our civilization, a form of bankruptcy for us all — even for those who are confident that they are right; that all of us, victors and vanquished alike, must emerge from it poorer than we began it and farther from the goals we had in mind; and that, since victory or defeat can signify only relative degrees of misfortune, even the most glorious military victory would give us no right to face the future in any spirit other than one of sorrow and humbleness for what has happened and of realization that the road is long and hard — longer and harder, in fact, than it would have been had it been possible to avoid a military cataclysm altogether.

But whoever said "no war" was obliged to suggest how the seemingly insoluble conflicts of outlook and aspiration that divided the United States and the Soviet Union were ever to find a tolerable issue. And to this my answer was: change — gradual, peaceful change — the sort of change to which no man and no government was immune — plus a positive example. If only the necessary alternatives could be kept before the Russian people, I wrote,

in the form of the existence elsewhere on this planet of a civilization which is decent, hopeful and purposeful, the day must come — soon or late, and whether by gradual process or otherwise — when that terrible system of power which has set a great people's progress back for decades and has lain like a shadow over the aspirations of all civilization will be distinguishable no longer as a living reality, but only as something surviving partly in recorded history and partly in that sediment of constructive, organic change which every great human upheaval, however unhappy its other manifestations, manages to deposit on the shelf of time.

We could not be sure that the changes we wished to see come about in Russia could be brought about without some violent break in the continuity of power there; but we could also not be sure that they couldn't and wouldn't. What was important was that our policy not be such as to discourage or impede a gradual development in this direction.

If it should turn out to be the will of fate that freedom should come to Russia by erosion from despotism rather than by the violent upthrust of liberty, let us be able to say that our policy was such as to favor it, and that we did not hamper it by preconception or impatience or despair.

These were the fears, hopes and convictions concerning our policy towards Russia which occupied my mind during that initial year and a half of respite from governmental service. If I have tried the reader's patience with their recital, it is because the strains of the ensuing period of official service, to be described in the next chapter, are not fully intelligible unless these differences of viewpoint are borne in mind.

6

The Moscow Ambassadorship

A T some point in the late autumn of 1951 I seem to recall receiving from the Secretary of State, Mr. Dean Acheson, word to the effect that Admiral Alan Kirk, our ambassador at Moscow, was about to retire from that position and that the President wished to appoint me as Kirk's successor. The suggestion was in some ways personally agreeable to me, in other ways not. I had just gathered around me at the Institute a group of younger scholars with whose collaboration I had hoped to do a study of the effect of existing internal trends of development in our country on the requirements we would be obliged to make in future on our world environment. I felt that I had incurred an obligation to these men in bringing them to Princeton for the year; and I was reluctant to leave them in the lurch. Beyond that, I still had freshly in mind the disagreements I had had with official policy in the period just prior to my departure on leave of absence, and had misgivings about undertaking to represent, in a capital as important and sensitive as Moscow, a policy I neither fully understood nor believed in.

On the other hand, I was still a career official of the government. I did not feel it proper to decline any assignment given to me, and particularly any in which the President was directly involved. And it was especially hard for me to turn down an assignment as ambassador to the Soviet Union — a task for which my whole career had prepared me, if it had prepared me for anything at all.

I therefore told Mr. Acheson that while I was of course at the government's disposal and would go anywhere they wanted me to go, I wished to suggest that the President look around and see if he could not find someone personally closer to him and more conversant with his own thoughts and policies, to take over this job. The reply, a few days later, was negative: the President still wished me to do it.

I therefore accepted. The appointment was announced on December 27, 1951. It was agreed, however, that I would not have to proceed to my post before May. While it was clear that the public effect of the announcement of the appointment, plus the necessity of many sorts of preparation for departure, would interfere seriously with the completion of the scholarly program at Princeton, this delay would at least give me a chance to be, throughout most of the remainder of the academic year, with the younger men whom I had brought there, and to take some interest in their work.

The appointment went before the Senate, for confirmation, in the middle of February and was considered by the Foreign Relations Committee in the middle of March. (This marked in effect the end of that initial period of my activity at Princeton. From that time on the preparations for assumption of the new duties went into high gear.) The appointment was unanimously approved in the Senate, although one West Coast senator subsequently said publicly that had he known what was going on he would have been present to vote against it — his reason being that three years before, in a secret session of the House Foreign Affairs Committee, I had said something to the effect that we did not need to be in panic about the advent to power of the Chinese Communists; they would not overcome in a day the backwardness of China; they would need trade with the industrialized West; we would still have strong bargaining power with them. This, the senator intimated, suggested a willingness to give aid to Communist China.

On April 1, being now duly confirmed, I went to Washington to pay my official calls. The first was on President Truman. He had just announced his intention not to run for the presidency again, and he was, as my diary notes of the time record,

in a relaxed and genial frame of mind. He indicated that he shared my views as to the motives and principles of behavior of the Soviet leaders, and had never believed that they wanted another great war. . . . Beyond this, he gave me no instructions of any kind.

For the remainder of the preparations for departure, I shall let the diary, less endangered than are my present recollections by the tricks of memory, carry the burden.

The following day I was sworn in, and lunched privately with Secretary Acheson. He, too, was cordial but very reserved; and he said nothing that could give me any clue to the basic line of policy I was to follow in my new capacity.

The next day, April 3, I went to the Soviet embassy, accompanied by Dick Davis (who now has the Soviet desk in the department) and lunched with Ambassador Panyushkin, and his counselor, whose name was something like Karavaev. They were cordial and pleasant and we had a reasonably amiable talk, keeping off the more painful issues of the day, concerning which neither of us had any instructions to say anything authoritative on the part of his government

Some days later (April 14) I made a similar call on Mr. Malik in New York. I found him much more bitter and sour, mouthing the same things he had said to me when I had occasion to talk with him nearly a year before. He professed to believe that American business circles wanted war. As proof of this he cited the frequent statements in the press that an abrupt backtracking on the rearmament effort would produce another major depression. He, too, asked why there was no reply to Stalin's statements. I told him that we did not wish to mislead people by making vague general statements. At the end of our talk he spoke of the

Soviet Union being threatened. "Are you sure," I asked, "that your government does not prefer to be threatened?" "Positively," was his answer.

Reflecting, back in Princeton, on this visit to Washington, as well as on the various evidences of Soviet willingness to enter on some new phase of discussion and negotiations with the Western powers, I became concerned to realize that I had had absolutely no real instructions of any sort either from the Secretary of State or from the President, or even any proper guidance as to their attitude with respect to the acute problems of the moment, such as Germany, the Korean armistice talks, the disarmament discussions in the United Nations, etc. I therefore telephoned Chip Bohlen and arranged for a meeting with the Secretary and his top advisors on April 18. The meeting took place immediately after lunch, and lasted only an hour — the Secretary having an appointment at the White House in midafternoon. I was disappointed to find that it was left entirely to me to set the trend of the discussion. The official attitude, so far as I could see, was: "You have asked to see us; we are obliging and have come together at your request; now what is it you want of us?"

I pointed out that in view of the sensitivity of my position in Moscow, every word I said there would be taken by the Soviet government as indicative of American policy, and since I had been away from the Department of State for a year and a half, I thought I ought to be thoroughly briefed on the rationale and objectives of our various policy positions.

I mentioned first the question of Germany. From the ensuing discussion, I could only gather, the diary records,

that our government did not want any agreement with the Soviet government about Germany at this time and wished if possible to avoid any discussion that would carry us along that path; we were staking everything at the moment on the attempt to get the new contractual arrangements with the West German government and the agreement on the European defense force both signed and "in the bag" before any discussions with the Russians could complicate matters. I said that this position worried me very much: I thought it likely that the Russians would press us mercilessly along the lines of their recent notes and would say in effect, "If you don't like our proposals then tell us and the world what your own ideas are for the unification of Germany." I thought we ought to state clearly the terms on which we could consent to unification but say that we would not hold up progress on the West German arrangements for a day in favor of negotiations on the four-power level.

The reply given to me was that unless we could achieve the signature of the new West German arrangements and the European Defense Community within the next few weeks, our whole European policy would suffer a grievous setback. Nothing should be said, therefore, which could possibly distract attention from these two projects. What this amounted to was, of course, that we now had no interest in discussing the German problem with the Soviet government in any manner whatsoever.

Turning to the Far East, I asked whether it was desirable to induce the Soviet government to join us as a guarantor of any settlement we might arrive at in the Korean armistice talks, or whether we wished it to remain formally detached. To this query, I could get no clear answer and could only conclude that this was a matter of indifference to official Washington.

Turning to the question of disarmament negotiations then being pursued from time to time at Geneva, and asking particularly about their relation to our political objectives, I was depressed to hear the Secretary say that it was our idea to get some real measure of disarmament first, hoping this would permit solution of the political problems. "If there is any one lesson," I noted in the diary,

to be plainly derived from the experiences we have had with disarmament in the past half-century, it is that armaments are a function and not a cause of political tensions and that no limitation of armaments on a multilateral scale can be effected as long as the political problems are not tackled and regulated in some realistic way. So far as I was concerned, therefore, I felt that our government could not be more on the wrong tack.

My diary also contains my own record of the remarks with which I concluded this discussion. "I had come to Washington," I said,

not to make suggestions about policy but to find out what I should know about it. Nevertheless I could not conceal my concern at the general pattern that seemed to me to flow from what I had been told. So far as I could see, we were expecting to be able to gain our objectives both in the East and the West without making any concessions whatsoever to the views and interests of our adversaries. Our position seemed to me to be comparable to the policy of unconditional surrender in the recent war. This position, I thought, would be fine if we were really all-powerful, and could hope to get away with it. I very much doubted that this was the case, and I thought we ought to reflect very carefully on these matters and see whether we were sure that it would not be better to attempt to solve at least some of these problems by accommodation with our adversaries rather than by complete defiance of them.

The discouraging impressions left by this meeting were deepened by conversations I had later in the day with friends in the department, concerning our policy in the development of nuclear weapons. Considering such weapons to be suicidal in their ultimate implications, destructive in a degree which no purely national objectives could ever justify, and wholly unsuitable as instruments of national policy, I had always opposed the basing of our defense posture upon them, and particularly the adoption of the principle of their "first use" in any major military encounter. I had pleaded in vain, only two years before, against the decision to proceed to the development of the hydrogen bomb before at least renouncing the principle of "first use" and then having another try at international negotiations looking to the outlawing of these and all other weapons of indiscriminate mass destruction. I had drawn attention to the dilemmas that would eventually present themselves for our policy-makers if there should be a competition of indefinite duration and extent in the development of weapons of this nature. Now, on the eve of my departure for Russia, I found even some of my closest friends captivated, as it seemed to me, by "the flat and inflexible thinking of the Pentagon, in which the false mathematics of relative effectiveness [in these weapons] was given a sort of absolute value and all other possible factors dismissed from the equation as of no demonstrable importance." The philosophic difference between this view and my own was, as I observed at the time, profound — so profound as to preclude any further intellectual intimacy even with people who in the past had generally shared my own views on world affairs and American policy generally.

The diary describes the upshot of this visit:

I returned to Princeton feeling extremely lonely. There was, it seemed to me, no one left in Washington with whom I could discuss matters fully, frankly and hopefully against the background of a common outlook and understanding. There would surely be no one of this sort in Moscow, for the doubts I had cut much too deep to be revealed in any way to junior members of the mission, for whom they would only be discouraging and demoralizing. It seemed to me that I was being sent on a mission to play a game at which I could not possibly win and that part of my obligation consisted of assiduously concealing from the world the fact that I could not win at all and taking upon myself the onus of whatever overt failures were involved. I imagined that I was not the first person who had labored under such handicaps in the strange profession of diplomacy, but it was with a very heavy heart that I set forth, thus empty-handed, uninstructed, and uncertain, to what is surely the most important and delicate of the world's diplomatic tasks at this particular juncture.

These words were all written, I may say, on April 22 and 23, 1952, hard on the heels of the events they describe, and naturally with no foreknowledge of the disaster that was eventually to overcome the mission on which I was embarking. Such, however, is the power of premonition.

I timed the arrival in Moscow for May 5, just after the May 1 celebrations. The family, or such of it as was accompanying me — in this case, my wife and the two-year-old Christopher — had to be left behind in Bonn, because the new baby was due any day. It made its appearance only five days after my departure for Moscow: a girl, born in a hospital at Bad Godesberg, situated on a hill called, somewhat disturbingly, the Mount of Venus. She was named Wendy Antonia. It was, in view of her appearance, some weeks before the others could join me.

The arrival in Moscow was a time of very mixed feelings. I was overwhelmed, on the drive in from the airport, by the familiar odor of the Moscow streets — a mixture, I always thought, of *makhorka* (Russian tobacco) and cheap perfume. I found it, having been for so many years an underling in Moscow, difficult to adjust to the reserve and deference of the officers who met me. Spaso House, the ambassadorial residence, into which I had once, in 1934, carried personally the first items of American governmental furniture, seemed now, despite the fact that a number of the rooms had been freshly painted, barnlike, empty, and a little sad. I was puzzled, at that first moment, by the fact that certain of the servants, still on duty in the residence, whom I had known and with whom I had had pleasant relations in earlier years, failed to greet me or, in some instances, even to put in an appearance, when I arrived. Nor did any of these who *were* present make a move to carry the luggage upstairs to the bedroom. When told to do so, they did so willingly enough; but they would not do it of their own initiative.

I was soon to learn that this last bit of behavior was only one small expression of a drastic deterioration that had taken place, since my last service in Moscow, in the entire atmosphere by which the diplomatic corps, and particularly our own mission, was surrounded. The elaborate guarding and observation of foreign representatives, their studied isolation from the population, their treatment generally as though they were dangerous enemies, there for

no good purpose: these had been standard features of Soviet practice in the past, as they had of the practice of the Grand Duchy of
Muscovy, three hundred years earlier. But it was clear that since
1946 they had been much intensified — ominously so. The outer
walls of the Spaso property (the house and garden were surrounded by high brick walls on three sides and a high iron fence on
the fourth) were now floodlit, like those of a prison, and patrolled
day and night by armed guards. At the entrance gate, where one
drove in and out, were stationed, night and day, not only one or
more armed militiamen but also seven other husky individuals in
plain clothes (picked officers, actually, of the police armed forces
— the Border and Internal Guards) who constituted, at any given
moment or hour, my personal bodyguard. Five of these accompanied me every time I left the premises. If my departure was by car,
they swung into line behind me with a car of their own ("Daddy's
other car," as my little boy referred to it). If I left by foot, three of
them paced along at my heels, and their own car, with the others,
followed at a pedestrian pace. If I went swimming, as I did two or
three times during the course of the ensuing summer, one of them
was in the water, swimming amiably alongside, wherever my
strokes took me. If I went to the theater, five unfortunate ticket-
holders in the row just behind us were relentlessly displaced, and
the "angels" (as they were ironically called in the diplomatic
corps) shared my enjoyment of the performance.

Eagle-eyed and taciturn, these men were correct in their behavior, and not unfriendly.* Their function, never explained to me or

---

* Only on three occasions, over the course of the months, do I recall having any
verbal communication with these companions.

Once, when driving in the countryside and encountering a railway barrier which
appeared to be permanently lowered, one of them suggested a suitable detour.

On another occasion, walking from the office to my home, I heard a low, almost
whispering, voice saying repeatedly, in Russian: "Mr. Ambassador, Mr. Ambassador." I first thought it was some misguided Soviet citizen who, not recognizing
the bodyguard for what they were, was trying to get into communication with
me: an undertaking which could easily have landed him in a concentration camp. I
therefore ignored it. It persisted, however, and when I finally turned around, I

to anyone else by the Foreign Office, was obviously a multiple one: partly to protect me from any form of harassment (unless it was one staged by the regime), partly to observe my comings and go- ings, partly to assure that no Soviet citizen came into contact with me without the knowledge of the regime. I was aware that they had been told they were to view me as the representative not just of *an* unfriendly bourgeois power but indeed of *the* most dangerous and most hated one, and thus, in a sense, as Public Enemy No. 1 within the walls of the Soviet citadel. But I felt they recognized, as the magnificently disciplined men they were, that I was doing my duty as they were doing theirs; and I sensed that they viewed me with respect and without personal dislike.

This guarding was, actually, the least unpleasant feature of the attentions given by the police to the Western diplomatic represent- ative — but particularly, at that time, to the American ambassador. There were others that were harder to take. It very soon became apparent that the Soviet servants in the residence were wholly ter- rorized. None, it appeared, would sleep there; none, in fact, wanted to be in the house alone with myself or any other of the Americans; they might, after all, be accused of having in some way conspired with us. None would accept any authority over any of the others — it was hard even to get any of them to pass an order along; they might, after all, be accused of constituting themselves the agents

---

found it was one of my guards, trying to advise me that my shoestring had come untied.

On the last of these occasions, I was taking a long walk alone but with my guardians faithfully behind me, late at night. We passed a bookstore window in which I observed a reproduction of a painting, the original of which I had seen in the Tretyakov Gallery in Moscow. Dating from the 1880s, it depicted a muddy little village street-crossing, with a church in the background. I knew that this was actually the representation of the little square in front of Spaso House, where my guardians spent most of their days and nights on lonely vigil, awaiting my sorties. I therefore turned to them, and, violating all the rules and traditions, asked them: "Do you know what that scene is?" Their faces reflected shock and consternation. They looked at each other, none wishing to be the first to speak. Finally one of them, the superior no doubt, nodded his head and replied, with a slight smile: "We know, we know." They were pleased, I suspect, that their knowledge of Russian art was equal to mine.

(or the "running-dogs," as the Communist phrase went) of the imperialists. None would take any initiative; every service had to be
specifically ordered; otherwise it might look as though one were
leaping to ingratiate oneself with the capitalistic masters. (Hence
the initial unwillingness, on my first arrival, to take the bags upstairs.) They would not report their presence on arrival in the
morning; nor would they tell you when they were leaving at the
end of day. They simply silently and mysteriously disappeared.
Some of them one never saw at all, in fact, unless one summoned
them.

A slight exception to this rule was provided (at some risk to
themselves, no doubt) by two elderly Chinese who had been at the
embassy in earlier years, knew me from these earlier times, and
could not free themselves from a concept of their calling somewhat
higher than that by which the Russians were animated. They were
the only ones who exhibited a limited measure of individual concern over the way things were going in the household. During the
first weeks, when I was living there alone, one of them — to my
lasting gratitude — would remain after everyone else had left,
bring my supper up to my study on a tray — trembling, I always
suspected, for the risk he was running in being thus alone, if only
for a moment, with someone so dangerous as myself. The supper
eaten and the tray removed, he too would vanish precipitately.
I would then be left wholly alone in the great empty mansion
through the long twilight of the northern summer evening. Looking out the window, I could see the Soviet citizens piously crossing
the street to avoid walking in the dangerous proximity of our fence.
I could hear, night after night, the testing of jet engines somewhere
off across the Moscow River. Sometimes I would wander around
the building without turning the lights on, go down into the great,
dimly lit white ballroom that rose from ground floor to ceiling, and
play the grand piano, or, having no one with whom to speak Russian, establish myself in one of the gilded chairs of the several living

rooms and read Russian aloud to myself just to indulge my love of the language. This state of solitude in the great nocturnal spaces of the building gave me no sense of anxiety. No Russian criminal would have been caught dead trying to enter the place: such an action would, after all, probably have been interpreted as an attempt to get into touch with *me*, and that, in official Soviet eyes, was a crime worse, and more severely punishable, than mere murder or robbery. So I wandered securely about in my gilded prison, comforting myself with the reflection that if this venerable building, with its unhappy history, had a ghost, the ghost was unquestionably I.

On a few occasions, chafing under my isolation, I went for evening walks in the great "Park of Culture and Rest," along the south side of the Moscow River. Here, the paths would be crowded with tens of thousands of Muscovites, strolling, taking the summer air, visiting the movie houses and other recreational institutions. Never did I long more for the privilege of being, if only for a time, a part of these people, of talking with them, of sharing their life. For more than two decades, now, Russia had been in my blood. There was some mysterious affinity which I could not explain even to myself; and nothing could have given me deeper satisfaction than to indulge it.

But this was not to be. My guards strode relentlessly at my heels. Even if they had not done so, I knew myself to be the bearer of a species of plague. I dared not touch anyone, for fear of bringing to him infection and perdition.

Our appearance — that of my guards and myself — on the paths of the park attracted no attention. The guards looked like any other Russians. I was casually dressed. We merged inconspicuously with the crowds. I could feel the very physical proximity of these inhabitants of a forbidden land — hear snatches of their speech, observe their faces and their behavior, detect the familiar and peculiarly Russian odor of their clothing. Yet I was separated from them by an invisible and insuperable barrier: so near, and yet so far.

I came gradually to think of myself as a species of disembodied spirit — capable, like the invisible character of the fairy tales, of seeing others and of moving among them but not of being seen, or at least not of being identified by them. Thus, I thought to myself, might life appear to someone from another age, or another planet, permitted to come to this scene and to observe the comings and goings of a life in which he had no part.

Particularly galling, in those first weeks of renewed residence in Russia, was the realization that while the embassy residence was ostensibly at our disposal, and specifically at my own, as ambassador — while it was, in fact, officially my home — it was really run by unseen hands, before whose authority I and all the rest of us were substantially helpless. Servants could be obtained only through the agency of a Soviet office, known as the Burobin, which, although nominally a section of the Foreign Office, was in reality a branch of the secret police. They, not we, decided who could and who could not work in the American embassy; and their decision was essentially final, because it was only through them that we could get anyone at all. If it did not suit their purpose to supply a "servant" or to comply with some other sort of request (they were the only agency authorized to supply servicing facilities of any sort to the foreign diplomatic missions), months could go by without even the courtesy of a reply. They had a monopoly. We had no alternative. The household personnel, who had of course to report to these unseen masters at regular intervals, were well aware of the situation; and we were made to feel it.

It was May when I arrived in Moscow. A few days after my arrival I noticed that although the growing season was now upon us, not a hand had been laid on the lawn and garden, all of which lay there in a state of total neglect. Inquiry of the embassy's administrative office elicited the information that there were three men on the residence payroll, very highly paid by Russian standards, whose title was that of yardman, and whose duty it was to keep lawn and garden in order. Having never seen them, and having no one to help me, I went on the search for them one morning, before leaving for the office. I found the three of them sitting on a bench in the mild spring sunshine, in the untouched garden. They neither responded to my greeting nor did they rise at my approach. I asked why nothing had been done about the grounds. The answer was curt and rude. "There are no tools. We don't know where the tools are." I simply walked away. I was helpless, and they knew it. If I fired them, I would get no replacement at all.

Finding that there was a man on the payroll as night watchman who was rarely there, even at night, and when there was incapable of doing any useful work, I fired him and filed with Burobin the usual request for a replacement. Months went by with no response. My family, in the meantime, arrived. One night in late summer my wife and I were wakened by hearing a slight noise on the gallery of the ballroom, just outside our bedroom. I arose and went out to see what it was. There, in the dim light of the gallery (we kept a single lamp burning in the ballroom, below), I suddenly found myself face to face with an apparition which I was able to identify as the figure of a large woman, taller than myself — or so it seemed. I said: "Who are you?" The answer came back: "I'm the new night watchman." Characteristically, Burobin (for which read: the secret police) had not even done us the courtesy of telling us she had been hired, nor had she made her presence in the house known. The idea of consulting us as to whether we wanted her had obviously never even entered the minds of our police mentors.

Things got better after the family arrived. My wife brought with her an excellent Danish cook and butler and later a capable Danish nurse for the child. These collaborators, being non-Soviet citizens, were relatively immune to police pressures. With their help and with my wife's presence and attention, things finally got moving, and even the Russian staff began to take an interest.

But irritations were never absent. The ones described above sound petty from the distance of nearly two decades. But the atmosphere of Moscow was, for "bourgeois" diplomats, a tense one anyway. One was constantly conscious of the suspicion and hostility with which one is viewed, of the elaborate secretiveness of the authorities, of the proximity of unseen but sinister eyes, ears, and hands — observing, eavesdropping, manipulating one's life from the shadows. For sensitive people this could, over the long run, tell on the nerves.

It was on the fourteenth of May, 1952, that I presented credentials. Nikolai Shvernik,* in his protocolaire capacity as Chairman of the Presidium of the Supreme Soviet, did the honors from the Soviet side. The ceremony was in the usual ballroom of the Kremlin palace. My mind naturally went back to the occasion, some eighteen years earlier, when I had accompanied our first ambassador to the Soviet Union, Bill Bullitt, on a similar errand to this same room. It was in the first euphoric days after our arrival in Moscow, in December 1933. I had received word, the evening before, that my beloved and respected father, from whom I had taken final leave only a fortnight earlier, was dead. Not wishing to burden the other members of our delegation with my own sadness at such a moment, I had kept the news to myself; but I had not slept at night, there had been no time for breakfast, and when I stood there in my cutaway behind Bullitt at the ceremony, in the middle of the vast, polished parquet floor, with nothing to lean against or hold on to for thirty feet in any direction, the whole room had begun to swim,

---

* Nikolai Mikhailovich Shvernik (1888–1970), old Bolshevik and prominent Soviet official, at that time Chairman of the Presidium of the Supreme Soviet of the USSR, in which capacity he functioned as titular head of state and received the credentials of foreign ambassadors.

and I had had to spread my feet and speak sternly to myself to keep from fainting. Bullitt, I recalled, had come with high hopes and enormous enthusiasm. I came, now, only with misgivings and premonitions. So much had we learned in two decades of contact with the Soviet government.

In my instructionless state, I had had to draft my own letter of presentation. I was damned if I was going to mouth any of the stock phrases, customary in such communications, about my zeal to maintain and to further "the good relations which so happily exist between our two governments." The armistice talks were still dragging on in Korea. The tone of the Soviet press was wildly hostile to us. Why pretend? The purpose of my government, I said, was "the peaceful adjustment of all those specific questions the solution of which requires agreement between the two governments." We also wished, I added, "to see the removal of the conditions which up to this time have impeded normal associations between the citizens of our countries." To these aims my activity would be devoted. I hoped it would meet with understanding and collaboration on their side.

After the formal ceremony, there was the usual private chat with Shvernik. Here, I expanded on my letter. Yes, I said, we did wish to see the early and peaceful adjustment of outstanding questions. But this did not mean "agreement at the cost of our own vital interests, or of the independence and security of third countries, or of the stability of entire areas of the world that lie between our two countries." Nor was it the view of my government, I went on, that an improvement could be achieved just by paper agreements alone. "For such agreements to be really effective they would," I observed,

have to be accompanied by changes in the attitudes and behavior of states as well as in their obligations and formal statements. The initiatives for such changes cannot be entirely one-sided; but I can assure you that my government will not be found lacking in readiness to show goodwill and to improve conditions for the conduct of our relations, if it sees any similar readiness on the other side.

Generalissimo Stalin has indicated that he believes in the possibility of coexistence between the system of government prevailing here and that which prevails in our country; and certain of your representatives seem to feel it necessary that we should assert publicly our own belief in this possibility. We find this suggestion a strange one. Of course we believe in this possibility. Had we not believed in it we would never have established relations with the Soviet government in 1933 nor continued to conduct those relations over a period of nineteen years under conditions which have generally been unfavorable and discouraging in the extreme. The question is not whether the two systems can coexist. They have already coexisted for thirty-five years; and we see no reason why they should not continue to coexist for thirty-five more, or three hundred and fifty more, for that matter. The real question is "how" — whether, that is, they are to continue in a state of tension and mutual suspicion bound to keep the world in uncertainty and anxiety, or whether they are to achieve a normal relationship based on mutual tolerance and respect and compatible with a constructive development of world society as a whole.

This was, so far as I can recall, the only statement of a political nature that I ever made to the Soviet government during the period of my incumbency as ambassador. Even this represented nothing but my own views, and I am not at all sure, in retrospect, that it was accurate. There were, I am afraid, a number of people in our own government, particularly on the military side, who had no belief at all in the possibility of an indefinite period of peaceful coexistence with the Soviet Union; and I cannot, on reflection, think of any major problem in which we were prepared to make any significant concessions in order to reach agreement with the Russians — certainly not with relation to Germany, or nuclear weaponry, or Japan. But I cannot reproach myself too severely. When one is without instructions, one has to say *something*.

I did not ask for an appointment with Stalin. The main reason was simply that, being effectively without instructions, I had nothing to say to him. Why, I thought, take up the time of a busy man for no good purpose at all and only invite embarrassment in case he opened up any serious question? Beyond that, my British colleague, Sir Alvary Douglas Frederick Gascoigne, had at that time been waiting several months in vain for a reply to his own request for such an interview, and I saw no reason to put myself in this position. But the failure to do so may have been a mistake. God knows what impression was produced by it on the aging and semi-mad dictator.

I seldom had occasion to visit the Soviet Foreign Office. When I did, the various officials there were correct, if reserved. We were accustomed to this. Their offices were obviously "bugged." They had to account to unseen superiors for every incautious or overly friendly word. One did not normally attempt to discuss political questions with them; and when one did, one got nothing but the familiar party line.

We were left, therefore, to derive our impressions of Soviet attitudes from the press and other public media of official expression. And here, the impression was shattering. For my arrival in Moscow coincided with a chorus of vituperation, directed against the United States, which for sheer viciousness and intensity has no parallel, so far as I know, in the history of international relations. The wartime anti-Allied propaganda of Joseph Goebbels paled, as I can testify, beside it.

Anti-American propaganda was of course nothing new at the seat of the Soviet government. To a considerable extent, it had always been present. In 1951, a little over a year before my arrival, it had taken on new and extreme proportions. After the issuance in February 1952 of the report of a committee of the House of Representatives, in Washington, on the Katyn Massacre,* a report which

---

* This refers to the deliberate execution of several thousand Polish officers whose bodies, interred in mass graves, were discovered by the Germans, and the deed revealed to the world public, in February 1943.

threw the blame for this incredible act of cruelty squarely on the Soviet police authorities, where it belonged, the anti-American propaganda was further stepped up. A high point of sorts had been reached in April, the main theme being already the charge that we were conducting bacteriological warfare in Korea. Now, immediately after my arrival in Moscow, a new crescendo was reached; and it continued through the summer. To the theme of bacteriological warfare there were added blood-curdling accusations of the mistreatment of prisoners in Korea. These, as I say, were the main themes; but it is difficult to think of any atrocity, even down to the bayoneting of the bellies of the pregnant women, of which we were not accused.

The impact of this campaign hit us from all sides. Not only was the press full of it — agitators beat the drums in the parks; it found its reflection in the theaters and movies; placards portraying hideous spiderlike characters in American military uniform, armed with spray guns and injection needles for bacteriological warfare, stared down at us from every fence throughout the city.

My friends in the government in Washington were not exposed to this barrage. To the extent they heard of it, they took it, accustomed as they all were to the general fact of anticapitalist Soviet propaganda, with a blasé indifference. But to me, as ambassador on the spot, it was a different thing. I spent much of my time, over those unhappy months, attempting to analyze the reasons for it. In a letter written to a friend in the department on June 6, when I had been for one month in Moscow, I tried to identify the conceivable hypotheses. I found four of them, which I adduce here in the language of the letter.

(1) That the Kremlin considers that the general state of popular morale throughout the Communist-controlled area, as marked by such things as the attitudes of the Communist war prisoners in Korea, the continued defections of individuals in the satellite area, the difficulty of raising reliable military forces in Eastern Germany, and the general

apathy of the Soviet population itself toward international problems, is simply not adequate for the strains of the situation in which Soviet policy is now proceeding, and has concluded that something drastic must be done to stir people up to a greater enthusiasm for the severe tensions which this policy involves.

(2) That the Kremlin foresees some more severe test of political morale in the Soviet and satellite areas looming up in the near future, and is setting about to steel the population for these anticipated eventualities, whatever they may be.

(3) That there has been some internal disagreement in influential circles here over problems of policy towards the United States and that the violence of this present campaign represents the characteristically crude and ruthless expression of the victory of one group over another; and

(4) That the campaign stands in some connection with my appointment and arrival here, and with the possibility that a time might be approaching when confidential discussions between our two governments on what would be considered here the "real" plane, as opposed to the plane of propaganda exchanges aimed at the grandstand, would be in order, or would at least be suggested by our side.

None of these hypotheses fully satisfied me at the time. None satisfies me completely today. From what we now know of the failure of the senior party bodies to meet in the period preceding my arrival, I think one may be fairly sure that the impulse to the campaign came directly from Stalin. It had begun at a time when, as we also know (see above, Chapter 5), Stalin had thought that war with the United States might well be imminent. Possibly he continued, through the summer of 1952, to hold to that view, although the papers he permitted to be published over his name in the magazine *Bolshevik*, in October 1952, do not suggest it. (If he did hold to it, the anti-American campaign may have been conceived as an effort to overcome the irrepressible pro-American tendencies in Russian mass opinion.) Stalin may also have mistaken publication of the House committee's report on Katyn for the beginning of a campaign on our part to discredit the Soviet Union in the Communist orbit, and particularly in Poland; and this may have been his way of replying. (He would not, in this connection, have been influenced by the fact that the charges about Katyn were true. In the Soviet view, the publication of anything discreditable to the Soviet leaders, even if it happens to be true and historically important, constitutes an unfriendly act.) However that may be, continued exposure to the violence and ubiquity of this propaganda, particularly for one who, in this case, represented in his person the President of the United States and the commander in chief of the American armed forces, added very materially to the harrowing impressions of those few short months in Moscow.

I would not like to give the impression that life in Moscow at that time consisted only of unalleviated strain and unpleasantness. Russia was still Russia; there were still occasional fleeting points of contact, or near-contact, with Russian life — not nearly as many as there had been during previous tours of duty in Moscow, but some; and for me these brushes were always fascinating, tantalizing, and enjoyable.

The Associated Press correspondent in Moscow at that time was Tom (Thomas P.) Whitney, formerly, during the war and just after, an attaché on the embassy staff. Obliged to leave the embassy because he had married a Russian girl, he had remained in Moscow as a journalist. He and his wife — the latter a musician and *chanteuse* of talent — had a cottage in one of the regular *dacha* communities, some miles out of Moscow. I drove out and visited them there on several occasions, usually on weekends.

The suburban community in question was a thoroughly Russian one. There were few, if any, other foreigners. It consisted, like other such communities, of small cottages, many of them log cabins, generously spaced among the pine trees along the long straight avenues of sand and grass, scarred here and there with wagon tracks and footpaths, that served as streets. My angels, apparently understanding (and, I suspect, even sympathizing with) my desire for a little privacy, would park their car at a discreet distance, so that I did not have the feeling that my presence was painfully conspicuous. Harrison Salisbury, then stationed in Moscow as correspondent for the *New York Times*, would also usually be present. We would sit in the garden under the birches, drink tea, and sometimes read aloud; and then there would ensue one of those glorious unhurried discussions, philosophical and political, which seem to be a part of the very air of Russia.

Here, once more, as on my various journeys around Russia in the 1930s and during the war, I could have the sense of Russia all about me, and could give myself, momentarily, the illusion that I was part of it. It was summer — the marvelous summer of central Russia, with its deep blue skies, its fields and ravines, its evergreens and birches and poplars, its straggling villages and onion-domed churches, its far horizons with always the dark dim line of distant forests. The common people, beginning now to recover to some extent from the horrors and privations of the war, and animated, in these final months of the Stalin era, by a fear of all political involvement and a revulsion to all thought and talk of internal politics, were digging in again, so to speak, with their characteristic patient, irrespressible vitality — creating a life for themselves, such as they could, within the rigid limits prescribed by the system. The collective farmers were permitted now to sell, at open outdoor markets, such surplus produce as they could grow on their own small private plots. The city suburbanites had likewise their kitchen gardens and sometimes even an animal or two. These various private activities tended to merge; and in this way there was growing up, particularly on the outskirts of Moscow, what might be called a form of petty free enterprise — a free enterprise strictly limited in the scope and forms it could take but active, busy and, in its way, hopeful.

There was, therefore, something old-Russian about these suburban communities in that last year of Stalin's life — an atmosphere of health and simplicity and subdued hope which I drank in, on my brief visits there, as one drinks in fresh air after long detention in a stuffy room. I tried to convey something of this atmosphere, and of the economic realities that made it possible, in a private letter, of July 15, 1952, to H. Freeman Matthews, then Deputy Under Secretary of State. Little garden plots existed around Moscow, I wrote,

by the hundreds of thousands, some leased out for the summer by the suburban municipalities from public lands (roadside strips, stream-bottoms, etc.) but without accompanying buildings, others leased out as the grounds of summer dachas, others belonging to what are, in effect, private suburban properties. These areas on the edge of the city virtually hum with activity, and the activity is one having little or nothing to do with the "socialized sector" of economy. Houses are built with family labor (log houses still, but stout and warm and not bad housing); gardens and orchards are laid out; poultry and livestock (individual cows and goats) are traded and cultivated in great number, though all trading must be done in individual animals, or at the most, pairs, not in herds.

I estimated the number of people engaged in these activities, just near Moscow alone, in the millions. And around their activities, I pointed out, there had grown up

a sort of commercial servicing establishment: people who make their living by growing seeds and hothouse plants, breeding animals, etc. All these people have to keep their operations to a small scale. They must be careful not to employ labor, or to be found owning anything so magnificent as a truck. Everything must be masked as individual, rather than highly organized commercial, activity. But there are ways and means of solving all those problems.

And the result of all this was, I wrote, a world of "miniature private interest" in which people devoted themselves to, and thought about, "everything under the sun except the success of communism," and appeared to be quite happy doing so. I knew, in fact, of no human environment more warmly and agreeably pulsating with activity, contentment and sociability than a contemporary Moscow suburban "*dacha*" area on a nice spring morning, after the long, trying winter. Everything takes place in a genial intimacy and informality: hammers ring; roosters crow, goats tug at their tethers, barefoot women hoe vigorously at the potato patches, small boys play excitedly in the little streams and ponds, family parties sit at crude wooden tables in the gardens under the young fruit trees. The great good earth of Mother Russia, long ignored in favor of childish industrial fetishes of the earlier Communist period, seems once more to exude her benevolent and maternal warmth over man and beast and growing things together; and only, perhaps, an American ambassador, stalking through the countryside with his company of guardians to the amazement of the children and the terror of the adults, is effectively isolated, as though by an invisible barrier, from participation in the general beneficence of nature and human sociability.

Well — the Whitney *dacha* was as close as I ever came to breaking, in that strange summer, the barrier to which this letter referred; and the hours there glow in memory. But I realize, as I look back on it today, that the magic of this atmosphere was derived not just from the fact that this was Russia but also from the fact that it was a preindustrial life that I was privileged here to observe: a life in which people were doing things with their hands, with animals and with Nature, a life little touched by any form of modernization, a pre–World War I and prerevolutionary life, agreeable precisely because it was not a part of, little connected with, in fact disliked and only reluctantly tolerated by, the political establishment of the country in which it existed. How much richer and more satisfying was human existence, after all, when there was not too much of the machine!

Nor was this the only pleasant experience of that summer. I arranged at one time to pay a visit, in company with my wife and our oldest daughter, Grace, to the Tolstoi estate, in the country near Tula, some hundred and twenty miles south of Moscow. I had been there once many years before; but that had been in midwinter, in a blizzard, and there had been limitations on what one could see. The journey was made, this time, by car. We had, for some reason, two vehicles following us, instead of the usual one; and we picked up more at the border of the Tula Oblast, where the provincial police authorities became involved. We arrived, therefore, as in a veritable cortege.

Nevertheless, I enjoyed the day greatly. The old house, despite the vicissitudes of the four decades that had elapsed since Tolstoi's death and despite the museumlike quality that now, unavoidably, hung over it, felt and smelled like any old American country house — musty and with a sense of apples under the porch floor — felt and smelled, I thought, as it must have done when my cousin, the elder George Kennan (1845–1923) visited the great writer there, many, many years ago. But what gave me greatest pleasure was that there was produced, to guide me, none other than the man who had been Tolstoi's private secretary in the final year of the great man's life: Valentin Fedorovich Bulgakov. Bulgakov had been there — not in the house but nearby — when the aged Tolstoi got up and fled secretly, in the night, from home and family, to embark on the short journey from which he was never to return. It was he, together with the youngest daughter, Aleksandra Lvovna, to whom it had fallen to frustrate the attempts by Tolstoi's frantic wife, Sofya Andreevna, to commit suicide, when she discovered what had occurred.

Of all this, and of many other subjects of common interest in nineteenth-century Russian literature, we talked with Bulgakov as we walked that day through the paths of the "park" at Yasnaya Polyana. He, I suppose, does not remember it; but I do. Our guardians walked behind us, but they did not interfere with our conversation. And it was as though I had entered, for that hour, into a different world, familiar from old times, yet long unseen. Not only was I charmed to encounter once again that peculiar combination of modesty and knowledge which Bulgakov shared with so many others of the prerevolutionary cultural intelligentsia, but I recall the pleasure I derived from hearing once again (I had heard it in some of my first Russian teachers, many years before) the authentic accent — rich, polished, elegant and musical — of the educated circles of those earlier times. So, I thought to myself, must Tolstoi himself have spoken.

Whether the assignment of Mr. Bulgakov to this task was a routine practice, or whether those in whose hands the arrangements lay on that particular day consented to recognize for this brief hour the existence of a sincere and serious interest on my part in Russian literature and culture, I shall never know. But here, once again, I was permitted to feel close to a world to which, I always thought, I could really have belonged, had circumstances permitted — belonged much more naturally and wholeheartedly than to the world of politics and diplomacy into which Fate had thrust me; and if the brief leniency of that day reflected an understanding of this fact somewhere in the tangled reaches of Soviet bureaucracy, my thanks go out with these words to whoever it was who authorized it. For so little could one, in the Russia of 1952, be grateful.

Finally, if I am to describe the pleasures of that generally unhappy summer of 1952, I must mention the Moscow theater — no greater a pleasure then, to be sure, than at any other time, and in some ways even less so, but a pleasure still. Here, in premises where we could not talk to them at all and they could talk to us only through the mouths of dramatic characters, we nevertheless came close, physically, to the members of that remarkable and talented group of Soviet people, the theatrical community; and in their acting, in the interpretations they gave to the parts they played, we were able to gain some idea of what they, and with them the generation to which they belonged, were like.

Did they know this? Were they aware of our presence, of our scrutiny, of our effort to understand them through the artificiality of what they were doing? We never knew. I attended one evening, in company with my friend Robert Tucker, now a professor at Princeton, a performance of Tolstoi's *Resurrection* at the Moscow Art Theater. We had seats in the second or third row, my angels arrayed in solid phalanx behind us. In the middle of the second or third act (I was sunk in one of those reveries one sometimes falls into even at the best of plays), I suddenly seemed to hear the leading man, who had advanced to the footlights and appeared to be looking right down on me, say, in the course of a long monologue, something to the effect that "there is an American by the name of George, and with him we are all in agreement." I was electrified. I could not believe my ears. Was this a message of sympathy? Was it some sort of disguised demonstration? I looked at Tucker. He had caught it, too, and looked equally startled. Together, when the play was over, we rushed back to the embassy, got out a copy of the novel from which the play was taken, and traced down the origin of the scene. To our great disappointment, there it was, indeed: a reference to Henry George, the advocate of the single tax. The line, then, was legitimate. But was the actor aware of the play on words? And did he enjoy it as much as we did? We shall never know. It was in just such faint signals, or fancied signals, that we foreigners, like astronomers listening for sounds from space that would betray life on another planet, were forced to try to gain our feeling for the Russian cultural world whose presence and vitality we felt all around us.

They were strange months: those summer months of 1952. We know more today than we did then about what was proceeding behind the scenes. But those of us who knew Russia were aware of the fact that all was not right. In Moscow, as in no other place of my acquaintance, political atmosphere can be sensed without being discussed. A curious deadness, caution, and feeling of uncertainty hung over the Russian capital that summer. Although Stalin's health was, to all outward appearances, good enough for a man of his age, things seemed to have come to, or to be approaching, some sort of end. There was no five-year plan, no great undertaking of the regime around which to whip up the semblance of popular enthusiasm. Stalin, contrary to his usual custom, appeared to have remained in Moscow; but even about this there was no certainty. The Stalin who was supposed to appear at the opening of the Volga-Don Canal, in midsummer, and for whose appearance tremendous fanfares of preparation had been undertaken and carried forward to the morning of the event, failed unaccountably to show up. Some time later, our armed services attachés, surveying the tribune at the Air Force Day parade (I myself declined to attend the occasion because the event was announced to the populace in advance by placards showing American planes being shot down over Hungary), had the distinct impression that the Stalin who appeared there was a dummy: the other members of the Politburo, in any case, seemed to pay no attention to him and talked unceremoniously past his face.

As compared with the years of my earlier service in Russia, two changes struck me sharply. One was the growing inner detachment of the people from the ostensible purposes of a revolutionary regime — their curious lack of interest in the professed ideological inspiration of those who commanded their obedience. The second was the growing extent and rigidity of stratification, both social and bureaucratic, in Soviet society. In the years prior to World War II Stalin had kept all of Russian society, but particularly the educated and politically active sectors of it, in a constant state of change and turmoil — with his programs of collectivization and industrialization and his sweeping, terrible purges. There had been no opportunity for internal relationships within Russian society to congeal: for friendships and loyalties to form in bureaucratic bodies, for vested interests to be created, for the advantages of the father to become the assets of the son. But since the war, there had been no further purges of general significance.* And the result was that these processes were now beginning to take place.

Both of these phenomena, I pointed out in the conclusion of the letter to Matthews mentioned above, were reflections of the life and works of a single man — Stalin.

The first is the reflection of his infinite jealousy and avidity for political power — qualities that carried him to his absurd pretensions to an earthly divinity and actually killed the ideological sense and function of the political movement of which he is the head. The second is the reflection of his increasing age and approaching death. No great country can be identified as closely as is this one with the life and fortunes of a single man — so bent and attuned to his personality, his whims and his neuroses — without sharing to a degree his weaknesses and his very mortality. The party has tried to rule out change; but the party is hoisted here on the petard of its own lack of genuine democracy, of the loss of organic connection with the emotional forces of the people themselves — of its dependence on, and beholdenness to, the life cycle of a single individual.

I did not see in this situation, I explained, any early revolt in the Soviet Union.

I see no likely dramatic or abrupt ending to the phenomenon of Bolshevism. Least of all do I see in the minds of the people any new or revolutionary alternative to the present system. I cannot rule these things out, but they are not in the cards as they appear to me today. I *do* see that the party has not succeeded in ruling out change. I see that there are great forces operating here which are not really under the control of the regime, because they are part of the regime's own failings and its own mortality.

I warned against drawing any "primitive and oversimplified conclusions" from these observations; but I did see in them reinforce-

---

* I think now that I somewhat underestimated the extent and importance of the purge of the Leningrad party apparatus that began with Zhdanov's death in the summer of 1948 and continued throughout 1949 and 1950; but even this was primarily a local operation and did not affect the population as a whole.

ment for my skepticism of the reality of George Orwell's nightmare of 1984. It was simply not true, I thought,

> that the Soviet leaders have somehow found some mysterious secret of
> infallibility in the exercise of power and that it is no problem for them
> to hang on indefinitely and to mold Soviet society to their hearts' desire.

Although I had not been able to detect in official Washington
any particular desire for my own views on American policy, my
position as ambassador left me no choice but to worry about it.
Trying to distinguish what might be the kernel of sincerity in that
great shell of exaggeration and distortion in which Soviet statements were normally included, I began to ask myself whether, even
accepting the disingenuousness of most of the Soviet propaganda
about the aggressive aims of the United States and NATO, we had
not contributed, and were not continuing to contribute — by the
overmilitarization of our policies and statements — to a belief in
Moscow that it was war we were after, that we had settled for its
inevitability, that it was only a matter of time before we would unleash it.

The Soviet press of that day was replete (as I suppose it has been
ever since) with stories of American or NATO military activities
which, if true, would indeed have suggested commitment on the
Western side to the inevitability of war. Americans, it was reported, were taking over various Yugoslav airports; the size of the
American military mission in Turkey had risen to the number of
twelve hundred; a strategic road of some seven hundred miles in
length was being built from the Turkish port of Iskanderun to the
Soviet-Turkish frontier (an undertaking which, if it was really
proceeding, would have clearly suggested offensive rather than defensive intent); American agents, one of them identified by name,
were intriguing with nationalist, anti-Soviet elements in Finland;
the United States was pressing Denmark for air bases; in Western

Germany and in Austria, vast tracts of land were being requisitioned by the American authorities for military use.

Some of these reports were obviously false or overdrawn. But were all of them so? I had no means of knowing. Our government never — but literally never — took the trouble to refute them. The Department of State itself probably did not know, in most cases, whether they were true or false. The Pentagon, if asked, would probably not have told. Military security would have been cited as the reason for this reticence. And besides, nobody at the Washington end cared. The Russian reports, they would have said, were "just propaganda."

I never agreed with this reaction. If the tales were false, I thought it dangerous to let them go without denial. If they were true, and if the actions in question were indeed creating the impression — and not just on the Russians — that we were pursuing a highly militarized policy, disbelieving in the possibilities for peace and concerned only with the shaping of our posture for a war regarded as inevitable, then, I thought, we should review these actions and see whether, judged from the standpoint of our overall interests, political and military, they were really worth pursuing.

It was not just from the columns of the Soviet press that this problem impinged itself on me. I was not long in discovering, after arrival in Moscow, that the facilities of the embassy were being abused, and the very usefulness of the mission jeopardized, by the service attachés (the military, naval and air attachés sent out by the Pentagon) for the purpose of gathering military intelligence. The Russians had always regarded military attachés, and indeed all diplomats, as spies; now ours were acting like them.

This led to ridiculous and undesirable situations. Our people, for example, mounted a sort of telescopic camera on the roof of our embassy chancery to photograph the Soviet planes as they flew over the city on the days of the major Red Square parades. The

Russians stood on the roof of the Hotel National, next door, and photographed our people in the process. We then, in turn, photographed the Russians photographing us. It had all become a silly and discreditable game, merely fortifying the Russians in their cynicism about the purpose of our embassy in Moscow and about the inspiration of our policies generally.

I strongly disapproved of all this. We were, for all our differences with the Soviet government, guests in the Soviet capital. We owed it not only to them but to our own standards of behavior to observe the rules of propriety and good taste, not to mention the laws of the host country. But beyond that, we were abusing the real diplomatic potential of the mission, and in some respects endangering its existence. And nobody in Washington, apparently, cared about this. The State Department was either too indifferent or too timid to make an issue of it. But I could not disregard it.

I gave orders that these abuses were to stop — that such activities were to remain within the limits normally permissible in international intercourse. During the brief period of my stay there, I believe there was a considerable improvement. But the situation continued to worry me. How was I to account for, or to explain, the overriding priority that Washington appeared to give to the gathering of military intelligence over whatever other usefulness, and particularly whatever usefulness in the task of *preventing* a war, the embassy might have had?

A particularly violent jolt was received one day when one of the service attachés showed me a message he had received from Washington concerning a certain step of a military nature that the Pentagon proposed to take for the purpose of strengthening our military posture in a region not far from the Soviet frontiers. I paled when I read it. It was at once apparent to me that had I been a Soviet leader, and had I learned (as the Soviet government would have been certain to learn) that such a step was being taken, I would have concluded that the Americans were shaping their preparations towards a target of war within six months. Since it had been freely bruited around Washington, in the 1949–1950 period, that our military preparations were being oriented towards a "peak of danger" supposed to arrive in 1952, it would have been all the easier for Soviet leaders to jump, here, to the most alarming of conclusions, with the result that *their* preparations, too, would have gone into high gear, and the situation would soon be out of control.

I was able, by dint of vigorous remonstrances, to spike this particular initiative; but I could not get over my concern at the recklessness — the willingness to subordinate everything to military considerations — that appeared to inspire official Washington. I knew that my government had no aggressive intent — that even such suggestions as the one I had just opposed were basically defensive in nature. But it was also apparent to me that the Pentagon now had the bit in its teeth, and that there was simply insufficient vigor, and insufficient understanding of the situation, on the political side of the Potomac to bring about a proper balance in American policy between military and political considerations. The coordination of these two categories of considerations has always been the weak point of our system of government; and never did this weakness seem more conspicuous, and more dangerous, than it did to me at that time.

It was these reactions that led me to undertake, in late August, the composition of a basic dispatch on the subject of the Soviet reaction to NATO. This document, drafted in Moscow many years before the "revisionist" challenges of the late 1960s to the propriety and integrity of American statesmanship in the postwar period were advanced,* constitutes unquestionably the strongest statement I ever made of my views on this general subject of our

---

* The reference is to a number of works on the origins of the "cold war" by American scholars (including Messrs. Gar Alperovitz, Walter Carl Clemens, David Horowitz, Gabriel Kolko, and Carl Oglesby) which have tended to assign to the United States government the major blame for the provoking or initiating of the various conflicts and complications that have marked Soviet-American relations in the postwar period.

responsibility for the deterioration of relations between Russia and the West in the late 1940s. I append, therefore, in the Annex, the main portion of the report (omitting only a section about Korea which would duplicate what has been said above in this present volume).

The document being available to the reader, I shall not summarize it in detail. The essence of what I had to say was that the Russians, many disagreeable and disturbing aspects of their behavior notwithstanding, had had no intention of attacking Western Europe in those postwar years, and thought we must have known it. For this reason, the manner in which NATO was formed and presented to the Western public, i.e., as a response to the "Soviet threat" and as a "deterrent" to Soviet aggression, mystified them and caused them to search for some sinister hidden motive in our policy.* This effect had been reinforced by our steps toward the rearmament of Germany and Japan, by the manner in which we ourselves had interpreted and presented our action in Korea, and by Leninist doctrine, which told them that as the social foundation of the capitalist order disintegrated in the West, the leaders of the exploiting class (i.e., the Western governments) would "go from one form of attack to other, sharper forms of attack."

I was careful to point out that of course not all Soviet professions of suspicion of ourselves were sincere. The evidence merely seemed to me to indicate

---

* The following item, which appeared in the news bulletin of the British embassy in Moscow on May 12, 1952, one week after my arrival there as ambassador, will serve as an example of the manner in which Soviet intentions were at that time generally depicted in the atmosphere of official Washington:

"In Washington the Foreign Affairs Committee of the House of Representatives has said there has been no lessening of the danger of Soviet aggression to justify the United States relaxing her defence efforts. This statement is made by the Committee in a report on the Foreign Aid Bill. It says that American military leaders and diplomats consider that Russia has not set a date for an attack on the West. It is quite likely, the report says, that the Kremlin has not yet decided that an all-out war with the Free World is inevitable. Nevertheless, vast Soviet forces, fully mobilized, are ready in Eastern Germany and other places to attack at a moment's notice."

that if one were able to strip away all the overgrowth of propagandistic distortion and maligning of foreign intentions which is the normal encumbrance of Soviet utterances and attitudes, one would find that there remained in recent years a certain hard core of genuine belief in the sinisterness of Western intentions and that this belief was in considerable part, though not entirely, the result of a misinterpretation on their part of Western policies in the years from 1948 to the present.

How far had this misinterpretation affected their policies? It had not yet brought them to consider war as entirely inevitable. For that, they were too much aware of the role of the unexpected and unforeseen in international affairs. But it had probably caused them to intensify their military preparations. It had also brought on in Russia an accentuation of the habitual preoccupation with questions of internal security, and a tightening up of the regime of control and observation applied to foreigners. It had, in this way, weakened what little usefulness might otherwise have been present in the institution of diplomatic relations between Russia and the West. It had, in other words, further impaired that cushion of safety that normally existed in the ability of governments to talk with one another over the diplomatic channel. Beyond this, the Soviet leaders had seen the advantages offered to them, by this American overemphasis on military preparations, for posing as the partisans of peace in contradistinction to the imperialist warmongers of Washington; and the rash of "peace congresses" now being organized by their agents in various parts of the world represented merely the effort to take best advantage of this opportunity.

For these reasons it seemed to me undesirable for us to let the misinterpretation go unchallenged and unresolved.

What, then, should we do to challenge it?

First, we should try to portray our military preparations as prudent minimal responses to the *political* threat posed by the power and attitudes of the Soviet leaders — not as responses to an alleged or implied Soviet intention to attack the West, and not as reflections of a conclusion on our part that the only possible outcome of our political differences with the Russians was a major war.

But secondly — and this was all-important — we should attempt to establish a proper balance in our policy between political and military considerations and should not let the prospects for the preservation of peace be diminished by pursuit of the ideal military posture in an imaginary and not inevitable war. I felt all the more strongly about this last, because I regarded any war between the NATO powers and Russia as a certain, final, and irremediable catastrophe. Our only hope — everyone's only hope — rested in the possibility of restricting the so-called East-West conflict to the political field. If it spilled over to the military field, we were all lost. To permit the chances for the successful pursuit of our interests by means short of war to be in the slightest degree damaged by the fatuous search for the best posture in a war that was not inevitable and from which no one could conceivably gain: this seemed to me the greatest and most terrible of follies.

I was aware, of course, that many of the military measures on our part that disturbed me were viewed by their authors as defensive in inspiration. But any given pattern of military preparations was always bound, I pointed out, to appear to others as the reflection of a given pattern of calculations and intentions. The building of the NATO structure ought to be shaped in such a way as to appear to others, I wrote, not as

the feverish preparations of people who regard war as inevitable and are working against a limit of time, but [as] the calm and judicious measures of people simply building a fence, not in the belief that someone else is likely to try to knock it down, but rather in the normal and prudent desire to have clarity on all sides.

Obviously, such a view would have disadvantages from the standpoint of the earliest possible achievement of the ideal military posture. But there was an incurable conflict between the ideal military posture and the goal of winning the political war — "a war which is still in progress and which we have no choice but to continue to fight."

The requirements of either of these approaches, the military or the political, would — if carried to extremes — be quite destructive of the requirements of the other. . . . Neither could be successful if the other were fully destroyed. If problems were to be faced only from the political standpoint, the degree of actual military preparation that would ensue would be quite inadequate. . . . On the other hand, if the professional military planner were to be given all that he desired . . . the results would be quite disruptive of the political resistance of the Western peoples.

What was needed, then, was "a reasonable and sensible compromise between these two requirements." And this should be a compromise that took full account of Soviet sensibilities. This applied particularly to activities by outside powers in areas adjacent to the Soviet borders, both land and maritime. The Soviet leaders were "quite naturally sensitive about being surrounded by a ring of air bases plainly grouped with a view to penetration of their own territory."

In this respect, too, I reiterated, I was not arguing for the abandonment by ourselves of all means of defense. Obviously, we had to cultivate a stronger military capacity.

But here again *le mieux est l'ennemi du bien.* Surely as one moves one's bases and military facilities towards the Soviet frontiers there comes a point where they tend to create the very thing they were designed to avoid. It is not for us to assume that there are no limits to Soviet patience in the face of encirclement by American bases. Quite aside from political considerations, no great country, peaceful or aggressive, rational or irrational, could sit by and witness with indifference the progressive studding of its own frontiers with the military installations of a great-power competitor. Here again, a compromise must be struck, and one which will inevitably fall somewhat short of the military ideal. This compromise must be struck with a view to the peculiarities of the Russian mentality and tradition. We must remember that almost the only language in which we can now communicate with the Soviet leaders is the language of overt military and political moves. If we still hope to have the ultimate decision confined to the political field and to win on that field, let us be sure the words we speak in this peculiar language do not operate to reduce the Soviet leaders to a state of mind in which for them . . . the only question is not "whether" but "when."

For me, as an individual inner-governmental advisor on problems of relations with Russia and the cold war, this dispatch was my swan song. It was the last thing I would ever have to say formally and in writing to my government, as one of its responsible professional servants, on this subject to which I had now given just twenty-five years of my life. The subject matter of which it treated went to the heart of the problems involved in the further development of our relations with the Soviet Union. Aside from minor questions of style, I would have nothing to change in it today; and if, in the light of the recent controversies about the relative guilt of the two sides for the origins and deepening of the cold war, I had to let public understanding of my views rest on any single document, it would probably be this dispatch, written even prior to such great intervening events as the acceptance of Western Germany into NATO and the arrival of the missile age.

As against those facts, gratifying so far as they go, I have to record that the document was utterly without effect — that it might, insofar as its influence on American or NATO policy was concerned, just as well never have been written. Instead of moving along the lines here urged, the United States government would move, for at least nineteen years into the future, along largely contrary ones. Far from attempting to avoid depicting its own and NATO's military preparations as responses to an alleged Soviet desire to attack the West, it would teach itself and its NATO associates never to refer to the most menacing element of our own military potential otherwise than as "the nuclear deterrent" — the unmistakable implication being that the Russians, longing for the inauguration of World War III, would at once attack, if not deterred by this agency of retribution. Year after year, nothing would be omitted to move American air bases and missile sites as close as possible to Soviet frontiers. Year after year, American naval vessels would be sent on useless demonstrative expeditions into the Black Sea — thus, by implication, imputing to the Russians a degree of patience which our own public and congressional opinion would have been most unlikely to muster had the shoe been on the other foot. Time after time, as in Pakistan or Okinawa, the maintenance and development of military or air bases would be stubbornly pursued with no evidence of any effort to balance this against the obvious political costs. Political interests would continue similarly to be sacrificed or placed in jeopardy by the avid and greedy pursuit of military intelligence; and when our failure to exercise any adequate restraint on such activities led, as it did through the U-2 episode, to the shattering of the political career of the only Soviet statesman of the post-Stalin period with whom we might conceivably have worked out a firmer sort of coexistence and to the replacement of his dominant influence by that of a coterie of military and police officials far more reactionary and militaristic in temper, there was only momentary embarrassment in Washington, no one was held to blame, and no one thought to conduct any serious investigation into the causes of so grievous an error of American national policy.

Whatever intellectual merit the dispatch in question had, it was a failure from the standpoint of its real purpose; and while this is a fate which it has shared with a great many other recommendations by a great many other American ambassadors, I have been moved at times to reflect on the possible causes, and to wonder to what extent my own failings may have contributed to them.

There were specific reasons why no dispatch of this nature

would probably have been read with any interest by anyone in a policy-making position in Washington at that time. Its impact would in any event have been blunted by the excitement attending my expulsion from Russia, soon thereafter. This was, furthermore, the end of a political epoch in Washington. The electoral campaign of 1952 was getting into high gear. However it came out, the days of the Truman administration were now strictly numbered. Neither the President nor the Secretary of State would have been in a mood to undertake the struggle with the Pentagon that would have been necessary if such a change in spirit and orientation of military policy as I was suggesting was really to be effected.

But even in normal times, it would have been most unusual had a dispatch from an ambassador on a subject as broad as this carried any particular weight with the two senior architects of American policy. Coming from an influential senator or a congressional committee chairman or from the AFL-CIO or from some other factor in domestic affairs, and particularly from a number of such people, views of this tenor would have been given serious consideration. But an ambassador represented, in the eyes of his own government, no one but himself. And his opinions, while sometimes engaging or amusing, had little value in the scales of Washington life. What was wrong with this effort to influence government policy was not the nature of the recommendation, or the way it was phrased, but the limitations of the platform from which it was put forward. The realization of this fact diminished my enthusiasm, in the ensuing months, for remaining in a profession where passivity, inscrutability and tactical ingenuity were valued so highly, and serious analytical effort — so little.

7

Persona Non Grata

I HAVE already mentioned the elaborate measures taken by the Soviet authorities to keep foreign representatives under observation and to isolate them from the population. While more extreme in 1952 than at certain other times, such measures were a standard feature of Stalin's practice.

There was one small episode, connected with this situation, which occurred in the early summer of 1952, and which should have been more of a warning to me than it was. To explain it, I must first say a word about its background.

During my previous tours of duty in Moscow, in the 1930s and during the war, there had always been two or three Soviet citizens, usually presentable and cultivated people from among the cultural intelligentsia, who were obviously cleared by party and police for normal social contact with members of the diplomatic corps, and with the senior personnel of our embassy in particular. These individuals would accept invitations to social functions and would associate in a normal way with those officers of the embassy who enjoyed their company and paid them normal social attention. It was obvious that they stood in some sort of special relationship to the police; otherwise they would not have been permitted to cultivate such associations. We always assumed that they were expected to report, and did report, to their police contacts whatever information of interest to the Soviet authorities these associations might yield.

But we did not discourage the arrangement — at least not when we felt that the American officials in question were sensible and experienced persons. It held advantages for us as well as for the Soviet authorities. For one thing, these Russians who were permitted to associate with us were for the most part intelligent and sometimes even charming people, whose company afforded both pleasure and profit. But beyond that, they provided a useful, if one-way, channel of communication to the higher Soviet authorities; and this was nothing to be sneezed at in a situation where communication generally was in such short supply. It was possible to say to these people, in the course of casual conversation, things one would not have wished to say to Soviet officials on the official level, where they would be made a matter of formal record; yet one could be reasonably sure that things said in this informal manner would, in the course of time, reach the ears of responsible Soviet officialdom. This enabled us to explain things which, if unexplained, could easily have led to misinterpretation and misunderstanding.

On arriving in Moscow, then, as ambassador, in 1952, I was disturbed to learn that this whole institution — the existence, that is, of a group of "tame Russians" (as we called them) with whom we could have normal contacts — had become a victim of the deterioration of Soviet-Western relations that set in during the late 1940s, and had thus ceased to exist. There was now no one of this character, indeed there was no Soviet citizen of any sort, with whom I could occasionally come together and talk in a normal social way and through whom I could at least convey something of the background and rationale of American policy. This troubled me particularly because of the tensions arising from the Korean War and the realization that unnecessary misunderstandings could, in these circumstances, easily lead to war.

I was anxious, therefore, to let the Soviet Foreign Office know of my regret over this situation. I could not do it formally, because this was, precisely, one of those matters of which cognizance could not be taken at the official level. The only occasions on which we met Soviet officials at all, other than at the official level, were the occasional diplomatic receptions. Even there, it was not easy to find anyone with whom my relations were such that I could mention a matter of such delicacy. It occurred to me that Boris Fedorovich Podserob, who was at that time Secretary General of the Foreign Office but whom Ambassador Harriman and I had known during the war when he was head of Molotov's personal chancery and with whom we had then had pleasant, if strictly formal, relations, might be such a person. Since he, unlike a number of other Foreign Office officials, spoke good French, and since I could not be sure that I would have opportunity to talk with him myself on any particular occasion, I told the counselor of embassy, Mr. Hugh Cummings, that if he, too, should chance to find himself talking with Podserob at one of these receptions, he might mention to him casually the fact that I regretted that there was not one Soviet citizen, and preferably one in good standing with the party, with whom I could occasionally meet in a normal social manner and take a cup of tea.

At the end of June, while I was briefly away from Moscow, Cummings, as it happened, did so encounter Podserob and communicated to him his understanding of what I had wanted him to say.

Not long after my return to Moscow, in the middle of a busy Saturday morning at the office, Cummings came to me and reported that there was a young man, a Russian, at the reception desk, who refused to give his name but had flashed a Communist Party identification card, and demanded to see me. The appearance of such a person in the embassy chancery was, of course, almost unprecedented. All visitors to the embassy were closely observed by the police guards stationed before the building; and it was clear that any Soviet citizen who attempted to enter without permission from the Soviet authorities would be sternly and grimly held to account when his visit was over.

I first said that if the young man would not give his name I would not receive him. When Cummings told me, however, that he was sure he had seen this person on some previous occasion in the Soviet Foreign Office, I concluded he must have some sort of official status and agreed to speak with him, albeit only in Cummings's presence.

The man was therefore admitted: a nondescript person, on the young side, pale and obviously very nervous. His tale was substantially this: He was the son of the Minister of State Security who, as he assumed I knew (actually I did not know), had recently been purged. The family had shared in, and suffered from, the father's disgrace. He, the young man, now found himself without prospects, and in a desperate situation. He had several young friends who were similarly situated. Together, they were in a position, through former connections, to know the comings and goings of the Soviet leaders. They needed only money and arms. It was implied — I cannot recall that he said so specifically — that they, if provided with these things, would be able to do away with the existing Soviet leadership.

I was naturally staggered by this weird approach. That it represented a provocation could not be doubted. That anyone could seriously have supposed that I would fail to recognize it as such could not be believed. I was at a loss for words to respond. I said, rather feebly, that I had no interest whatsoever in any such suggestions; I had not come to Russia to violate Soviet laws or to interfere in Soviet internal politics; I could not help him; I was obliged to ask him to leave the premises at once. Putting up a show of great disappointment and terror, my visitor asked how he was to leave the building without attracting the attention of the police. I asked him how he had come in. He said he had just darted in past the police guard. How, I asked him, had he expected to get out? He had hoped, he said, that I would place at his disposal an embassy car in which he could conceal himself and make his getaway. I told him there could be no question of anything of that sort: he was responsible for his coming there; the consequences of his departure were his own affair. He therefore left again, on foot, and we were able to observe from the windows how he was picked up by the plainclothesmen and followed as he disappeared up the street.

That, on the face of it, was the episode. It had an equally bizarre epilogue. Some days later Cummings, who had been in touch with our British colleagues, brought me a photograph, unearthed in the British embassy, which had been taken at the presentation of credentials, a year or so before, by my British colleague, Sir Alvary Gascoigne. The photograph was one of the entire group of officials, British and Soviet, who were in attendance at that event. And there, in the background, just behind and between the heads of the two leading figures, Shvernik and Gascoigne, there loomed up dimly, as a sort of plasma apparition, the face of the young man who had paid me the strange visit. To this day, I do not know who he was or what his face could have been doing in this position.

Pondering this curious episode, I thought I knew what was meant by it. It was typical Stalin. I had said I wished there was at least one Soviet citizen with whom I could occasionally meet and talk. The visit I had received was Stalin's reply. What he was saying by it was this: "I know, you miserable capitalist scoundrel, for what purpose *you* wish to meet with Soviet citizens: subversion, terror, and the overthrow of the Stalin regime. All right — I am sending you the proper sort of fellow. Let us see what you do with him."

To understand the plausibility of this explanation, one must recall that in the public purge trials of the 1930s any opposition to Stalin's leadership was equated by the prosecutor with the intention to overthrow it; but since, as the prosecutor pointed out, the regime was not prepared to submit peacefully to its overthrow just to please the opposition, this meant the intention to overthrow it by force, and this, in effect, was "terrorism." Well, the United States government included people who talked about "liberation." What did this mean if not the overthrow of the Soviet regime? And what was the endeavor to accomplish this overthrow, if not the use of terrorism? He would, therefore, send me the right man.

Aside, however, from this rationale, the connotations of the episode were distinctly disturbing. It suggested exceptional personal hostility towards me in high quarters. And not only hostility but also deep suspicion. The visitor, it will be recalled, had claimed to be the son of the Minister of State Security "who had recently been purged." The last Minister of State Security of whom we then had knowledge was Beria's creature, Abakumov.* He had indeed, as we were soon to learn, recently been purged — probably in the last weeks of 1951. His fall from grace appears to have been one of the first developments in that intensive round of inner-party intrigue, unleashed by the visible signs of advancing age and declining powers in Stalin, which was destined to gather momentum in the coming months and to find its early culmination in the announcement of the "Doctors' Plot" and the ensuing death of Stalin. I, at the time, knew little of all this, though I sensed that something unusual was going on; but the young man's statement made it clear that some highly placed person in Moscow thought I knew more than I did. There may, I think, have been some suspicion that my approach to Podserob was an attempt to get into touch with opposition elements, involved in the intrigues against Stalin or at least attempting to sew up for themselves the preeminent places in the succession.

Did Stalin have other reasons for personal bitterness against me? It is impossible to know. It was impossible to make any judgment at the time. How could any foreign representative in that city know what tales and falsehoods about himself were being dished up to

* Viktor S. Abakumov, Minister of State Security from 1946 to 1951. Executed in 1954.

Stalin by his secret police? The foreigner residing in Moscow was utterly helpless to defend himself from malice from that quarter; for he could at any time be made the victim of slander and false denunciations of which he had no knowledge at all.

I was then the senior diplomatic representative in Moscow in point of length of service in Russia and knowledge of the Soviet scene. My views were often consulted by other diplomats. It was a sultry, uneasy summer. A new party congress was in course of preparation. Changes were in the air; and changes, in terms of Soviet politics, always meant some degree of danger. If people exaggerated, as they appear to have done, my knowledge of what was taking place behind the scenes, was it impossible that some of them should have come to the conclusion that it was undesirable to have me around?

There was one other possible, even probable, reason for resentment against me, particularly, I suspect, on Stalin's part. In the earlier volume of these memoirs I have recounted the circumstances that caused me, on Victory Day, 1945, to stand on the pedestal of a column in front of our embassy chancery, and to say a few friendly words to a cheering and enthusiastic Soviet crowd. How intensely this rankled in the higher reaches of the Soviet regime was evident from the fact that there had been published in Moscow, in the late 1940s, an entire anti-American propaganda book based primarily on a distorted version of this episode. Even in 1952 it had not, as will be seen shortly, been forgotten. Stalin was not accustomed to sharing with anyone, least of all with a bourgeois diplomat, the demonstrative enthusiasm of Soviet crowds on which he had something resembling a political monopoly.*

---

* It may be worth noting in this connection that the only other bourgeois diplomat who had, so far as I know, had the experience of being the center of the friendly enthusiasm of a Soviet crowd was Mrs. Golda Meir, in 1948, when she was serving as Israel's first ambassador to the Soviet Union. I have been told that on the occasion of a visit to the Moscow synagogue, she found herself surrounded suddenly by great crowds of Russian Jews who had learned of her identity and gave her a great and moving ovation, many of them kneeling before her,

However that may be: the summer ran its course and began to draw to an end. On August 20 it was made known that a new party congress, now a decade overdue, would take place at the beginning of October. It was clear that Stalin had long opposed the calling of such a congress. There were signs that this had been, for some time, a delicate and painful issue in the senior ranks of the regime. The fact that Stalin had now been brought to assent to the election and convening of such a body was already a sign that things were coming into motion in the internal affairs of the party.

Eight days later *Pravda* published a set of "theses" for a report to be delivered at the forthcoming congress on a proposed revision of the party statutes. The changes proposed included ones of the greatest magnitude and sensitivity, including the abolition of the Politburo and its replacement by a body to be called the Presidium of the Central Committee. Particularly bewildering was the fact that these theses bore the signature of none other than Nikita Sergeyevich Khrushchev. The latter had generally been considered, up to that point, the least influential member of the Politburo and the Secretariat. Why should it have been his signature, and none other, over which this remarkable document saw the light of day? Plainly, strange things were now taking place in the bosom of the party.

Just before the new party congress was scheduled to convene, it fell to me to make a journey to Western Europe. In connection with my dispatch about the impact of NATO on the Soviet leader-

---

weeping, and kissing her clothing. I have often wondered whether there was any connection between the fact of my expulsion in late 1952 and the expulsion of the entire Israeli embassy (Mrs. Meir was no longer there) some weeks later, in early 1953. Stalin was, of course, wildly anti-Semitic in the final months of his life (to a certain extent, even sooner); and the expulsion may perhaps be attributable simply to that. But the similarity of the two episodes is striking.

That the incident of the Victory Day demonstration was by no means forgotten at the time of my appointment as ambassador is clear from the fact that it was brought up, in the usual distorted propaganda version (see pp. 244–245 of the first volume of these memoirs), by one of the controlled Soviet orators at a "peace" meeting in Moscow, only three or four days before I presented my credentials.

ship I had expressed to the department the hope that I might have opportunity, at some point, to discuss with those of our people who were concerned with NATO the questions I had treated in that dispatch. Whether in response to that suggestion or otherwise, the department arranged that there should take place in London, from September 24 to 27, a conference of certain of our chiefs of mission in Europe, to which I was also invited. I left Moscow, primarily for this purpose, on September 19.

On the eve of my departure, however, there occurred another incident which may well have heightened whatever ill will existed in higher Soviet circles, and particularly police circles, against my person. I had been somewhat shocked, when I arrived in Moscow in May, to learn that the interior of Spaso House had been redecorated just before my arrival, in the interval between ambassadors, and that the work of redecorating had been done under Soviet supervision by Soviet painters provided by Burobin, without the presence of any American supervisory personnel. In the old days, when those of us who knew something about Russia also looked after matters of this sort, I doubt that we would have permitted this. Now, however, things in our Foreign Service had become bureaucratized: we now had a professional administrative service, divorced from the substantive branches of Foreign Service work. The administrative section of the embassy lacked Russian-speaking personnel to supervise work of this sort, but had gone ahead and had it done anyway. And this, of course, had left the field entirely clear for the Soviet police authorities to take advantage of the redecorating in order to perfect their wiring of the house for other, less aesthetic and more political, purposes.

The "bugging" of foreign embassies and other official premises had of course been for many years, even back into the 1930s, a standard practice of the Soviet government, and not of that government alone. We had long since taught ourselves to assume that in Moscow most walls — at least in rooms that diplomats were apt to frequent — had ears. Still, we had supposed in earlier days that one did not want to make it easier for curious people than it needed to be made. Yet this was precisely what, in the redecorating of the building, we had now contrived to do.

In the first months after my arrival in Moscow, nothing untoward was noted. The ordinary, standard devices for the detection of electronic eavesdropping revealed nothing at all. The air of innocence presented by the walls of the old building was so bland and bright as to suggest either that there had been a complete change of practice on the part of our Soviet hosts (of which in other respects there was decidedly no evidence) or that our methods of detection were out of date.

In recognition of this last possibility there arrived from Washington, just before my scheduled departure for London in September, two technicians detailed by our government to give Spaso House a more searching and technically competent going-over. After one or two days of fruitless effort, these gentlemen suggested to me that their efforts might be more successful if I would arrange, on a given evening, to go through the motions of performing some sort of official work in the premises of the residence, instead of at the office. I saw no reason not to do this; and on the evening in question I summoned a secretary to the residence (it was the loyal and devoted Dorothy Hessman, who had already been with me in Washington and was destined to remain with me off and on, in government or outside it, for more than a decade into the future) and proceeded to dictate to her, in the large upstairs living room–study, a body of prose which was intended to sound like a diplomatic dispatch in the making, and must indeed have sounded that way for all but a historically schooled ear, because it was drawn word for word from just such a dispatch sent from Moscow in earlier years and now included in one of the published volumes of American diplomatic correspondence.

This worked. And what followed was an eerie experience. The family, for some reason, was away that evening — my wife was, in any case. I have the impression that the great building was again substantially empty, except for the technicians, Miss Hessman, and myself. I droned on with the dictation, the technicians circulated around through other parts of the building. Suddenly, one of them appeared in the doorway of the study and implored me, by signs and whispers, to "keep on, keep on." He then disappeared again, but soon returned, accompanied by his colleague, and began to move about the room in which we were working. Centering his attention finally on a corner of the room where there was a radio set on a table, just below a round wooden Great Seal of the United States that hung on the wall, he removed the seal, took up a mason's hammer, and began, to my bewilderment and consternation, to hack to pieces the brick wall where the seal had been. When this failed to satisfy him, he turned these destructive attentions on the seal itself.

I, continuing to mumble my dispatch, remained a fascinated but passive spectator of this extraordinary procedure. In a few moments, however, all was over. Quivering with excitement, the technician extracted from the shattered depths of the seal a small device, not much larger than a pencil, which, he assured me, housed both a receiving and a sending set, capable of being activated by some sort of electronic ray from outside the building. When not activated, it was almost impossible to detect. When activated, as it was on that evening, it picked up any sounds in the room and relayed them to an outside monitor, who presumably had his stance in one of the surrounding buildings.

It is difficult to make plausible the weirdness of the atmosphere in that room, while this strange scene was in progress. The air of Russia is psychically impregnated, anyway, as ours is not. At this particular moment, one was acutely conscious of the unseen presence in the room of a third person: our attentive monitor. It seemed that one could almost hear his breathing. All were aware that a strange and sinister drama was in progress.*

The device in question was of course packed off to Washington a day or so later. It left, if my memory is correct, on the same American Air Force plane that carried me out to Western Europe for the conference at London. It represented, for that day, a fantastically advanced bit of applied electronics. I have the impression that with its discovery the whole art of intergovernmental eavesdropping was raised to a new technological level.

The following morning the atmosphere of Spaso House was heavy with tension. I had thought it best to close and lock, temporarily, the room where the device had been found. The Soviet servants, their highly trained antennae positively humming with vibrations, sensed serious trouble, and cast terrified glances in the direction of the locked door, as they passed along the corridor, as though they suspected the place to contain a murdered corpse. The faces of the guards at the gate were frozen into a new grimness. So dense was the atmosphere of anger and hostility that one could have cut it with a knife.

Had I been right, I wondered, to lend my person to this deception? Was it proper for an ambassador to involve himself in this

---

* This episode was not without its amusing side. Earlier in the summer, before the arrival of my family, when I was living in the building alone, I had wanted to keep up my Russian, and particularly my fluency of vocabulary and pronunciation. Since there were no Russians with whom I could talk, I hit on the idea of reading a certain amount of Russian aloud to myself each evening. For purposes of vocabulary I wanted particularly to read material which had relation to current international problems, so that I would be fully conversant with the manner in which events and institutions were referred to in current Russian usage. Looking around for material of this sort, my eye fell on the scripts of Voice of America broadcasts to Russia, which were sent to me regularly for my information. On several occasions, therefore, I took the foreign-political commentaries from these scripts, vigorous and eloquent polemics against Soviet policies, and read them aloud to myself precisely in that upstairs study where the listening device was placed. I have often wondered what was the effect on my unseen monitors, and on those who read their tapes, when they heard these perfectly phrased anti-Soviet diatribes issuing in purest Russian from what was unquestionably my mouth, in my own study, in the depths of the night. Who, I wonder, did they think was with me? Or did they conclude I was trying to make fun of them?

sort of comedy? Or would I have been remiss, in the eyes of my own government, if I had refused to do so?

I am not sure, even today, of the answers to these questions. The political sky, in any case, as I left Russia for the conference in London, was dark and menacing.

There is one other small incident, occurring on the eve of my departure, that must also be mentioned.

It occurred on a Sunday, as I recall it, one or two days before I left. For some reason I was alone at home, that afternoon, with my two-year-old boy. It was a pleasant late summer day — so far as Nature, at any rate, was concerned. The little boy and I spent part of the afternoon in the front "garden," as it was called (jolly few flowers grew in it), between the house and the high iron-spike fence that separated the garden from the sidewalk and street. The child was playing in a little sand pile we had provided for him there. I was reading a book.

Tiring of the sand pile, the boy wandered down to the iron fence, gripped two of the spikes with his pudgy little fists, and stood staring out into the wide, semi-forbidden world beyond. He was, even if I embarrass him by saying so today, an endearing little fellow. No one could resist his charm. Some Soviet children came along the sidewalk on the other side of the fence, saw him, smiled at him, and gave him a friendly poke through the bars. He squealed with pleasure and poked back. Soon, to much mutual pleasure, a game was in progress. But at this point my guardians at the main gate, becoming aware of what was going on, rushed up and shooed the Soviet children sternly away. Their orders were, after all, that there was to be no contact — no fraternization.

It was a small episode, but it came at the end of a difficult and nerve-wracking summer. And something gave way, at that point, with the patience I was able to observe in the face of this entire vicious, timid, mediaeval regime of isolation to which the official foreigner in Moscow was still subjected. Had I been the perfect ambassador it would not, I suppose, have given way. But give way it did; and it could not soon be restored.

I left Moscow, as I say, on the morning of September 19 — in the official plane which the United States government then placed at the disposal of the ambassador in Moscow for the purpose of his travel into and out of Russia. (The plane was not permitted by the Soviet authorities to come there for any other purpose or to remain there in the intervals between such journeys.)

How ironic can be, on occasions, the workings of Fate! As the plane approached the Tempelhof airport in Berlin — its first stop in what was in reality "the West" — I reflected that there would certainly be reporters at the airport who would wish to interview me; and I said to myself: "Why don't you, you boob, for once in your life prepare yourself for this sort of ordeal? Why don't you try to anticipate their questions, and have your answers all prepared?"

No sooner thought than done. I took out a pocket notebook, dreamed up several of the questions I thought they might ask me, and jotted down the proposed answers: nice, cagey, diplomatic answers that would give them something to write, and yet get no one in trouble. I still have the little book somewhere, with this pathetic record of the failures of human foresight.

It was as I had foreseen. The reporters were indeed there, at the airport. They asked the expected questions. I reeled off the prepared answers. But then one young reporter — from the Paris *Herald Tribune*, if my memory is correct — asked me whether we in our embassy had many social contacts with Russians in Moscow. The question itself annoyed me. Had the man been born yesterday? The regime of isolation applied to Western diplomats in Moscow had been in existence for at least two decades. How could a reporter not know that? Why, I thought to myself, must editors send people of such ignorance to interview ambassadors at airports?

"Don't you know," I asked, "how foreign diplomats live in Moscow?"

"No," he replied. "How do they?"

I should of course have let it go at that. But there welled up in me, at that point, the whole dismal experience of the past four months, ending with the experience of seeing my little boy's playmates chased away from him, lest they be contaminated by his proximity. Being again in Germany, I was reminded at that moment of the five months I had spent in internment as a prisoner of the Germans, in 1941–1942. There, too, the building had been surrounded by guards. There, too, fraternization had been forbidden. There, too, people had got into trouble for having anything to do with us. There, too, the local servicing personnel had functioned only under the watchful and suspicious eye of the police guard. There, too, we had been, officially, "the enemy."

"Well," I said, "I was interned here in Germany for several months during the last war. The treatment we receive in Moscow is just about like the treatment we internees received then, except that in Moscow we are at liberty to go out and walk the streets under guard."

A faint but wholly unreliable recollection suggests to me that before making that statement I had tried to indicate that what I was about to say would be off the record. But I am not sure. There was a lot of airplane noise; and obviously, if I said it at all, I did not say it loudly enough. I have never, in any case, tried to make this an excuse. I took then, and must take today, full responsibility for the statement. Correct or incorrect, accurate or inaccurate, it was an extremely foolish thing for me to have said.

I have no record of what I said to my colleagues at the London meeting. I have drafts of things I *intended* to say. How much of it I actually said I do not know, and it is not important. The proposed statements were of course mostly along the lines of my recent dispatches from Moscow. I did intend, however, to add a word about our manner of dealing with the Soviet government. We had not made up our minds, I thought, as to what we were trying to achieve in our relations with that country. On the one hand, we maintained diplomatic relations and claimed to be pursuing the quest for an ordered, peaceful, constructive relationship. On the other hand, we were not talking with the Soviet leaders. We were

treating them at arm's length and never closing with them on the constantly recurring instances where their propaganda and statements give us just cause for complaint. If we really mean business about diplomatic relations with them, then I should be down there in the Soviet Foreign Office at least three or four times a week complaining violently, loudly and publicly about things they say, proving these things are false, getting publicity for my complaints and proofs, keeping after them incessantly and saying to them, in effect: "You simply cannot do things and say things like this." I am not sure that this would not have some effect. They are stubborn and pigheaded people. To influence them you have to scold them and keep after them like recalcitrant children. Perhaps with sufficient self-assurance and resolution and persistence, and with a determination to keep our own skirts clean, so that we could approach them from a higher plane, we might have some chance of influencing them, or at least of embarrassing them to a point where their behavior would be modified.

But if we have given up all hope of taming the shrew, and if we are really going to center our effort on the subversion and destruction of Soviet power, then I believe we would be more effective, and happier in our own minds, and our hands would be freer, if we were to give up in large measure the farce of maintaining normal diplomatic relations with the Soviet government. I am not saying that we should break diplomatic relations entirely or have no mission at all in Moscow; but I am saying that in this case, if we appoint an ambassador to Moscow at all, I do not think he should normally reside there.

These passages, drafted on the eve of the meeting, will give some idea of my frame of mind as this conference began, just before the falling of the major blow that now awaited me.

I listened, of course, with intense interest, to what was said by the others there present, whose number included one of the senior American officers connected with NATO. What they said came to me, as I recorded in my private notes at the end of the second day's sessions, "as a great shock." I realized, I wrote, that my dispatch about NATO

had fallen on stony soil; that there was, and would be, no understanding here for the sort of things I had written about; that the NATO people, as well as our own military authorities, were completely captivated and lost in the compulsive logic of the military equation. From now on, logic would press them continually to do those things which would make war more likely and to refrain from doing those things that would tend to stave it off. For this, they were not really to blame. The fault lay with the failure of the political authorities to provide a firm line of guidance. . . .

Secondly, I was extremely disturbed by the statements . . . about our policy with respect to Germany. I had hoped that . . . we might be approaching a time when we would be prepared to contemplate negotiations for a unified Germany based on the possibility of an eventual withdrawal of United States forces. I had been urging since 1948 that we state this as our objective and make clear to others the terms on which we would be prepared to consider such a solution. These terms did not need to be ones which would deliver Germany up to the Soviet Union. . . . This line of thought had always been rejected in the department. I thought our position might now have softened. But what I learned at the meeting showed that this was anything but the case. Our people . . . were basing their entire hopes on the ratification of the German contractuals and the European Defense Community, and they were unwilling to contemplate at any time within the foreseeable future, under any conceivable agreement with the Russians, the withdrawal of United States forces from Germany.

Our stand meant in effect no agreement with Russia at all and the indefinite continuance of the split of Germany and Europe. . . . But the split was bound to become increasingly dangerous and onerous both to ourselves and to our allies; and to put ourselves in this awkward and difficult situation, with the only hope for overcoming it lying in a possible collapse of Soviet power in Eastern Europe, would be to embark upon a path the logic of which would eventually bring us squarely to the view of John Foster Dulles: that the accent of our policy should lie on an attempt to subvert and overthrow Communist power. . . . I could see no end to such a policy but failure or war.

I left the meeting, that second day, profoundly depressed. For the first time, after years of resistance, my diary notes recorded, it seemed to me that war had to be accepted as

inevitable, or very nearly so — that the only alternative to it lay in the collapse of our political position in Europe. . . . And to think that I would have to return to Moscow and live through further weeks and months of exposure to foul, malicious, and insulting propaganda and yet realize that there was just enough in it (because we *were* actually following . . . the false logic that would lead to war in one way or another) — this reflection seemed to me as bitter a one as a representative of our country could ever have had.

Fate, however, as it turned out, was about to decide things in a different, if scarcely less unpleasant, manner. On the following morning, September 26, came the news of a sharp editorial attack on me by the Moscow *Pravda*. The editorial took off from the interview given at the Tempelhof airport. I was a slanderer, the paper said. I had "lied ecstatically." I was an enemy of the Soviet Union. The editorial ended, significantly, with a recounting of the distorted version of the incident of the demonstration before our embassy on V–E Day, 1945.

The news of this attack completed my misery. I had few illusions about its portents. "What the United States government started one day," I recorded bitterly in my diary, "the Soviet government finished on the next." Between the two of them I felt hopelessly caught, totally helpless. I was afflicted, I wrote, by a

loneliness greater than I had ever conceived. . . . Nowhere would I be likely to find full understanding for what I had done, or full support;

there would never be any tribunal before which I could justify myself; there would be few friends whom I could expect ever wholly to understand my explanations. By being tossed into this impossible position between the two worlds, I had entered an area into which none could be expected to follow in his thoughts or his imagination. From now on I had nothing to look to but my own conscience. The realization, while hard, was not intolerable; but I think that with that moment I lost the last shred of any desire to be associated with public life for any moment longer than was absolutely essential.

In the light of this attack, I could scarcely conceive of myself returning to Moscow, nor did I wish to. Actually, as I wrote to my friend Bohlen the following day, I did not favor our keeping an ambassador there at all; and if there had to be one, I did not favor its being me. This problem, however, was soon resolved by the Soviet government itself. On Saturday, October 3, the second in command at our embassy in Moscow, Mr. John M. McSweeney, serving in my absence as chargé d'affaires, was summoned to the Soviet Foreign Office and presented with a third-person note of the following tenor:

As is known, the Ambassador of the United States of America in the USSR, Mr. Kennan, on September 19 at Tempelhof airport in Berlin made a statement before representatives of the West Berlin press and American correspondents in which he made slanderous attacks hostile to the Soviet Union in a rude violation of generally recognized norms of international law. In this statement, published in a number of West German papers, Mr. Kennan allowed himself to compare the situation of Americans in Moscow with that which he allegedly experienced when in 1941–1942 he was interned by Nazis in Germany, and stated that "if the Nazis had permitted us to walk along the streets without the right to converse with any kind of German, that would have been exactly the same situation in which we must live today in Moscow."

This statement of Mr. Kennan is completely false and hostile to the Soviet Union.

In view of the foregoing, the Soviet government considers it necessary to state that it considers Mr. Kennan as *persona non grata* and insists on Mr. Kennan's immediate recall from the post of Ambassador of the United States of America in the Soviet Union.

McSweeney asked whether I might be permitted to return to Moscow to fetch my family. The answer was "no." He then, with much presence of mind, asked whether the official American plane might be permitted to return to take out Mrs. Kennan and the family, and this request was granted.

I was, at the time, in Geneva, visiting my daughter Joan Elisabeth, who was in school there. The news of my expulsion was relayed to me by our government that same Saturday, even before it had been made public, through the agency of the American consulate at Geneva. I was not authorized to reveal it to outsiders, but I was warned that an official announcement would be made in Moscow almost immediately. Realizing that the moment the announcement was made I would at once have the whole world press about my ears, and anxious to have a few moments to compose myself before this happened, I walked out of my hotel and, not knowing what else to do, went to a movie. There, sitting in the darkness and trying to come to grips with the measure of the catastrophe, I found myself, to my disgust, becoming absorbed in the damned film, and can recall the struggle I was obliged to conduct with myself to get my eyes off the silly picture and to make myself comprehend the whole incredible reality of what had occurred.

The first victim, and the only hero, of this episode was my wife. Still in Moscow, she was of course informed at once, that same Saturday morning, of what had happened, but she, too, was not at liberty to reveal it before the official announcement was made. Aware that she had only a matter of hours, or one or two days at best, in which to liquidate an entire household of some twenty-two servants, get everything packed up, say her goodbyes, and vacate both the building and the country, she proceeded, without a sign of discomposure, to entertain at an official luncheon that noon, and then to attend, as guest, a diplomatic dinner that evening, all without betraying by word or glance the sickening knowledge of which she was the possessor. Then, when the news was released, she went through the ordeal of hasty *déménagement* with a dignity and composure that was the admiration of everyone in the embassy and the diplomatic colony. When she left from the Moscow airport, on October 7, the attachés of our armed services, God bless them, were all in attendance in full uniform; and if the feelings toward myself and the reasons for my banishment were mixed ones, affected by the knowledge that I had done a very foolish thing, the tears that were shed for my wife, as she boarded the plane with the children and the Danish staff, were unfeigned and unreserved in their admiration. Whether or not I had been up to my job, she had been up to hers.

There remained for me the task of coming to terms with this disaster. Reactions were initially, of course, somewhat defensive. What I had said, after all, was not wholly inaccurate. I could see no reason why I was under obligation to conceal from the American public the conditions under which American diplomats in Moscow were obliged to work and to live. And surely, I tried to convince myself, the airport incident was only a pretext. The real reasons for my expulsion were deeper, and much more creditable to me. The demand for my recall had been made on the day before the opening of the party congress. They had been afraid, I suggested to myself, to have me in town. They had thought that I knew too much. They had feared my influence on the other diplomats in the interpretation of the events of the congress. They had feared that my presence would give encouragement to moderate elements within the regime.

It was with such thoughts, and others like them, that I tried, initially, to salve the wounded ego. But this was all, of course, bravado. At heart, I was deeply shamed and shaken by what had occurred.

And I have had to ask myself many times, over the course of the years: was I really fit for the task to which I had been assigned?

The answer, I suppose, is both yes and no. I was a good reporting officer. I *think* (what chief ever really knows?) that I gave good leadership to the staff of the embassy — that they respected me, enjoyed working under me, and learned something from it. Despite Mr. Acheson's reference, many years later, to my being instructed, after the event, to observe "such taciturnity as he could muster," gaffes of this sort were not a common occurrence in my life. I had served in a number of other positions, and was later to serve as ambassador to Yugoslavia, without any comparable breaking of the crockery.

A part of my trouble, too, came from a failure on my part to understand exactly what was wanted of me by my own government. I should, no doubt, have understood, when I was sent to Moscow, that what was wanted of me by the President and the Secretary of State was only that I should keep the seat warm in the brief remaining interval before the next election, for which purpose I should put up stoically with all the insults and embarrassments of my position and not worry my head over problems of policy. A little more clarity on this point might have saved me from asking too many questions and helped me to accept more philosophically the irritations of the situation into which I had been placed.

But even had such instructions been given me, I was probably too highly strung emotionally, too imaginative, too sensitive, and too impressed with the importance of my own opinions, to sit quietly on that particular seat. For this, one needed a certain phlegm, a certain contentment with the trivia of diplomatic life, a readiness to go along uncomplainingly with the conventional thinking of Washington, and a willingness to refrain from asking unnecessary questions — none of which I possessed in adequate degree.

All this being so, I think it probably fair to say that I was not wholly fitted for the task I had been given. The manner in which this was finally made evident was painful; and the memory of it remains painful to this day. When I reflect, however, that it was part of a process of change in my own life which I have never regretted but which I would never have encompassed on my own initiative, I realize that I must not protest this turn of fate too much. God's ways are truly unfathomable. Who am I to say I could have arranged it better?

8

Retirement

ON October 7, three days after the announcement that I was no longer welcome in Moscow, I met my hard-pressed wife, with the little children, at the Cologne airport. I had been instructed to remain, for the time being, at the seat of our High Commission in Bad Godesberg. The presidential election of 1952 was now only a month off. The President and Mr. Acheson had concluded that it would be undesirable for me to return to the United States before the election. Just what dangers my presence in the country would have added to the fortunes of the Democratic party I was unable then to imagine; nor can I easily picture them today; but I was thoroughly humbled by what had just befallen me, and was in no mood to argue. The High Commissioner, the late Mr. Walter Donnelly, placed at our disposal a handsome flat in the official American ghetto. There, in this faithful, pathetic replica of a Midwestern suburb, the ostentatious Americanism of which was thought to be essential to the well-being of our personnel on duty there, we stayed until the election had taken place and the Republicans had completed their triumph.

The weeks at Bad Godesberg constituted a relatively happy interlude between the miserable months at Moscow and some scarcely less harrowing ones that lay just ahead. Unhappy as I was about the manner in which my liberation had been achieved, I was secretly pleased to be absolved of further service in Moscow. I enjoyed being back in Germany, where I had spent so many earlier years of my life. I took long walks along the towpath of the Rhine, and derived an enduring comfort from the spectacle of the immense flow of waterborne traffic which that great stream carried. There was something reassuring in the powerful, never-failing rhythm both of the stream and of the uses men were making of it.

Having plenty of leisure, I devoted my spare time to the preparation of a careful analysis of what was generally called "Stalin's paper on economics." This was a series of papers which had appeared, over Stalin's signature, in the Moscow magazine *Bolshevik*, on the eve of the party congress, just as I was leaving Russia. I did not believe that Stalin actually wrote this monograph (there is mounting evidence, today, that he did not); but I tried to put myself into the mind and mood of a political leader who was prepared, as he had shown himself to be, to take responsibility for it. My study (it was a long one) makes interesting reading today, in the light of our present knowledge that Stalin had, at that time, only some four months to live. I came to the conclusion that the theses put forward in this document reflected a certain senility of outlook — the mentality of a rapidly aging man who had lost the ability either to learn or forget. The regime in Moscow was, as I wrote on the basis of this analysis,

an old man's government, ruthless and terrible to be sure, but insensitive to the deeper experiences of its own subject peoples, living in its own past, and determined to give validity and fruition to its past concepts, even if this means flying in the face of the logic of change and defying the evolution of human society by destroying the very society in which the evolution could take place.

I was pleased, some months later, when a team of German physicians, studying the medical reports on Stalin's last illness, came up with an analysis of the probable state of his mind in the final months of his life that read almost word for word like this one.

A few days after the election, my presence in the United States being finally acceptable to a Democratic party which was now beyond embarrassment, the family journeyed, on the High Commissioner's private train, to Bremerhaven, and embarked on the old S.S. *Republic* for New York.

I had at that time, of course, the status of a Foreign Service Officer on active duty, reporting to Washington for reassignment. We had, however, no home in Washington; and it was clear that there was not likely to be any reassignment at the hands of the outgoing Truman administration, now wearily living out its last dragging weeks. We took up residence, therefore — my wife, the two small children, the Danish nurse, and myself — at our farm in southern Pennsylvania, some eighty-five miles north of Washington, and settled down there to await the government's decision as to what it wanted to do with me. I went, of course, to Washington, soon after our arrival, and paid courtesy calls on the outgoing President and Secretary of State. Both were courteous and cordial; but it was plain that neither had any particular interest in what was now to become of me, or even in what I might have to tell about Russia. Both had in their eyes the faraway look of men who know that they are about to be relieved of heavy responsibilities and who derive a malicious pleasure in reserving their most bitter problems for those who are about to displace them. The question of my future was not even mentioned; it was tacitly understood that this would be one for the new administration.

I was reasonably well acquainted with both the President-elect, General Eisenhower, and with his Secretary of State–designate: Mr. John Foster Dulles. I rather expected that one or the other of them would get into touch with me prior to their assumption of office and that we would have opportunity to discuss the problems of the Moscow ambassadorship and my own future. But the weeks passed; nothing was heard from them; and I, over-proud and over-shy as usual, was reluctant to make the first move.

So I continued to live on the farm. Christmas came and went. My paychecks, happily, continued to arrive. But not a word from Washington either about my present status or my future. No one there showed any interest in discussing with me the background and implications of what had befallen me in Russia. Whenever I appeared in the Department of State the subject of my expulsion was in fact studiously and significantly evaded by friends and colleagues. I found myself treated with the elaborate politeness and forbearance one reserves for someone who has committed a social gaffe too appalling for discussion. Nor did anyone undertake at any time to discuss with me the subject of conditions in Russia — a country I had just left and about which I was supposed to know something. It was as though my objective judgment had been somehow discredited together with my discretion.

I had received, meanwhile, an invitation to address on January 16 — i.e., four days before the new administration was to take office — the annual meeting, at Scranton, of the Pennsylvania Bar Association. I saw no reason why I should not accept this, and did. I drafted a speech for the occasion. Bearing in mind my recent service in Moscow and the fact that this was to be the only public statement I would make on the subject of our relations with the Soviet Union while still officially ambassador to that country, I naturally attached a certain importance to it, and meant it to be a constructive treatment of the problems of this relationship. Since I was still a Foreign Service Officer on active duty, I submitted the speech to the Department of State in the usual manner for clearance. The department cleared it without a murmur; and on January 16 I duly appeared at Scranton and delivered it.

I began, that evening at Scranton, by attempting to identify the deeper sources of our conflict with Soviet power. I found them primarily in the ideological preconceptions of the Soviet leaders and particularly in the image of an ineradicable hostility between the "bourgeois" and "socialist" worlds which they had built up in their own minds. I then turned to the various views as to what we could and should do about it. I explained why the policy of ignoring the Soviet Union, which had been followed for twelve years under the last Republican administrations (1921–1933), was no longer feasible. I pointed out what was wrong with the idea, held by many people during the past war, that things could be set to right if only we would exhibit goodwill, show "trust" in the Soviet leaders, and hope that they would reciprocate one-sided concessions and favors on our part. I explained why I also felt we must reject every thought of war as a solution to this problem.

I then turned to the suggestions that we should try to solve the problem by promoting the overthrow of the various Communist regimes, and I said the following:

Finally, there are those who point to what they believe to be the unhappiness of the various peoples under Soviet rule, and advocate a policy which, placing our hopes on the possibility of internal disintegration of Soviet power, would make it the purpose of governmental action to promote such disintegration.

Gentlemen, it is right that individual Americans should stand for their beliefs and do what they can to make them understood and respected elsewhere. I do not underrate the competitive power of freedom in the struggle of political ideas. I hope it will always be on our side. I think time and circumstances will tend to prove its strength. I think the arts of totalitarian despotism will prove in the end to be self-destructive.

But I would be extremely careful of doing anything at the governmental level that purports to affect directly the governmental system in another country, no matter what the provocation may seem. It is not consistent with our international obligations. It is not consistent with a common membership with other countries in the United Nations. It is not consistent with the maintenance of formal diplomatic relations with another country. It is replete with possibilities for misunderstanding and bitterness. To the extent it might be successful, it would involve us in heavy responsibilities. Finally, the prospects for success would be very small indeed; since the problem of civil obedience is not a great problem to the modern police dictatorship.

Let us by all means take pride in our institutions and our political ideas. Let us do all we can to commend them by their successful application in our own country. Let us certainly not make of ourselves the allies and guarantors of despotism anywhere. But beyond that, let us not commit ourselves.

I ended this argument with the now well-known passage from one of John Quincy Adams's speeches (I had myself unearthed it, from his published but forgotten papers, some years back) about America being the well-wisher to the freedom and independence of all, but the champion and vindicator only of her own.

The remainder of the speech was devoted largely to the need for unity here at home, particularly in the face of the then rampant anti-Communist hysteria. To that I shall have to return shortly.

The *New York Times*, already committed to a policy (destined to be pursued long into the future) of publishing anything trivial that I might have to say and ignoring everything of importance, did not mention the Scranton speech at all — at least not in the edition I saw. The *Washington Post*, however, took a different view of it. That paper came out the following day, to my great surprise and consternation, with a front-page story from the pen of my good friend Ferdinand Kuhn headlined: "Dulles Policy 'Dangerous,' Kennan Says." (The word "dangerous," incidentally, had not occurred anywhere in the pertinent passage of the speech, nor had Mr. Dulles been mentioned.) "George Kennan, probably the foremost government expert on Russia," wrote Mr. Kuhn,

sounded a warning last night against the John Foster Dulles policy of encouraging the liberation of captive peoples in Europe and Asia.

In a speech to the Pennsylvania State Bar Association . . . the former ambassador to Moscow showed that he was out of sympathy with the attitude of Dulles, the incoming Secretary of State.

Dulles had told the Senate Foreign Relations Committee on Thursday that the government must use "moral pressure and the weight of propaganda" to weaken the Soviet hold on satellite peoples.

Kennan, on the other hand, argued that such a course would be dangerous.

The story went on to quote from the passages of my speech cited above and then continued:

But his blast against one of Dulles' favorite policies raised new questions about Kennan's future under Dulles at the State Department.

A similar story, from the pen of John M. Hightower, appeared the following day in the *Washington Star*. Here, the alleged difference was declared to be "an open break over policy toward Russia and its satellite countries between the Secretary of State–designate . . . and the State Department's top expert on foreign relations."

To say that I was shocked and surprised by this press reaction would be to put it mildly. I had not conceived, actually, that there was any great difference between Mr. Dulles's views and my own on this particular subject, and had not had him in mind when I made these statements. I felt very badly about it. We were now within three days of his taking office. The last thing I had meant to do was to embarrass him by public criticism on the eve of his assumption of his new duties.

As usual, I overreacted. Full of horror, I tore down to Washington to see what could be done to mend the situation. Mr. Dulles was not there. No one could tell me where he was. I therefore addressed a note to my friend H. Freeman Matthews, then serving as Deputy Under Secretary of State, and asked him to show it to Mr. Dulles when the latter arrived. I pointed out, in this letter, that

(1) the speech had been intended as "the first, last, and only

major statement by myself on Soviet-American relations during the period of my incumbency as Ambassador to the USSR";

(2) the speech had been written and distributed to the press before I knew anything of Mr. Dulles's statement before the Foreign Relations Committee;

(3) that I had seen no important difference between our respective views and did not have him in mind in what I said — "rather certain editors, legislators, professional propagandists for minority groups," etc. — and

(4) I had deliberately chosen a time prior to the inauguration to make a public statement on this subject "in order that there could be no question of any responsibility of the new administration for the views expressed."

Appalled, furthermore, at the thought that I had inadvertently put the new Secretary on the spot, I included in the letter what was meant as an offer to resign, if this was what was needed to make things right. Unfortunately, whether out of false pride or what I do not know, I obscured the motives of the offer. I said that it was my desire to retire to private life when I reached the youngest possible retirement age, which would be about a year hence. Meanwhile, I would be glad to take any job suitable to my rank in the service. I also offered to make a public statement to the effect that I had not thought there was any important difference between Mr. Dulles's views and mine on the subject in question.

There was no response to this communication. I remained, in fact, for many weeks under the impression that Mr. Dulles had not seen it at all. He did, however, call me in, together with his press secretary, Mr. Carl McCardle, on the third day after his assumption of office. I made my explanations. He listened noncommittally. The result was that the official spokesman of the State Department, Mr. Michael J. McDermott, made a statement to the press that afternoon to the effect that the Scranton speech had been "prepared by Mr. Kennan, cleared in the normal fashion in the Department of State, and distributed to the press before Mr. Dulles's appearance before the Senate Foreign Relations Committee and had no relation to Mr. Dulles's remarks." He added that I had conferred with the Secretary and that the latter wished it to be known "that he considered the episode closed."

This disposed, formally at least, of the matter of the speech. But nothing had been said about my future. Once again, weeks went by with no word from Washington. February passed. The wild doves returned to the farm — as always, the first optimistic harbingers of spring. The baleful month of March (regularly, I have discovered, a low point in my fortunes) made its appearance. It was now five months since I had been regularly occupied; and still no word from anyone in the government about my future. I must, as I realize today, have been quite a problem for people. The press had repeatedly published speculation on the subject. The *New York Times* had me appointed, at various times, as chief of mission to Cairo, to Switzerland, and to Yugoslavia. I read these stories with interest, but knew of no confirmation of them. Finally, on March 13, the *New York Times* came out with a story "from high administration sources" that I was to be retired in the near future; but of this, too, I had no direct word from Washington.

This last event, apparently, forced Mr. Dulles's hand. He summoned me to Washington the same day, called me into his office and took up, finally, the question of my future. Without ceremony or preliminary he said, quite simply, that he knew of "no niche" for me, in department or Foreign Service. He feared difficulties with regard to my confirmation if I should be appointed to a position requiring senatorial approval. He thought it was not worth risking such difficulties for an appointment to a minor post. It was clear, by implication, that he had no intention of appointing me to a major one.

Too stunned to prolong the discussion, I agreed to retire, only warning him (in the words of a memo written by me on the heels of the event) that "I would not be able to conceal from my friends or the public the fact that no position had been offered to me."

The Secretary having made this decision, I supposed that it was up to him to find some way of announcing it. I had, after all, not declined to serve. I sat back, therefore, and waited for the announcement to appear. But he had other ideas. Further weeks passed — still no announcement. I continued my life at the farm. But the uncertainty was wearing. I found it increasingly embarrassing to respond to the inquiries of friends and members of the press. I learned, again from the newspapers, during the month of March, of the appointment, confirmation, and finally the swearing-in, of my successor at the Moscow post, Charles Bohlen. This meant that I was no longer ambassador to Moscow. But what was I?

Finally, at the beginning of April, I went to Washington to seek clarification. I was received by Mr. Dulles on the morning of the seventh. Once again, I explained to him that if there was any way that I could be of service to the government in any significant capacity, I would not decline it, even though it might involve a certain personal sacrifice; but I did not want to be given an assignment "just to be taken care of." He said he hoped I would continue to serve the government, but in some other way than as an official of the Department of State. He hoped particularly that I would accept the position his brother Allen had long and very kindly been holding out to me, as an official of the Central Intelligence Agency. But this, I had already decided, I did not want to do. I felt that if I was not wanted where I had grown up and belonged, i.e., in the State Department, I would rather not be anywhere; and I told him so.

With this, the matter was settled. On the following afternoon Mr. Carl W. McCardle, the new official spokesman, read out, at the department's regular press conference, a communication of the following tenor:

Mr. Kennan expects to retire from the Foreign Service in the near future and to return to private activity in the academic field. He hopes to be able to make arrangements which will permit him to function, following his retirement, as a regular consultant to the government.

These plans are the result of discussions between him and the Secretary and are agreeable to both.

It should be added that under the legislation then governing the administration of the Foreign Service, anyone with the rank of ambassador who, upon leaving one ambassadorial post, was not reappointed within a period of three months, would be retired automatically. This clause, inserted with the evident intent of making it possible for successive Presidents and Secretaries of State to disembarrass themselves painlessly of incompetent or otherwise undesirable ambassadors, had — so far as I am aware — never before been invoked. It was clear, however, that it would, in the circumstances, be operable in my case.

As I look back today on this confused contest of wills between Mr. Dulles and myself, he determined to get me to resign voluntarily or to pawn me off on his brother, I equally determined that he should take public responsibility for not offering me a post, it seems to me that it ended as a draw of sorts — and one that afforded a certain rough justice to both parties.

Mr. Dulles, for his part, did not want to have me around. He knew very well that whatever he might say publicly, he was going to have to pursue in reality in this coming period pretty much the policy toward the Soviet Union with which my name had been often connected. But he did not at all wish things to appear this way, particularly in the eyes of the Republican right wing. He feared that if I were in the picture at all, he would be tagged as the implementer of my ideas. For this reason he wished to disembarrass himself of me, and succeeded in doing so.

But this is not to say that it did not cost him something. The newspapers, by and large, spoke kindly of me, professed to deplore my leaving, and portrayed me as a victim of partisan politics. A cartoon that appeared in several papers even depicted Mr. Dulles seated on an elephant, setting out alone into the impenetrable jungles of international affairs with the woebegone figure of Kennan left forlornly behind, and all this under the title: "What a Spot to Fire a Guide." I suspect, however, that Mr. Dulles still thought it was worth it, even at this price.

As for me: my desires were admittedly confused and in part contradictory. I was in the position of the man who does not really wish to attend the party but insists on being invited. I could have wished for a happier way to terminate what had, on the whole, been a successful and creditable Foreign Service career. It was not easy to recognize in oneself the first person to be retired under a legislative provision designed to permit the government to divest itself of incompetent ambassadors. On the other hand, I deserved some punishment for the folly of my performance at the Berlin airport. I would have been intensely unhappy in any position under Mr. Dulles's authority — not so much because of differences over policy (these would have been scarcely worse than those that had divided me from Messrs. Truman and Acheson) but because of the outrageous regime of internal security introduced by that administration into the department and Foreign Service under the pressure of the McCarthyist hysteria in right-wing Republican circles. And finally, retirement at this young age not only gave me a certain financial independence such as I had never before had, but it made it possible for me to embrace scholarship as my main dedication and career and to do so at an age when I was still capable of learning and progressing in this new field of endeavor: a necessity I have never regretted. Looking at it from the perspective of two decades I see that Fate, as so often in the hardest moments of life, was more

just to me than I at the time, in my own vanity and shortsighted-
ness, would have been to myself, had circumstances permitted me
to shape things according to my heart's desire.

This was, nevertheless, in the uncertainties it involved as well as
in the attendant buffeting of the ego, a harrowing winter. If it was
made tolerable at all, it was partly by virtue of the various ironies
that attended this whole process of parting between Mr. Dulles and
myself. Several of them stand out in my memory.

I recall, in the first place, that Mr. Dulles, after informing me, on
March 14, that my career in the Foreign Service was at an end,
went ahead to expose to me his views on the circumstances of
Stalin's recent death, and then inquired my own. Pulling myself
together as best I could, I said what I could say on the subject.
"That's very interesting," he said. Then he added, reflectively:
"You know, you interest me when you talk about these matters.
Very few other people do. I hope you'll come in from time to time
and let us have your comments on what's going on." It was, I told
my wife that night, as though I had said to her: "You know, I'm
divorcing you as of today, and you are to leave my bed and board
at once. But I love the way you cook scrambled eggs, and I wonder
if you'd mind fixing me up a batch of them right now, before you
go."

Then, on the following day — on the heels, that is, of Mr.
Dulles's statement that he feared difficulties with regard to my confirmation if I were appointed to any post requiring senatorial confirmation, I received word, at the farm, that Senator Ferguson, of
Michigan, whom I had never met, wished to see me. Senator Ferguson was a pillar of the conservative Republican forces in the Senate
and a member of the Senate Foreign Relations Committee. Much
puzzled as to what he could want to talk with me about, I went
down to Washington to see him, and discovered that what he
wanted was to ask my advice as to whether he should vote for
Bohlen's confirmation as my successor at Moscow. When I had fin-

ished telling him, as I did, why there should be no question at all of Bohlen's confirmation (and he did vote for confirmation, when the question came up), he asked me what I was doing living on a farm up in Pennsylvania. I could not resist divulging to him that I had been told by Mr. Dulles that my name could not be submitted to the Senate for any diplomatic job for fear of difficulties over confirmation. To this, the Senator's reply was: "Why hell, you wouldn't have had any trouble getting confirmed."

When, on April 7, we finally came down to the question of getting out a press release on my retirement, I found the Secretary of State's press officer, Mr. McCardle, quite at a loss to know how such an announcement ought to be phrased. I, feeling somewhat like a man being asked to write his own death sentence, went off alone to lunch, took out a piece of paper, and drafted then and there at the luncheon table the text of an announcement. After lunch I took it back and showed it to McCardle. His reaction has remained vivid in my memory. "Geez, Mr. Ambassador," he said, generously, "that's elegant; I couldn't have written that."

Finally, and of greater seriousness: if President Eisenhower knew anything of the true circumstances of my retirement, which is doubtful, he never betrayed that knowledge. (He wrote me, later in the year, a cordial letter blandly deploring my decision to resign and saying the usual nice attendant things.) In the late spring of 1953, however, while waiting for my three months of grace to expire, I was both startled and amused to receive from him an order to report to the White House staff for service over the ensuing summer in connection with a highly secret and responsible project known as the Solarium Exercise. Although this undertaking has subsequently been mentioned both in the press and in historical literature, I am still not sure how much I am authorized to reveal about it. Suffice it to say that its purpose was to clarify the various alternatives conceivable for American policy toward the Soviet Union in the coming years. I was chosen, on the President's orders, as director of one of the three teams by whose competitive efforts the exercise was to be carried through. Day after day, in the heat of midsummer, we slaved away in the basement floor of the National War College where, seven years before, I had introduced and conducted the first courses of political instruction for officers of the armed services. When the exercise was completed it was the concept propounded by my team that received the presidential approval. This had the ironic consequence that I found myself, one fine day at the end of summer, standing at a podium in a room in the White House basement, briefing the entire cabinet and other senior officials of the government on the rationale and the intricacies of the policy toward Russia which, it was decided, the government should now pursue. At my feet, in the first row, silent and humble but outwardly respectful, sat Foster Dulles, and allowed himself to be thus instructed. If he then, in March, had triumphed by disembarrassing himself of my person, I, in August, had my revenge by saddling him, inescapably, with my policy.

Having said all of this, I think I ought perhaps to add a word about my own view of Mr. Dulles as a statesman, lest what I have said create a misleading impression.

Of all the men in our public life in that postwar period whose names were mentioned as possible candidates for the position of Secretary of State, there was none who wanted the position more (which I do not regard as anything in his disfavor) and none who was better qualified for it by knowledge and experience than John Foster Dulles. His interest in international relations, and in many respects his experience with this field of activity, spanned the entire three decades that had elapsed since the Paris Peace Conference. Temperament and family tradition combined to reinforce his interest in the subject. His legal training had given him much ingenuity in argument; and he was nothing if not flexible — some would have said devious — in his tactics. Add to these qualities a very considerable depth of historical understanding and wide knowledge of the international scene and it will readily be seen that American foreign policy reposed during his incumbency as Secretary of State in what were, in many respects, uniquely qualified hands.

Informed by a wealth of observation that probably went back to the experience of himself and his uncle, Secretary of State Robert Lansing, with Woodrow Wilson at the Paris Peace Conference, Foster Dulles was intensely aware of the dependence of a Secretary of State on senatorial support for the success of his policies, and he leaned over backward to assure it. His senatorial fences were tended with an anxious and no doubt exaggerated care. This solicitude for senatorial opinion was matched, as it was almost bound to be, by a reduced concern for the feelings and opinions of those — his subordinates in government but also, on occasions, his opposite numbers in diplomacy — whom he considered unlikely to exert any significant influence on his senatorial patrons. He acquired in this way a reputation for coldness and ruthlessness, particularly in the treatment of subordinate personnel. I would think it more accurate to say that his attitude toward them was impersonal. This was not in itself a fault. General George Marshall, too, had been largely impersonal in the treatment of his subordinates in the Department of State. Where the two men differed was in the motivation for this attitude. And even here, the difference was subtle. The General's impersonality was prompted by a rigid sense of duty, supplemented by a small dose of that personal ambition which no man is totally without. In Mr. Dulles's case, the admixture was rather the other way around. It was everyone's misfortune that he was Secretary of State just at a time when the Republican majority in the Senate, under the spell of the very myths it had itself invented and cultivated, was calling for blood sacrifices in the State Department as a form of self-vindication. Had there been no victims in that quarter, this would have suggested that the whole vendetta had been unjustified. A warmer man than Mr. Dulles, and one who had had more in the way of personal experience within a career organization, might have felt a greater impulse to loyalty with relation to the men under him, and a greater disposition to resist pressures of this nature. But if Mr. Dulles ever experienced stirrings in this direction, they fell an easy victim to his conviction of the importance of placating senatorial opinion; and it was here, I think, that many of us were most critical of him. He had the reputation of being a pious man; but I, a fellow Presbyterian, could never discern the signs of it in his administration of the State Department.

With his policies I was partly in agreement, partly not so. The differences between his policies and those of the Truman administration lay less in their substance than in the rhetoric and style with which he pursued them. I liked neither the rhetoric nor the style, but in the policies themselves I could find little more to disagree with than in the policies of the old administration. I disagreed with Mr. Dulles about nuclear weapons, about Germany, and about Japan. On all these points I had disagreed no less with Mr. Acheson. The militarization of policy toward the Soviet Union under the Dulles regime was no smaller, but also not much greater, than it had been in the final two or three years of Mr. Truman's presidency. I considered shameful and indefensible Mr. Dulles's neglect of his normal collegial relations with the British; and I still feel that the state of Anglo-American relations at the time of Suez, aside from being veritably tragic in the paralysis it inflicted on Western policy toward the Hungarian rebellion, represented a low point in the entire development of American policy in the postwar period.

If, then, I had to sum up my view of Mr. Dulles as a Secretary of State, I would have to say that his weaknesses lay in the personal rather than in the intellectual and professional field. They flowed not so much from any dislike of others or malignancy of spirit toward them as from a simple lack of interest in them, or concern for them, as human beings. He tended to overintellectualize and to underpersonalize the exercise of his high office. Whether he was fully aware of the price he paid for this in its effect on the attitudes of others, I have no means of knowing; I suspect that he would, in any case, have considered the price not inordinate with relation to the goals he wished to achieve.

Dwight Eisenhower, endowed with personal qualities that were in many respects almost the exact opposite of those of his Secretary of State, was a more difficult man to understand. He was in fact, and remains in the light of history, one of the most enigmatic figures of American public life. Few Americans have ever had more liberally bestowed upon them the responsibility of command; and few have ever evinced a greater aversion to commanding. His view of the presidency resembled more closely the traditional pattern of the European head of state than that of his own country. In manner as well as in concept of the presidential office — the concept of the President, that is, as the supreme mediator, above politics, reconciling people, bringing them together, assisting them to achieve consensus, softening the asperities — he would have made an excellent crowned head. He incorporated, in personality, manner and appearance, all that Americans liked to picture as the national virtues. He was the nation's number one Boy Scout. No royal personage ever possessed to a higher degree the art of repulsing, with a charming, baffling evasiveness, any attempt on the part of a casual visitor to come to grips with him over a serious political subject.

He had the reputation — and I dare say it was correct — of never reading anything he could possibly avoid reading. His recreations, for which he always seemed to have ample time, were healthy ones but seldom reflected any serious intellectual preoccupations. I sometimes suspected that he, like many retired people who have grown up in the Army, was a lost man, socially, in civilian life. He had, "stateside," no established home — no natural place to turn in. There was no street on which it was normal for him to live. He was respected around the Gettysburg region, where he had bought his farm, but was never a real member of the community. Accustomed to the abundant amenities of senior military command, he, like other generals, gravitated naturally after his retirement from the Army, as though not knowing where else to turn, to the company and avocations of the heavy-spending tycoons of the business world: the expensive resorts, the celebrated golf links, the plush country clubs. He was used to power; such people seemed to have the attributes of it; one felt comfortable in their company. There was something helpless and pathetic, it always seemed to me, in this clumsy choice of a social milieu.

For all these reasons, there was a tendency in some quarters to view Dwight Eisenhower as an intellectually and politically superficial person whom chance, and the traditional love of the American voter for the military uniform, had tossed to the apex of American political life. The impression was quite erroneous. He was actually a man of keen political intelligence and penetration, particularly when it came to foreign affairs. Whether he used this understanding effectively is another question; but he had it. When he spoke of such matters seriously and in a protected official circle, insights of a high order flashed out time after time through the curious military gobbledygook in which he was accustomed both to expressing and to concealing his thoughts. In grasp of world realities he was clearly head and shoulders (this required, admittedly, no very great elevation) above the other members of his cabinet and official circle, with the possible exception of Foster Dulles, and even here he was in no wise inferior.

Dwight Eisenhower's difficulties lay not in the absence of intellectual powers but in the unwillingness to employ them except on the rarest of occasions. Whether this curious combination of qualities — this reluctance to exert authority, this intellectual evasiveness, this dislike of discussing serious things except in the most formal governmental context, this tendency to seek refuge in the emptiest inanities of the popular sport — whether this came from laziness, from underestimation of himself, or from the concept he entertained of his proper role as President, I would not know. But it is my impression that he was a man who, given the high office he occupied, could have done a great deal more than he did.

These observations will serve, perhaps, to show that it was not in any spirit of contempt for the leaders of the new administration that I accepted, in 1953, the exclusion from the Foreign Service which I suffered at their hands. I am persuaded, nevertheless, that it was best for all of us that I left. It would not have been easy for me to observe that particular sort of "positive loyalty" which Mr. Dulles demanded of his subordinates, so decidedly unfavorable to independent thinking and questioning at lower levels. And most difficult of all, as we shall see shortly, would have been the crises of conscience I would certainly have suffered over the regime which the new administration was about to apply under the heading of "internal security." In all likelihood, I should soon have felt obliged to resign anyway, in protest against certain of the measures that were taken in this field; and this would only have concealed, rather than clarified, the differences on questions of foreign policy that divided me in those years not just from this particular administration, but from the entire ruling establishment of American political life.

I have deviated a bit from the account of my departure from government. What remains may be briefly told.

The appointed three months of grace — or of ill-grace, if you will — began with the termination, in mid-March, of my status as ambassador to Moscow. I spent those intervening weeks working voluntarily with some of the lower-level government experts who were then occupied with the study of the political background of Stalin's death. This required my presence in Washington; and a vacant desk was found for me, as I recall it, somewhere in the vast reaches of the New State Department Building.

Finally, the day arrived — a day in June — when the three

months were up and the retirement became formally a fact. I busied myself that morning in the department, collecting such personal papers as I had about me and making arrangements for the receipt of my appointed pension. By early afternoon, I had completed these final chores and was ready to leave.

It occurred to me, then, that one would normally, on completion of twenty-seven years of service with a great organization, say goodbye to someone before leaving it. My connection with it had, after all, been something more than wholly casual. I had enjoyed the most rapid advancement, as a Foreign Service Officer, of anyone of my generation. For two years, in the exciting days of the Marshall Plan and the rescue of Europe, I had occupied the office next to that of the Secretary of State. Only three years before, I had been Counselor of the department and president of the American Foreign Service Association.

I cast around, in my mind's eye, to discover someone to whom I might suitably say goodbye. At first, I was unable to think of anyone. The friends from earlier Moscow days had either left the service entirely or had been sent to posts abroad. The housecleaning conducted by Mr. Dulles's minions as a means of placating congressional vindictiveness had been thorough and sweeping. The place was full of new faces — many of them guarded, impassive, at best coldly polite, faintly menacing. But I persisted in my quest. Surely there must, I thought, be someone somewhere in this great building — the institution that had been the center of my professional life for twenty-seven years — to whom it would be suitable and proper for me to say goodbye on this occasion.

Then suddenly a light dawned on me: there was Mrs. Mary Butler — the receptionist who guarded the approaches to the offices of the Secretary and his senior aides, on the fifth floor. A Southern lady in the finest sense of that term, beautiful, courteous, warm and competent, her lovely face and cheerful greeting had heartened me on many a morning, in the years of incumbency as head of the

Planning Staff, and strengthened me for the trials of the day ahead. She had happily survived the purge that followed upon Mr. Dulles's assumption of office. I did not know her really very well; but I knew she would be interested, and possibly even sorry, to know that I was leaving for all time.

I went up, therefore, and took leave of her. I then went downstairs, clutching a briefcase full of personal papers, got into my car, and drove slowly northward, for the last time, through the familiar meandering byroads of central Maryland, to the farm. Again, I had a feeling — misleading, of course, as on the occasion of arrival in Princeton three years before — that the great effort of life had now come to an end, that nothing of consequence remained, that there was now plenty of time for everything.

The farmhouse was deserted when I arrived. The family, as I recall it, had gone off for the afternoon. Without even bothering to remove my bags from the car I strolled around the house, seated myself on the open front porch, and sat there an hour or two, and, looking out over the two lovely fields that stretch off below the house to the east, tried to take stock of the change that had, that day, been wrought in my life.

There was plenty to think about; but someone else, I knew, would have to strike the balance, if one was ever to be struck, between justice and injustice, failure and accomplishment. I myself could not. I cannot today.

9

"McCarthyism"

THE circumstances just recounted — of my gradual separation from government in the period from 1950 to 1953 — were sobering and disillusioning to some extent (and they should have been more so) with relation to myself: my judgment, my capacities, my fitness for government service. This would have sufficed in any event to make for a difficult time. But the strain thus imposed was heightened by the fact that these experiences ran parallel with another set of stresses, also conducive to sobriety and disillusionment, but this time with relation not to myself personally but to the government I had now served for a quarter of a century and to the society which it represented and reflected. I refer to the occurrence of, and my own involvement with, the curious wave of political vindictiveness and mass hysteria that came soon to be known as "McCarthyism."

I put this term in quotation marks, because I find it a very inadequate one. What was involved here was a phenomenon that existed well before the prominent appearance of Senator Joseph McCarthy on the national scene. It outlasted his abrupt and ignominious disappearance from it. He was its creature, not its creator. It was, as I say, a wave, of sorts — a wave of feeling and reaction experienced by a great many people; and Joe McCarthy, peculiarly (if unhappily) fitted by nature for just such an adventure, rode for a short time, recklessly and giddily, on its malodorous waters, contributing at one time to their ascent, at another — to their decline. It is a pity that his name came to be given to this episode in American political life. It deserved a wider and less restrictive designation.

The penetration of the American governmental services by members or agents (conscious or otherwise) of the American Communist Party in the late 1930s was not a figment of the imagination of the hysterical right-wingers of a later decade. Stimulated and facilitated by the effects of the Depression, particularly on the younger intelligentsia, it really existed; and it assumed proportions which, while never overwhelming, were also not trivial.

Those of us who served in just those years in the American embassy at Moscow or in the Russian Division of the Department of State were very much aware of this situation — aware of it at an earlier date and much more keenly than were most of our fellow citizens. It was more readily visible to us, through the circumstances of our work, than it was to others. Our efforts to promote American interests vis-à-vis the Soviet government came into conflict at many points with the influences to which this penetration led; and our own situations were sometimes affected by it.* We yielded to no one, therefore, in our feeling that this was a state of affairs which deserved correction.

It is also true that the Roosevelt administration was very slow in reacting to this situation and correcting it. Warnings that should have been heeded fell too often on deaf or incredulous ears.

The situation underwent a partial and temporary improvement in late 1939 and 1940 by virtue of the effects of the Nazi-Soviet Non-Aggression Pact, which caused many American liberals to shy off from the Soviet leadership and its American followers in the

* We were inclined to suspect, for example, that the sudden abolition of the old Russian Division of the Department of State, in 1937, was the result, if not of direct Communist penetration, then at least of an unhealthy degree of Communist influence in higher counsels of the Roosevelt administration.

Communist Party. But when, in mid-1941, we found ourselves fighting on the same side as the Soviet Union in the war against Hitler, the shock of the Non-Agression Pact was quickly forgotten; and by the end of the war, so far as I can judge from the evidence I have seen, the penetration was quite extensive — more so, probably, than at any time in the past, particularly in the hastily recruited wartime bureaucracies, the occupational establishments in Germany and Japan, and certain departments of the government normally concerned, for the most part, with domestic affairs and unaccustomed to dealing with problems of national security.

This penetration was less important, though by no means nonexistent, in the State Department, even during wartime; and never at any time did I see reason to believe that it was of such dimensions as to lead to any extensive Communist influence on the formulation of policy. Its importance there was presumably increased, to be sure, when, in the aftermath of the war, certain of the wartime agencies went into liquidation and considerable portions of their personnel were blanketed into the department. But this situation was met at a relatively earlier point by drastic tightening of security rules and standards. And the Foreign Service itself, as distinct from the Department of State, being a disciplined career organization entry into which had been largely governed in recent years by strict competitive examination, had at no time been importantly affected by the problem of foreign penetration.

By 1947, at the time I came into the State Department, this problem, as it seemed to me then and seems to me now, was well on the way to being mastered, to the extent it ever can be. In part this was the consequence of the higher security standards. In part it may be attributed to the fact that many people who had previously considered themselves friends or followers of the Soviet leadership were given cause to hesitate and to reconsider their positions as evidence increased of the brutal and undemocratic conduct of Soviet troops and authorities throughout Eastern and Central Europe, of extensive use by the Soviet secret police of foreign Communists for espionage purposes, and of growing political conflict between the Soviet Union and the United States — conflict which meant that it was no longer possible to be a follower of Soviet leadership without placing oneself in a position of disloyal opposition to one's own government. In the face of all these developments I gained the impression by the late 1940s that Communist penetration, whatever might have been its importance in earlier years and whatever importance it might still have had from the standpoint of military espionage, was no longer a serious problem from the standpoint of its influence on American foreign policy.

All this being the case, it was with amazement and incredulity that I took note, in the years 1948 and 1949, of the growing virulence of the attacks now being launched against the administration over just this point. Even allowing for the obvious domestic-political motivation for the exploitation of an issue that held out extensive possibilities for embarrassing the administration, it seemed to me that these attacks, vastly exaggerating as they did a waning danger and throwing discredit on a great many honorable people together with a few dishonorable ones, were not only unjustifiable but misleading and destructive.

In mentioning these matters I would, I know, not be doing justice to the more serious and responsible of the people who associated themselves with these attacks unless I also took note of the importance of the Hiss case in stimulating, and often confirming, their suspicions.

The development of this case I viewed, at the time, with a detached and skeptical wonderment. I had never had more than a nodding acquaintance with Mr. Alger Hiss. I had met him once casually in 1945 when he and others from our delegation to the Yalta Conference passed through Moscow on their way home. I met him once again, in equally casual circumstances, if my memory is correct, in Washington, after my return to this country in 1946. I cannot recall ever talking with him. Our careers had followed wholly different lines. I did not like what I suspected to be his cast of mind or his approach to international problems; and I was not alone, I suppose, among Foreign Service Russian experts in experiencing a slight tinge of resentment over the fact that a man who had never served abroad and who had, in particular, no firsthand knowledge of Russia should be serving as senior advisor to the Secretary of State in Washington and journeying to Yalta as a member of the official American delegation, whilst others of us, who had long experience in international affairs, pursued our routine Foreign Service duties.

On the other hand, I saw no reason (and see none today) to suppose that the President or the Secretary of State had been importantly influenced by Hiss's presence at the Yalta Conference, and particularly not in connection with the Far Eastern matters on which suspicion centered. I was aware, also, that he had enjoyed the personal confidence of many people whom I respected, including some whom I numbered among my friends. I was prepared, therefore, to reserve judgment with regard to the attacks against him, until all the facts should be available. And I was at all times convinced that even if proof were to be forthcoming of an alleged involvement with the Communist movement in the 1930s, the case would be a most unusual one, from which no wider implications, and particularly no inferences of extensive Communist influence on the formulation of policy in the postwar period, could justifiably be drawn.

Unfortunately, I must say, the facts of this case were never to become fully available. Even today it is impossible for anyone, as I see it, with no more to go on but the statements of Mr. Hiss and his accuser, Whittaker Chambers, the transcripts of the congressional hearings, and the records of the trials, to form any conclusive judgment on the essential question as to whether Mr. Hiss had or had not had, in the mid-1930s, connections with the Communist movement which he was subsequently unwilling to reveal. I am not a "buff" of this case; but I have read a good deal of the material relating thereto; and I may say that I am as little inclined, even after the passage of twenty-some years, to believe that what Mr. Hiss had to say about this question represented the entirety of what could have been told as I am to accept the jury's conclusion that it was really he who filched from the State Department the famous "pumpkin documents," produced from Chambers's farm, and caused them to be typed on the Hiss family typewriter. There is a great deal, both in the habits of professional intelligence services and in the circumstances of the moment, that speaks against the likelihood that Alger Hiss, whatever his relations to the Communist movement, would have performed these particular actions.

For the effect which this inconclusive and, in many respects, still mysterious matter came to have on public opinion, and for the great extent, in particular, to which it served to pour oil on the flames of the aroused anticommunism of the time, it seems to me that one must place much of the blame directly on the Truman administration itself, and specifically for its failure to conduct a proper and exhaustive administrative investigation of its own into the question of Mr. Hiss's alleged earlier Communist connections. The American people had a need, in the face of the doubts that had been raised, to know all that it was possible to learn with relation to this question. Neither the congressional hearings, sensationally conducted and encumbered with many emotional overtones, nor the court proceedings, designed to test merely whether Mr. Hiss had perjured himself in two specific statements he had made under oath, were in any way adequate as a response to this need.

I emphasize this because it was, as we shall see shortly, not the last time that the executive branch of the government would show itself unhappily remiss in just this way. I wonder, in fact, whether one must not take cognizance of a certain congenital ineptness on the part of the United States government when it comes to the clarification of major mysteries of our public life. The tendency of the political parties to scratch around for ways of taking political advantage of such situations; the corresponding tendency of administrations to evade responsibility by pawning off embarrassing questions on the courts; the extent to which litigation once in progress then tends to interfere with administrative investigation (an example is the situation of Jack Ruby after the Kennedy assassination); the suffocating and disrupting attentions of the press; and the parochial interests of American intelligence services which cause them (sometimes legitimately) to be more interested in the concealment of information than in its revelation: all these make it seemingly difficult in the extreme for the executive branch of the government to conduct anything resembling a proper and searching administrative investigation even into matters where both that branch of the government and the public at large have every reason to wish to know all that can be known about the facts of the case.*

To return, however, to my own involvement with these problems of internal security in the late 1940s: when, during the course of my visit to South America in the late winter and spring of 1950, I read in the official news bulletin of one of our embassies there that Senator McCarthy had made a radio speech in which he said he "held in his hand" the evidence of the existence of two hundred and some "card-carrying Communists" in the State Department, I received this news not only with head-shaking wonder but also with a

---

* While this concerns a period into which these memoirs do not reach, it is not my impression that any of the three great and tragic political assassinations of the mid- and late 1960s ever received the sort of clarification the American public was entitled to expect. I never had the slightest doubt of the integrity of the members of the Warren Commission; but even their investigation of the first Kennedy murder seems tó me to have been in several respects inadequate, or unsuitable, to the task at hand.

certain satisfaction. "Now," I thought, "he will have to prove it. Then we will have an end to the matter."

How naïve I was! Had anyone told me then that he would never prove a single one of these cases, but that his charge would nevertheless be a great political success — that millions of worthy people would be running around for years to come saying: "We don't like his methods, but we think what he is doing needs to be done and he deserves great credit for it" — I would have found this hard to believe. Least of all did I suspect that while I was reading these words there were beginning to happen thousands of miles away, in Washington, particularly with relation to a subordinate of mine on the Policy Planning Staff, things, intimately associated with the Senator's efforts, that were designed to destroy this subordinate's career and to sadden both his life and, I may honestly say, mine.

But before I got into the matter of my own involvement with the Davies case and other manifestations of the wave of feeling and action to which this chapter is addressed, I ought, I think, to be more explicit about my own attitude as of that time with respect to the phenomenon of Communist penetration in American life, generally.

In the spring of 1951, while living and working in Princeton, I was nominated (and later elected) to the position of Alumni Trustee of Princeton University. Soon after my nomination was announced, I received a letter from an anxious alumnus, who placed before me what was, in the light of the preoccupations of the time, a not unreasonable question. "Since we are now at war," he wrote, "it seems quite in order to ask you this question: namely, just where will you stand on communism, if elected?"

I accepted this as a fair demand, and replied (at some length, because the matter was a serious one, close to my experience and my concerns) in a letter of May 16, 1951, the substance of which was

published, shortly thereafter, in the *New York Times Magazine*.*
Pointing to the length and character of my own involvement with
Soviet communism, I went on to treat the question, successively,
with relation to three groups of people: (1) the Communist Party
itself; (2) the fellow travelers and sympathizers; and (3) the rest of
us.

As for the Communist Party (then, of course, a completely
Stalinist organization, under close Soviet control, and without any
serious rival in the revolutionary radical-socialist camp in the
United States): I thought we would be morally and politically justified in outlawing it, but I doubted that it would be wise or expedient for us to do so. We would be better advised, I thought,

to keep it in the open where it can be seen and its activities observed,
where its very freedom of action demonstrates how little afraid of it we
are, and where its outward activities provide anyone who cares to see
with ever fresh and current demonstrations of its extremism, its remote-
ness from the feelings and ideals of our people, and the extent to which
it is beholden to its cynical and contemptuous foreign masters.

As for the fellow travelers, I thought they presented a problem;
that it was inadvisable for various reasons to have them in responsible and delicate governmental positions; but that in holding them
away from such positions or removing them from them, we ought
to be careful not to damage their reputations or their occupational
possibilities. They were not criminals. Their attitudes were in many
cases passing phases of outlook, which time would correct. What
they required was "a certain forbearance and firm intellectual resistance . . . not public humiliation and ignominious rejection." It
was more important to help them become useful citizens than to
make out of them "embittered outcasts."

The presence of people with strong pro-Soviet and Marxist sympathies in the educational process represented a special problem.

* May 27, 1951.

Persons really committed to the Soviet ideology had no place in that process, I thought, because they could not simultaneously be committed to that rigid dogma and total intellectual discipline, on the one hand, and to the freedom of the mind in the quest for objective truth, the first requirement of any proper educational experience, on the other. But with the uncommitted sympathizers, it was a different thing. Here, cases could only be decided individually, on the basis of common sense and human feeling. One had to beware of prejudicing one's own principles for minor causes. It would be a serious thing if we had to conclude that sound teachings could not stand the competition of one or two challenging voices. Our purpose, after all, was not to shelter youth from destructive and ill-founded ideas but to equip them for recognizing such ideas when they saw them, for resisting them and helping others to resist them. I recalled in this connection the words of Milton's *Areopagitica:* "He that can apprehend and consider vice with all her baits and seeming pleasures, and yet abstain, and yet distinguish, and yet prefer that which is truly better, he is the true warfaring Christian." We had no more reason than did Milton, I thought, to wish to see cultivated in our youth "a fugitive and cloistered virtue, unexercised and unbreathed, that never sallies out and sees her adversary."

But the most serious passages of this letter were reserved for the last question: the question of the possible effects upon ourselves — "the rest of us" — of an exaggerated and hysterical anticommunism. We must learn, I urged, to put this problem in its place. The greatest danger we could run would be to yield to the temptation to ascribe all our troubles to this one cause. It was not just the political danger of misestimating the phenomenon of Communist penetration; it was a question of something much more important:

our ability to meet effectively the many and heavy problems we have before us which have nothing to do with . . . communism . . . , in which we would not be materially aided if every Communist Party member and every sympathizer were to be deported from our shores tomorrow. . . .

The Communist Party, after all, was only an external danger, and now a minor one.

But the subjective emotional stresses and temptations to which we are exposed in our attempt to deal with this . . . problem are not an external danger: they represent a danger within ourselves — a danger that something may occur in our own minds and souls which will make us no longer like the persons by whose efforts this republic was founded and held together, but rather like the representatives of that very power we are trying to combat: intolerant, secretive, suspicious, cruel and terrified of internal dissension. . . . The worst thing the Communists could do to us, and the thing we have most to fear from their activities, is that we should become like them.

America, after all, was not just territory and people, it was something in our minds that caused us to believe in certain things and to behave in certain ways. It was what distinguished us from others. If that went, then there would be no America to defend. But that could easily go if we yielded to the temptation "to escape from our frustrations into the realms of mass emotion and hatred and to find scapegoats for our difficulties in individual fellow-citizens who are, or have at one time been, disoriented or confused." Better than this would be to forget the Communist problem entirely.

These, then, were the views with which I was obliged to face my own various involvements with the problems of "internal security" that so agitated the opinion of that time and so unsettled both society and government.

Of these various involvements (and they had to do, in one way or another with several of the most prominent cases of the time) the most extensive was my connection with the long ordeal suffered by Mr. John Paton Davies, Jr. He and I had been colleagues in

Moscow from 1944 to 1946. He was then, after return to Washington, attached in 1949 and 1950 to the Policy Planning Staff, of which I was director.

Even before coming to this position on the staff, Davies had been heavily under attack from former Ambassador to China Patrick J. Hurley and other persons close to the China Lobby, because of differences arising out of his service in China, and notably his service on the staff of General Joseph W. Stilwell, in 1942–1944. His reporting on the situation there in those years, and particularly his drawing attention to the grievous weaknesses of the Chinese Nationalist government and the improbability of its success in any prolonged further conflict with the Communists, had drawn upon him the ire of that government and its friends in the United States. Its influence in American political circles, by no means insignificant, was brought to bear against him; and he soon found himself under attack — an attack vociferously supported by Ambassador Hurley — on the strange charge of desiring the very misfortunes against which he had attempted to warn.

This charge — that Davies was pro–Chinese Communist and thus the bearer of left-wing sympathies — was simply untrue. He respected the seriousness and competence of the Chinese Communists. He warned Washington against underrating their abilities and their political prospects. But he shared nothing of the ideological doctrines which had inspired the rise of their movement.

There was, in the fact that Ambassador Hurley figured so prominently among Davies's detractors, a foretaste of the curious irony that was to bedevil the later and more tragic stages of Davies's career; for Hurley himself was already then on record as boasting, in 1945, that he was "the best friend the Chinese Communists had in Chungking" * and as maintaining that these latter were devoted to

* *United States Relations with China* (generally known as the China White Paper), page 103. Washington, 1949.

principles little different from our own.* He would have seemed, in the light of such statements, to be a more natural target than was Davies for just the sort of attacks the latter had to endure. But this, in the peculiar atmosphere of American political life, was largely ignored, whereas the charges advanced against Davies were eagerly seized upon by persons anxious either to find scapegoats for the miseries now being suffered by the Chinese Nationalist regime or to prove the dire extent of Communist penetration into the Roosevelt administration and the State Department.

These early attacks, however, were as nothing compared to what was now, in 1950, about to begin. And for this last, I must acknowledge a share of the blame.

Addressing ourselves, in 1948 and 1949, to the problem of how to frustrate Communist efforts at penetration and subversion of the governmental systems of Western Europe and other continents, some of us in the United States government, including myself, my friend the late Allen Dulles, later deputy director and director of the Central Intelligence Agency, and certain members of our respective staffs, came to the conclusion that the government had need of some sort of facilities through which there could be conducted, from time to time as need arose, operations in the international field for which it would not be proper for any of the regular departments or agencies of the government to take responsibility, or for which the regular procedures of the government were too cumbersome. We needed, in other words, an agency for secret operations.

The thought was entirely sound. It was not a question of establishing what came later to be referred to as "a department of dirty tricks." It was the question of creating a facility designed to give greater flexibility to the operations of a government, now involved in a global cold war, whose traditional arrangements for the appropriation and use of public funds were wholly unsuited to such a role

---

* Herbert Feis, *The China Tangle*, p. 261. Princeton: Princeton University Press, 1953.

in world affairs. The need was real; and many things subsequently done under the aegis of the facilities eventually established were constructive and effective actions.

However, one difficulty was present at the start: and this was the insistence of higher governmental circles that this undertaking be coordinated with the operations of the military establishment in the conduct of what the military had taught themselves to call "black propaganda" — a device inherited from the military operations of two world wars. I should, of course, have declined resolutely to let these two things be merged, even if the whole project of secret operations had to be sacrificed; but in such matters one is often wise only after the event, and I, in my folly or my effort to be cooperative, did not do so. The result was that we were forced to struggle along with our well-meaning military colleagues, acquiescing in something called "programs" — programs for each year and for each country — which forced us to conduct such operations even where and when none were needed, and attempting to contribute to undertakings which struck us as childish and for which we had little enthusiasm. And for this purpose, committee meetings were held, in the usual Washington fashion.

I, having a number of other duties, could not attend all these meetings personally, and I delegated various members of my staff to deputize for me at them. One of these members, assigned — in view of his experience — to such of them as concerned Far Eastern matters, was Davies. These meetings, I should add, were all, for obvious reasons, of a top secret classification; and it never occurred to any of us that things said or done in them would be divulged to anyone except the immediate superiors, in the departments and agencies involved, of those who took part.

In the course of this work, Davies, pressed to come up with ideas as to how certain kinds of informational material could be conveyed to the Chinese Communist intellectuals, despite the severity of the censorship in Communist China, advanced a number of ideas.

Some weeks later a request came from the CIA side that he eluci-
date one of them. A meeting was held, on November 16, 1949, attended by two individuals, ostensibly members of the CIA — men
whose names and official connection were previously unknown to
us and the circumstances of whose assignment to this work have
never, so far as I know, been fully clarified. Davies elaborated on
the project, which was a highly imaginative if not fanciful one, expecting that the matter would be discussed at the meeting. No discussion, however, took place. The CIA men listened in silence and
left, presumably to report back to their superiors. If their subsequent testimony before a congressional subcommittee is to be believed, one must conclude — and it would be the most charitable
conclusion possible in the circumstances — that they had a very
poor understanding of what the meeting was all about and of
Davies's status in particular, and came away with a most dreadful
misunderstanding of what he had been trying to say, not to mention
dire suspicions of his motives.

In the normal course of things, the observations and impressions
of these gentlemen would have been simply reported to their superiors, and the latter, if as puzzled and disturbed as their subordinates
professed to be by what Davies was understood to have said, would
have taken the matter up with the State Department at a higher
level (in this instance presumably with myself) and given people in
that department a chance to explain and to clarify. Had Allen
Dulles then been head of CIA, I am sure this would have been done.
The fact is, however, that it was not. Instead, a report was filed, if I
am not mistaken, with the FBI, which report then came, in the
normal course of things, to the attention of such of the congressional committees as were interested. Of these, the most interested,
certainly, was the Internal Security Subcommittee of the Senate
Committee on the Judiciary, the so-called McCarran (later the
Jenner) Committee, a body which made itself the center for the
investigation of suspected instances of Communist penetration and

influence in the executive branch of the government and elsewhere. In this committee, the report of Davies's supposedly subversive proposals appears to have been pounced upon with triumphant enthusiasm, and from here on out, the fat was in the fire. Charges and denunciations were at once addressed to the State Department. The latter, presumably to protect itself, allowed Davies to be subjected to a long series of formal loyalty investigations, conducted by boards appointed in some instances by itself, in others by outside bodies. All of these without exception (there were seven or eight of them, if my memory is correct) found no reason to question Davies's loyalty and exonerated him, I believe, on all counts. But this made no difference to the Internal Security Subcommittee. On August 8 and 10, 1951, Davies was haled before those of its members who cared to be present and subjected to much hostile and suspicious interrogation. Conscious of his obligation to official security, he loyally declined to describe those details of the incident which would have laid to rest the suspicions it aroused, because he had no authority to reveal them to outside parties. The man who had denounced him was then similarly summoned and questioned; and when differences were developed, as was not unnatural, between the two sets of testimony, the Subcommittee approached the Justice Department with the request that a grand jury be summoned to determine whether Davies should not be indicted for perjury. Some two years thereafter were spent in a vain effort by the chairmen of that subcommittee and its parent body to overcome the resistance of the Justice Department to taking this action. Meanwhile, of course, there had been a great deal of publicity, controversy, anguish to Davies and his family, suspensions, transfers, and harassments of every sort; and very little of this was alleviated by the fact that he was never, so far as I am aware, found guilty on any of the numerous charges.

Finally, in the year 1954, the new Republican Secretary of State, John Foster Dulles, appointed a special "Security Hearing Board," composed of five officials of other departments and agencies of the government (their chief qualification for this task appeared to have been their common lack of any sort of experience with, or knowledge of, diplomatic work) and charged them with investigating the case all over again in the light of the new security standards of the Eisenhower administration. Davies testified before this board, being assured that he would be given an opportunity to see the unclassified portions of the transcript of the hearings before any decision was arrived at. Before he could even see the transcript, however, or give his comments on it, the board, unbeknownst to him, reported to Secretary Dulles that his further employment was "not clearly consistent with the interests of the national security"; and on November 5, 1954, Davies, having never been found guilty on any charge against his loyalty, having had nothing but excellent efficiency reports from his Foreign Service chiefs for at least a decade back into the past, and having rejected the efforts of the department to induce him to resign voluntarily, was dismissed by Mr. Dulles from the service for "lack of judgment, discretion and reliability" (the Board's words) — after which the department exerted itself for several years, though unsuccessfully in the end, to deny him the pension rights to which he would normally have been entitled.

Such, then, were the bare facts of the Davies case. My own involvement in it was not extensive, but it was also not negligible; and the matter weighed on my conscience and my thoughts for years.

The incident with CIA first came to my attention soon after its occurrence, when a journalist friend in Washington came to see me and told me, in terms that left no doubt as to the date and place of the occurrence, that Davies had endeavored to infiltrate Communists into the employ of CIA. Since it was clear that there had been an egregious and deliberate violation of security, I took the matter up with CIA. An investigation ensued. It was not difficult to establish the identity of the man who had leaked the information; his case was indefensible, and I was given to understand that he was at once dismissed.

With this, I naïvely supposed the episode to be closed. But this was only the beginning.

There now ensued the first round of Davies's loyalty investigations. I returned from Europe in the summer of 1951 (at my own expense) to testify on his behalf before the State Department's Loyalty Board. I testified similarly, as I recall it, when the case came before the President's Civil Service Loyalty Review Board. In both of these hearings, the CIA matter, I believe, came up; but the circumstances were such that it was impossible to give a complete clarification of what had occurred.

In the summer of 1952, when I was serving in Moscow, I received letters from Davies about the efforts of the Subcommittee to have him indicted for perjury. These letters disturbed me greatly, and for a special reason. Throughout the whole period of the loyalty investigations, against Davies and others as well, I had strongly disapproved of the manner in which the congressional and other outside charges against people in the State Department had been handled by the senior officials of the department. Instead of conducting first their own independent investigations of such charges, and then either exonerating the man or taking action against him as their own investigation might warrant, these officials simply took any charges that came to them from outside, however absurd or implausible, haled the officer before a loyalty board, and said to him, in effect: "Here is what you are charged with. Defend yourself if you can. We, the department, have nothing further to do with the matter." It was then left to the accused officer to unearth evidence, sometimes from the department's own files, to establish his innocence.

It seemed to me that this procedure represented a clear evasion of the department's own responsibility. Pride, ignorance, stress of mind, or any one of a number of other causes, might have rendered the officer unwilling or unable to defend himself, even when the facts spoke for his innocence. In this case the department, having conducted no independent administrative investigation of its own, would never have known for sure what actually occurred, or even whether justice had been done to the man in question. Yet this is the way matters were handled — in Davies's case and in others. One of the charges brought against Davies from the congressional side, for example, was plainly disprovable on the basis of evidence in the department's own files, which showed the charge to rest on a clear case of mistaken identity — it was another Davies who was involved. The department, nevertheless, instead of consulting its own files and explaining to the congressmen that the charge was baseless, solemnly charged Davies with the offense before its own loyalty board, and left it to him to have the wit to unearth the evidence that cleared him. The same was done in other cases — why? I never knew. I would have suspected pusillanimity, except that this was the last thing one could suspect in Dean Acheson. I can only conclude that he was badly advised.

For me, in any case, faced with the persecution to which Davies was now being subjected, this raised a difficult problem. It meant that I had no opportunity to come to Davies's defense in a proper, secret administrative hearing before our common superiors in the department and to clarify both my own responsibility and the motives of his conduct. And now that there was a danger of his being indicted, I knew no way of helping. I immediately drafted a letter to the Secretary of State, to make my position clear.* Pointing out that I was Davies's superior at the time he performed the actions over which he was being attacked, I said that "I could not stand by and see an officer suffer injury to his career or to his status as a

---

* The signed draft of this letter was sent not directly to the Secretary but to friends in the department, with the suggestion that they show it to him and deliver it to him formally unless they thought it better not to make it a matter of formal record, in which case they could just show it to him. This last, I believe, was what was done.

citizen by virtue of actions performed by him in good faith as part of his best effort to carry out duties laid upon him by myself.

"The purpose of this letter," I continued, "is to tell you that in case this matter should have any unfortunate consequences for Davies. . . . I would not be able to feel that my own position, and my usefulness generally to the government, could remain unaffected." I suggested that the Secretary might wish to tell this to the President, as well as to the Attorney General and Senator Mc-Carran.

None of this, however, did any good. When I came back from Moscow, the matter was still roaring along. With every attack against Davies in the press, my own conscience winced. In November 1952, *Time* magazine ran a story charging Davies with being a member of a State Department group who worked up a policy paper which misrepresented General MacArthur's advice about withdrawing our troops from Korea. The allegation was quite untrue; and I at once wrote a letter for publication in the columns of the magazine. Davies, I wrote,

had no responsibility for the preparation of the paper you mention or any other papers on this subject.

It was I, after all, not Davies, who was at that time head of the Policy Planning Staff. I was responsible for its work and its recommendations. While I am not in a position to discuss the part played by the Staff in the preparation of individual governmental decisions, I have no interest in evading my responsibility as its Director or in seeing that responsibility diminished in the public eye at the expense of any of my subordinates.*

Two weeks after the appearance of that letter, I was myself subpoenaed to appear before the McCarran Committee. (I see no reason to doubt that there was a connection.) Puzzled and angered by the use of the subpoena to bring me there (I had never failed to respond to any normal invitation to appear before a congressional

* *Time*, December 29, 1952.

body, and would as a matter of course have responded to one in this instance), I duly appeared, on the afternoon of January 13, in the small and cluttered room which the Subcommittee used for its hearings. The experience was a traumatic one. I was not told who was present in the room, nor was I informed of the identity of the man who was questioning me. I did not know, at first, as I recall it, whether my interrogator was a senator or some other individual. (He was, as it proved, one of the two attorneys for the Subcommittee, Mr. J. G. Sourwine.) Nor was I told what the subject of the hearing was, or even the reason why I had been summoned. Only gradually did it become evident to me that the affair was in connection with the Davies case. I was placed under oath; and in this condition, wholly without preparation, without counsel, without the possibility of forethought, yet vulnerable to a charge of perjury if I made the slightest slip, I endured an hour or so of cryptic and carefully prepared questioning. It included, at one point, what I could only take to be a deliberate attempt to entrap me, one of them so shameless and egregious that I could hardly believe it. (It was a matter of dates, in which point I have one of the world's worst memories; and only the presence of some real but invisible guardian angel can have saved me from falling into the apparent snare.)

I survived the ordeal. I never heard anything further from the Subcommittee. There were no formal consequences. But the experience, falling as it did in that wretched winter of puzzlement and uncertainty over the mystery of my own situation vis-à-vis the new administration, was Kafkaesque. (The appearance before the Subcommittee was only three days before my Scranton speech and a week before the new administration took office.) I could expect, in the circumstances, no help from the State Department; and I was obliged to recognize that I had arrived at a point where my fate, as an officer of the government, was at least partially in the hands of people for whom a record of twenty-five years of faithful and honorable service meant nothing whatsoever; where one would be given no credit for it, no consideration, and no mercy — on the contrary. And not one of one's superiors in the executive branch of the government would lift a finger to help. It will not be difficult to understand that the desire to serve further a government in which such things could happen was not enhanced by this realization.

The difficulties over the Davies case were not yet at an end. With the change in administration, the Internal Security Subcommittee came to be headed, in place of the Democratic McCarran, by Senator William Jenner. His zeal in the ferreting out of hidden Communists in the State Department appeared to be no smaller than that of his predecessor. Discovering, to his evident disappointment, that the new Deputy Attorney General (the future Secretary of State, Mr. William P. Rogers) had still not moved to the indictment of Davies for perjury, he wrote (on June 11, 1953), asking for information on the status of the case. Mr. Rogers replied (on July 6) that the Davies case, together with others inherited from the previous administration, was under review "solely by appointees of the present Attorney General" and that the review had not yet been completed. All this came to my attention when, on August 28, the magazine *U.S. News & World Report* carried the excerpts of a lengthy report by the Subcommittee entitled *Interlocking Subversion in Government Departments*, in which the Davies case figured prominently.

It was obvious from this report that the ghost was still far from being laid, and my sense of frustration was now greater than ever. I could not forget that no independent administrative investigation had ever been carried out. I had had no opportunity either to acknowledge the degree of my own responsibility or to put on record my own knowledge of the case. The State Department, now in Republican hands, was less likely than ever to make any move in Davies's defense. I therefore got in touch independently with the Attorney General's office, telling them that I had information that ought to be taken into consideration before any decision prejudicial to Davies's interests was taken, and offered to come to Washington for the purpose. The Attorney General replied, naming a deputy with whom I might discuss the matter. But efforts to arrange an appointment with the latter came to nought; and we were soon back where we started.

Several more weeks passed. Then, on December 9, 1953, the *New York Times* printed lengthy excerpts of the testimony of Davies and others before the Internal Security Subcommittee, and two days later *U.S. News & World Report* followed suit, devoting nineteen pages of its issue to what it called, in a cover headline, "The Strange Case of John P. Davies."

This was too much. Left unclarified by any explanation from Davies's superiors, the bare bones of this testimony — the record of exchanges in which he, testifying under oath and concerned to protect governmental security, had been at a decided disadvantage — failed seriously to do justice to his position. I had restrained myself, to that point, from coming out publicly because the State Department had always discouraged me from doing so, professing confidence that Davies's interests would be best served if the matter were left to the operation of the judicial, or quasi-judicial, procedures. But it was now evident that he was being helplessly pilloried before public opinion, and could do nothing further in his own defense.

I therefore sat down and wrote a letter to the *New York Times*, the draft of which I sent, as a courtesy, to the Department of State, with an accompanying letter to the Deputy Under Secretary. Something had to be done, I wrote in this covering letter, to correct the unclarities and misapprehensions which Davies's testimony, taken by itself, would leave. "If the department," I added, "were prepared to do this, I would be happy to remain silent; but on the assumption that the department is not contemplating such a step, I propose, as Davies's former superior, to speak out."

The reply was again discouraging. People in the department

failed to understand, it was said, why I wished to "rush into print."

I wrote once more, on December 14. I respected, I said, the opinions of the senior officials of the department, but "I do not feel that I can or should permit the steady damaging of Davies's public reputation to proceed further without doing what I can to help him." As for "rushing into print":

For more than two years I have been repeatedly on the verge of coming out publicly . . . but have been restrained each time by the hope that the government itself would take the necessary steps to protect Davies's reputation. My own fear now is that my action has been delayed too long.

The letter appeared in the *New York Times* on December 17. After recounting, along the lines described above, the nature of the CIA episode, my own relation to it, and the reasons why neither Davies nor I had ever been able to give a detailed public account of the whole story, I pointed out that the matter had been reported to the security authorities before I had been able to offer any explanations or make any clarification; and this had led, I said, to

a seemingly endless series of charges, investigations, hearings and publicity — an ordeal which has brought acute embarrassment to Davies and his family, as well as a great sense of helplessness and concern to his friends and colleagues.

I had never, I added, had the slightest reason to doubt the honesty or integrity of his motives.

Since, however, there was a tendency to question Davies's judgment "even in quarters where the unsubstantiality of the loyalty and perjury suspicions is freely conceded," I wished, I wrote, to add the following observations on that point:

Mr. Davies served under me for several years, both in Moscow and in the department. In addition to this I had opportunity to learn something of his subsequent work in Germany. He is a man of quick and intuitive intelligence, great enthusiasm for his work and an unfailing devotion to duty. He did not come into this world, or even into the Foreign Service, endowed by nature with wisdom and maturity, but like many others of us . . . developed his powers of judgment over the years through the process of trial and error, and outstandingly through the ability to acknowledge and analyze his own mistakes. I would rate him today . . . as a talented and devoted public servant who has already suffered a unique measure of adversity for his efforts to be useful to his country and whose departure from the governmental service would be a serious loss to the public interest.

I hope that his difficulties may be a lesson to us all, and that we may learn from them how to protect our public servants in future from the sort of occupational hazard Mr. Davies has encountered.

With the publication of this letter, my possibilities for usefulness in the matter were exhausted. Davies was never indicted (I think that here my letter and other efforts may have done some good), but shortly after this Mr. Dulles placed in motion his own investigating procedures with the result already described. I had no influence with Mr. Dulles, and further intercession with him would have been quite useless.

If I have recounted the episode in such detail here, it is partly to illustrate the viciousness of the pressures directed against individual Foreign Service officers in the atmosphere of the time and the unsoundness of the procedures by which the leaders of the executive branch of the government reacted to these pressures, but also to make clear the bearing of such experiences on my own hesitations and vacillations with respect to the question of whether to accept passively my separation from government or to fight it and attempt to remain. I was never sure that I belonged in a government where such things could happen to one's subordinates, and where one could be so powerless to defend them from obloquy and injustice.

The Davies case was, as it happened, by no means the only one of these celebrated security cases with which I was personally concerned. I testified, similarly, at the loyalty hearings of two other "old China hands" — John Stewart Service and Oliver Clubb. I also appeared before the board headed by Mr. Gordon Gray which, in April 1954, sat in judgment on the question of Robert Oppenheimer's fitness to be a consultant for the Atomic Energy Commission, and passed there as sad and tragic a morning as I can recall experiencing. There were a number of other cases where I felt obliged to intervene privately (though usually futilely) within the walls of the State Department on behalf of one or another of my acquaintances who fell afoul of the various razzias which, by 1952, were in progress — razzias that sometimes involved the most outrageous sort of investigation into the private intimacies as well as the political opinions and associations of the victims.

These other involvements need not be recounted here. The Davies case will serve as a sufficient example. But there were two of them in which questions of principle were involved which ought perhaps to be noted.

One of these was the Service case. John Service, whom I had never previously met, came to me one day in 1950, when I was serving as Counselor of the Department of State, and asked whether I would consent to read the various reports he had submitted from China in the 1943–1944 period (his activity in that period now being under investigation), and then, if I found that these reports did not reflect pro-Communist bias, to appear before the State Department's Loyalty Board as a witness on his behalf. Among the charges levied against him by the department was one, presumably emanating from congressional circles, to the effect that his reports from China in that period reflected such a bias.

The very levying of such a charge by the Department of State was of course another instance of the improper manner in which that department handled charges of this nature originating with outside parties. The department was itself the recipient and custodian of Service's reports. It had had them in its files for years. It was quite capable of judging them. It had, in fact, been its duty to judge them, at the time they were filed. If it considered that they reflected a pro-Communist bias, it was at liberty to remove Service from further political work or, if it liked, from the Foreign Service. If, on the other hand, it considered that the reports did not reflect such bias (and this, one had to assume, was the case, for it had repeatedly rewarded him with letters of commendation for their excellence), then it had the duty to defend him from outside attacks. There was nothing to stop them going back at the congressional critics and saying: "We are better qualified to judge these reports than you are. The suggestion that they reflect a pro-Communist bias is absurd; and we emphatically decline to make ourselves the sponsors of such a suggestion by advancing it as a charge against the officer before our own Loyalty Board." Instead of doing this, the department raised its hands in pious detachment, let the charge be preferred against the officer, and said to him in effect, once again as in the case of Davies: "Here's what people say about you. Defend yourself if you can. We won't lift a finger on your behalf."

I said to Service, in reply to his request, that I would be glad to read his reports if requested by the department or the Loyalty Board to do so, and to give either of them my honest opinion, but I wanted the request to come from one of them, not from him, and I did not want to come before the Board known to it in advance as a witness for or against anybody. It was the department that was bringing the charges against him. I was a senior official of the department. If it wanted my opinion (which it should properly have solicited before it brought the charges), let it ask me.

Service was doubtful, initially, that the Board would consent to ask me. The Board would recognize, he said, only witnesses for the prosecution and witnesses for the defense. I insisted, however; and finally the Board (as an exception, I was told) consented to invite my opinion.

I took the reports (there were several hundred pages of them) to my home in the country and spent several days in their perusal. Then I appeared before the Board. After describing the nature, content and background of the reports, I went on to say that I had tried, in judging them, to ask myself what should now be the central point of our inquiry — what it was that was most important for us, at that juncture, to determine; and this, it seemed to me, was whether the reports represented Service's honest opinion and proceeded solely from a desire to give the department that opinion, or whether they had resulted from the workings of some ulterior motive or purpose. I had concluded that Service, in writing these reports, had reported honestly and conscientiously the views at which he had arrived on the basis of an open-minded examination and analysis of all the facts he had before him. It was out of the question that such reports could have emanated from anyone with a closed mind or with ideological preconceptions. It was up to his superiors at the time to tell him if they found his judgments faulty, his reports unhelpful, and his performance inadequate to the function he had been asked to fulfill. They were then at liberty to transfer him to other work. But if instead of this they encouraged him to go on with them, and commended him repeatedly for the quality of his work, then, it seemed to me, he could only conclude that for him to continue this work was his wartime duty and that he would not be subject to reproach at a later date for having done it to the best of his ability.

The Board accepted, I believe, the logic of these considerations, but asked me to comment on the charges advanced by General Hurley and others that Service had opposed policies then being pursued by the United States government and that this amounted to disloyalty. I had found in his reports, I replied, nothing more than a desire to make plain to our government what, in Service's opinion, our policy ought to be. That, I said, had never been considered in governmental practice to be in itself improper. What would have been improper would have been only an attempt to influence our government in policy matters not on the basis of his own honest judgment but on behalf of some outside party or from some other motives the nature of which he was not willing to reveal. Within those limits, there was no objection to his making known to his government, in confidence, his disagreement with any of the policies it was pursuing. I would feel alarmed for the future of the Foreign Service, I said, if we were ever to permit the inference to become established that a recommendation contrary to existing policy was a sign of disloyalty.

One of the most excruciating aspects of these attacks on individual officials was the feeling on the part of those of us who were *not* attacked that it was only chance, rather than any superior wisdom or virtue on our part, that saved us from this fate. It gave one something akin to a sense of guilt to see other people pilloried for things that might just as well have happened to oneself. I tried to give public expression to this feeling when, in October 1951, the nomination of Philip C. Jessup, a distinguished authority on international law and more recently a most effective negotiator for the State Department as American delegate to the United Nations General Assembly, was rejected by a subcommittee of the Senate Foreign Relations Committee because of some alleged statement or association (I forget what) in his political past. I drafted a letter to the *New York Times* (it failed to see publication only because my colleagues in the State Department, as usual, advised against its submission), in which I referred to the senatorial action and went on to ask:

If humiliation and rejection are to be the rewards of faithful and effective service in this field, what are those of us to conclude who have also served prominently in this line of work but upon whom this badge has not yet been conferred?

We cannot deceive ourselves into believing that it was merit, rather than chance, that spared some of us the necessity of working in areas of activity that have now become controversial, of recording opinions people now find disagreeable, of aiding in the implementation of policies now under question; for we know that not to be the case. We cannot comfort ourselves with the thought that a difference in casual personal associations of the remote past might justify this distinction, for we know that there could scarcely be a criterion less relevant, in itself, to the problem of a man's present fitness for service in government. Finally, we cannot believe that even differences in cast of opinion could provide an adequate answer. In no field of endeavor is it easier than in the field of foreign affairs to be honestly wrong; in no field is it harder for contemporaries to be certain they can distinguish between wisdom and folly; in no field would it be less practicable to try to insist on infallibility as a mark of fitness for office. Differences of outlook, themselves the reflection of health and vigor in the process of policy formulation, are frequently many-sided; and even where some of us might not have agreed in specific policy matters with Mr. Jessup and others of our associates who have suffered public criticism, there is no reason to assume that we would have been any more in agreement with their critics.

All these cases I have mentioned were of course only individual instances of this sort of persecution — and ones with which I just happened to be personally involved. It was only natural, in view of the sensitivity of my place in government, that they were, almost without exception, celebrated ones. But I was never for a moment unaware that they were part of a far wider pattern of error and injustice, stretching all across the nation and involving in one way or another the outlooks, behavior and experiences of great numbers of people. Everywhere, at that time, reputations were being attacked and damaged. Blacklists were being prepared. Innocent people were being removed from, or denied access to, employment for which they were qualified. Well-meaning citizens, normally humane and decent people, were busy purging libraries and screening textbooks for evidences of Communist influence. The records of faculty members were being combed over by zealots for signs of past heresy; and stern efforts were being exerted to see to it that the lecture platforms were denied to any who might be suspected of being the insidious agents, or the unconscious dupes, of the "Communist conspiracy." Thousands of good people were lending themselves in one way or another, as were large portions of the press, to this savage enthusiasm. And as is always the case in such movements of mass hysteria, the pack was led by the professed converts from the other side, the renegades from that which was feared, those who claimed to have been intimate with the devil and to know his ways — in this case, the allegedly reformed and penitent ex-Communists.

Europeans, reasoning from their own experience, tended to see in McCarthyism a sort of neofascism and to picture those who suffered from it as people experiencing the same dangers and hardships as those who, in the 1930s, figured among Hitler's opponents or his chosen victims. I was amused to find English friends who had happened to read my Notre Dame speech (to be mentioned below) commenting on how much courage it must have taken on my part to say such things. They were quite misjudging the situation. McCarthy had no police forces. The American courts remained almost totally unaffected. Whoever could get his case before a court was generally assured of meeting there with a level of justice no smaller than at any other time in recent American history. Indeed, the entire McCarthyist phenomenon was, viewed from the standards of a later day, markedly nonviolent.

But what Senator McCarthy and others had discovered was simply that there was a caste of persons in American society — intellectuals, professors, career government officials, foundation executives, etc. — who, in the circumstances of the modern age, could be punished just as cruelly by having their reputations damaged and their possibilities of employment reduced as by being put into prison. These were people whose ability to carry on successfully in their chosen pursuits depended on a certain minimum of public confidence and respect. They could, as a rule, be attacked with impunity; and there was, in the prevailing atmosphere of the day, political "mileage" to be obtained from the attacking of them. It enabled you to pose as the vigilant, farseeing, and dedicated patriot, determined to root out from ill-gotten positions of power all those who were the representatives of an alien and hostile culture. It afforded, if you were sufficiently devoid of scruple, the illusion, and to some extent the reality, of power. It was a great opportunity for those so constituted that they tended, as the Marquis de Custine once put it, to "fancy themselves strong when they create victims."

But if "McCarthyism" was not the sort of fascism Europeans had experienced, there were several aspects of it that sufficed to cause me great anguish and to affect deeply my view of my own country.

The phenomenon reflected, in the first place, a massive failure of public understanding with relation to some of the greatest of our problems of international affairs. At the very heart of it all was the thesis, peddled not just by McCarthy and his followers but also by many reputable publicists, political figures and prominent citizens across the country, that our greatest postwar problems, including outstandingly the falling to the Communists of Eastern Europe and China, were the result not primarily of the outcome of the military operations against Germany and Japan, and not of the serious but relatively innocent and understandable human errors by which that outcome had been determined, but rather of the fact that the United States government had been insidiously infiltrated by dia-bolically clever and successful Communist agents, that Alger Hiss had sat at Franklin Roosevelt's elbow at Yalta, that a virtuous and vibrantly anti-Communist Chinese Nationalist regime had been "sold down the river" and China thereby presented to the Commu-nists "on a silver platter" by the crafty machinations of such Soviet sympathizers (and perhaps even worse) as Davies and Service. In the wide acceptance of this thesis — in the fact that it could attain sufficient currency and plausibility to support a movement of such dimensions — I was obliged to recognize the failure of the effort, in which I had personally taken a prominent part, to convey to the

American public a realistic understanding of the origins and the nature of our postwar position.

Secondly, the fact that such things as those I have just described
could take place on the scale they did showed that our society was,
as a whole, incapable of assessing soberly at its true worth, and then
coping sensibly with, the phenomenon of domestic communism —
the existence in our midst, that is, of a very small group of very
uninfluential people committed (usually for reasons of temperament) to a foreign ideology, prepared to accept the political discipline of the leaders of a foreign government, and able at one time to
infiltrate numbers of their followers into the governmental apparatus and other sensitive areas of our national life. That this was a
problem, was clear; no sensible person would have denied it. But
the first requirement of a successful attack on this problem was the
recognition of its true dimensions and importance; and it was precisely this that was lost in the preposterous exaggerations and over-
simplifications of the McCarthyist pretense.

This was dangerous not just because it was a poor way to tackle
the problem of domestic communism itself — a way that could
easily create martyrs and win sympathy for the Communists by the
very force of comparison. It was even more dangerous because it
blinded people to the real nature of our national problems and interfered with their ability to face these problems successfully. To
exaggerate the importance of one factor in your problems meant
inevitably to underrate certain of the others. It was a form, as General Marshall liked to put it, of "fighting the problem." And this
was particularly dangerous when the factor you were overrating
was an external one. For the tendency to the total externalization of
evil represented, in bodies of people just as in individuals, a failure
of the critical faculty when applied to oneself — a failure of self-
knowledge; and there was nothing more dangerous than this,
psychically and practically.

I tried to make these points in a lecture given in my native city of

Milwaukee in May 1950,* while I was still in government. "If you permit yourselves," I said,

to attribute to contemporary causes which are shallow and fleeting and of dubious substance, developments which are in reality part of the cumulative effect of the behavior of whole peoples and groups of peoples in the past, you will be abusing your clarity of insight into the realities of this world. . . . We must learn to recognize the true causes of our difficulties.

Added to the political implications of what was going on under the name of McCarthyism were the cultural and spiritual ones; and these, while more difficult to define, were no less disturbing. For the political intolerance was accompanied by a comparable one in other fields: a rousing anti-intellectualism, a mistrust of thought, a suspicion of education, a suspicion of the effect of foreign contacts and foreign influences on the individual personality, a demand for uniformity within the framework of a cheap provincial chauvinism. Here, the phenomenon of McCarthyism fed on more traditional geographic reactions: on the Western-populist suspicion of a supposedly effete and decadent East, on the aversion toward people who "put on airs" and toyed with dangerous ideas. There were plenty of McCarthy supporters, of course, in the East as well; but McCarthy himself was from my native state of Wisconsin; he seemed to find his most vociferous and undiscriminating support in the regions that lay between there and Southern California; and the forces he symbolized fed on many of the endemic neuroses that affected people in these regions.

It seemed to me that I sensed, in these tendencies, a primitivism and an underlying brutality that threatened not just freedom of

* The occasion of this speech, delivered on May 5, 1950, was a meeting of the Institute on United States Foreign Policy. Milwaukee was, as it happened, suffering that evening from the greatest windstorm it had experienced in decades; signs were falling from buildings all around us; doors were banging; and the speech (in my own opinion a good one) was received with polite ennui by an audience half comprehending and half distracted by what was going on outside.

thought in the political sense but the cultural progress of the country generally. This was not the soil in which a greater culture could grow, or the existing one even be maintained.

I tried to express these thoughts when, in the spring of 1953, amid all the miseries of separation from government plus the various security problems, I was invited, much to my pleasure and surprise, to receive an honorary degree and deliver an address on the occasion of the dedication of a new center for the fine arts at the University of Notre Dame. What led to this invitation, I shall probably never know. But in the circumstances of the time I appreciated it intensely; and I cannot recall ever having a more heartening and reassuring experience.

I chose the occasion as an opportunity to make what was certainly the strongest anti-McCarthyist speech of my entire career. Describing the forces of militant anticommunism much as I have just described them in these preceding pages, I went on to predict that my hosts, in undertaking to maintain a center for the fine arts, would someday have to contend with these forces, as many of us in political life were already doing, if they were to make their project a success. Why? Because the forces in question were narrowly exclusive; they tended to stifle cultural exchanges; they pictured America as able to get along without the stimulus of cultural contacts; they "looked with suspicion both on the sources of intellectual and artistic activity in this country and on impulses of this nature coming to us from abroad"; and thus they tended to draw about us the same sort of iron curtain that we resented when we saw it surrounding our Communist adversaries.

But beyond this, I said, a distinguishing feature of these forces was their intolerance.

They claim the right to define a certain area of our national life as beyond the bounds of righteous approval. This definition is never effected by law or by constituted authority; it is effected by vague insinuation and suggestion. And the circle tends to grow constantly narrower. One has the impression that if uncountered, these people would eventually reduce the area of political and cultural respectability to a point where it included only themselves, the excited accusers, and excluded everything and everybody not embraced in the profession of denunciation.

Drawing attention to the importance attached, by many of the witch-hunters, to the ritual of denunciation — to their demand, that is, that people demonstrate the sincerity of their anticommunism by joining in the exposure and denunciation of others, I went on to deal particularly with this phenomenon. "What sort of arrogance," I asked, "is this?"

Every one of us has his civic obligations. Every one of us has his moral obligations to the principles of loyalty and decency. I am not condoning anyone for forgetting these obligations. But to go beyond this — to say that it is not enough to be a law-abiding citizen — to say that we all have some obligation to get up and make statements of this tenor or that with respect to other individuals, or else submit to being classified as suspect in the eyes of our fellow citizens — to assert this is to establish a new species of public ritual, to arrogate to one's individual self the powers of the spiritual and temporal lawgiver, to make the definition of social conduct a matter of fear in the face of vague and irregular forces, rather than a matter of confidence in the protecting discipline of conscience and the law.

I would know of no moral or political authority for this sort of thing. I tremble when I see this attempt to make a semi-religious cult out of emotional-political currents of the moment, and particularly when I note that these currents are ones exclusively negative in nature, designed to appeal only to men's capacity for hatred and fear, never to their capacity for forgiveness and charity and understanding. I have lived more than ten years of my life in totalitarian countries. I know where this sort of thing leads. I know it to be the most shocking and cynical disservice one can do to the credulity and to the spiritual equilibrium of one's fellowmen.

These anxieties look small today. One of the more refreshing aspects of the student radicalism of another decade would be pre-

cisely its rejection of the reactions against which I was here fulmi-
nating, precisely its receptivity to aesthetic, if not intellectual,
stimuli from other times and other places. But I cite these passages
because they may illustrate how broad and deep were the anxieties
occasioned by the atmosphere of McCarthyism — how they bor-
dered on, and tended to merge with, many of the more permanent
and familiar negative aspects of American civilization.

There was one more aspect of McCarthyism which must be mentioned — one which had, perhaps, a stronger effect than any other
on my own view of my country and my time. This was the dismal
failure of the American government, both in its legislative and its
executive branches, to cope with this phenomenon: to analyze it, to
portray it to our people as it really was, and to put a stop to it.
When first confronted with its true outrageousness (as when I
learned, in South America, of McCarthy's boast about the alleged
Communists in the State Department), many of us looked to the
leaders of our government to step in and to put things to rights. In
this expectation, we were dismally disappointed.

On Capitol Hill, most of the legislators were already so deeply
involved in the ritual and semantics of anticommunism — they had
either tried to make political capital out of it themselves or were
afraid to oppose it for fear of putting themselves in a wrong light
with their constituents — that they were helpless to deal even
with those antics of the Wisconsin senator that embarrassed them
acutely and discredited the legislative body to which they belonged. In the entire composition of the Senate, only three persons
could be found — William Benton of Connecticut, the elderly
Ralph Flanders of Vermont and Margaret Chase Smith of Maine
— who, to their everlasting credit, would muster the courage to
challenge McCarthy head-on and to oppose him uncompromisingly
for what he was. Elsewhere, there was only embarrassed wriggling;
and it is significant that when his behavior finally became unendur-
able and something had to be done, the skids were put under him

only indirectly and he was discredited on irrelevant side issues. Never could sufficient support be mobilized for a condemnation of him by the Senate as a whole for those things in his conduct that really represented his greatest disservices to the public life of the country.

And the executive branch of the government was not much better. One by one, the departments and agencies capitulated ignominiously to the forces that were now at work: introducing new security procedures, boasting of their success in the ferreting out of security risks, falling over themselves in their eagerness to prove to the congressional zealots their vigilance and their sterling righteousness of thought. We have already seen, in the example of the State Department, the evasion of responsibility, the failure to stand up for hounded subordinates, the confusion of concepts, that marked the reaction of its leading officials. It is sad to observe that neither of the two Presidents under whom these disgraceful things occurred gave fully adequate leadership in opposing them: Harry Truman not, God knows, because of any lack of courage, but rather because he tended to attribute them to the normal political partisanship of his Republican opponents, ignoring their deeper roots and consequences; Dwight Eisenhower because of some curious bewilderment in his own mind about the true responsibilities and possibilities of the presidency.

In the face of this failure, the phenomenon of McCarthyism was never decisively rejected by the political establishment of the country. McCarthy was of course encouraged and permitted, with the aid of the television cameras, to defeat and discredit himself, which he handsomely proceeded to do; but the movement of which he had taken advantage was not really discredited with him. It faded, gradually and partially, with the passage of time. But it left a lasting mark on American political life. For two decades into the future, as we shall see when we turn shortly to the problem of relations with Yugoslavia, there would not be a President who would not stand in a certain terror of the anti-Communist right wing of the political spectrum and would not temper his actions with a view to placating it and averting its possible hostility.

I myself, by luck rather than by any just deserts, survived the ordeal of these tendencies better than did others. They played a role in bringing to an end my Foreign Service career, but they did not cost me my reputation or my livelihood. I was sometimes attacked, sometimes even called a "socialist" or a "Marxist"; but the attacks made little impression; and I was never obliged to suffer the sort of humiliating personal experiences that Davies, for example, had to suffer, as a result of the tremendous unfavorable publicity his case produced.

What the phenomenon of McCarthyism did do, in my case, was to implant in my consciousness a lasting doubt as to the adequacy of our political system, and the level of public understanding on which it rested, to the role of a great power in the modern age. A political system and a public opinion, it seemed to me, that could be so easily disoriented by this sort of challenge in one epoch would be no less vulnerable to similar ones in another. I could never recapture, after these experiences of the late 1940s and early 1950s, quite the same faith in the American system of government and in traditional American outlooks that I had had, despite all the discouragements of official life, before that time.

10

The 1957 Reith Lectures

THESE memoirs were conceived primarily as an account of my involvement with the great problems of what is called the cold war — an account the writing of which seemed to me to find justification in the wide publicity given to some of the views I had occasion to put forward from time to time and in the many questionings and misunderstandings these views aroused. By its very nature, such an account had to be centered on my activity in government. This was after all the main source and scene of the involvement. The account might therefore logically be expected to cease with my retirement from the governmental service in 1953. There were, however, two later episodes — the delivery of the 1957 Reith Lectures, in England, and service as ambassador in Yugoslavia in 1961–1963 — that would seem to warrant a place in this account, the latter because it involved a further period of governmental service, the former because it was intimately concerned with those same problems of governmental policy, and because it represented an extrapolation to the public scene of differences with colleagues and others that had arisen during, and out of, my previous governmental service. Of these two episodes, the Reith Lectures came first and deserve precedence in this account.

There has long been, at the University of Oxford, a special chair called the Eastman Professorship (endowed many years ago by the late George Eastman, founder of the Eastman Kodak Company) to the occupancy of which a different American professor is invited each year. In 1955, I received and accepted an invitation to fill this chair, and my tenure of it was fixed for the academic year 1957–1958.

At the beginning of 1957, however, I received another invitation, which was to deliver in London in the fall of that year, over the facilities of the Home Service of the British Broadcasting Corporation, the annual series of talks known as the Reith Lectures.

The suggestion was a seductive one. I was going to be in England anyway at that time; no special journey was involved. The series was the finest thing the British media had to offer. It consisted of six talks, to be delivered "live" over six successive Sunday evenings, at the prime listening time — just after the nine o'clock evening news. The talks had been given in the past by an impressive list of distinguished people, including Bertrand Russell, Arnold Toynbee, Oliver Franks, and Robert Oppenheimer; and I was flattered to be considered for inclusion in such company. Viewed from a distance of several months ahead, the talks seemed short — just under a half-hour each. I assumed, with the usual casual optimism, that I could always find something to say when the time came. I did not anticipate any great pressure of publicity. And I had successfully met other lecture challenges, which also involved strains. Why, I thought, should I quail at this one? So I accepted.

The first inkling of the gravity of what I had let myself in for came to me when, in the spring, nearly a half a year before the scheduled beginning of the talks, the BBC sent all the way to Princeton from London one of its most talented editors, Miss Anna Kallin, to discuss them with me and to give me such advice as I might need and be willing to accept. The association was from the start a pleasant and fruitful one. Miss Kallin had been born and raised in the old Russian Empire. We had much in common, including a number of mutual friends. Her editorial judgment and sensitivity were of the highest order; and I could not have been better advised. The ordeal of the lectures, I often thought, would have been worthwhile if it were only for the privilege of this friendship. But her arrival brought home to me the importance attached to the talks in England, and I began to understand what I had let myself in for.

The greatest problem, from the start, was that of subject matter. I toyed for a time in that spring, as I recall it, with the idea of talking about Anglo-American relations, but soon realized that I did not have enough to say on this topic to fill six lectures, and that this was not what people wanted to hear from me, anyway. On arrival in Oxford, in late summer, the nearest thing I had to an idea for a subject was a vague and resigned feeling that I probably ought to retread, in some way, the familiar paths of Russia and the cold war. When the time came for delivery of the first of the lectures I had produced, as I recall it, drafts of only one or two of them. The rest remained to be written as we went along.

Given the circumstances in which I had now involved myself, the task of writing presented difficulties I had never imagined. The talks began in late October. I was by this time well installed in Oxford. The academic term had begun. I had undertaken to lecture twice a week at the University on the history of Soviet foreign policy. These academic lectures represented a serious commitment. They were my principal reason for being in England. They were in fact the primary commitment. Delivered with all traditional formality in the imposing premises of the "Schools"— the great University lecture halls on the High Street — in an atmosphere of spacious Victorian decorum, they turned out to draw academic audiences much larger and more distinguished than I had been led to expect.* This increased the responsibility, and the demands they placed for care and time of preparation. These lectures, too, of course, I

---

* These lectures were later embodied in the volume entitled *Russia and the West under Lenin and Stalin,* published in 1961 by the Atlantic Monthly Press–Little, Brown and Company.

had not found time to prepare in advance. With one or two exceptions they had to be written, about ten thousand words of finished copy a week, as I went along. Not only did they have to be written, but the research for them had to be done on the spot from the resources of the Oxford libraries, the holdings of which were rich enough, but scattered, not centrally indexed, and, compared to our American libraries, inconvenient to use. I was caught, then, between the formidable amount of work engendered by the Oxford lectures and the fantastic pressures which the weekly radio talks, as will be seen shortly, turned out to produce.

Things were complicated by the fact that Balliol, the college to which the Eastman Professor was automatically assigned, was able to supply that professor neither with an office nor with secretarial help. I was obliged, in these circumstances, to try to make an office out of the dining room of the flat in Merton Street where we were installed. Here English secretaries, hired by myself, banged cheerfully and loyally away on their typewriters; and I, between endless excursions down the hall to answer the telephone, attempted simultaneously to keep the coal grate going and to produce finished lecture copy, for both Oxford and London, in the amount of some thirteen thousand words a week (and since each lecture went through at least three drafts, this was actually closer to forty thousand), while my poor wife, servantless in accordance with the customs of the modern age, tried to mind the children and the household and serve meals in these same turbulent premises. When I think back on the strains this involved, at a time, incidentally, when the entire family was just recovering from the ravages of the Asian flu which had swept through Oxford earlier that fall and taken its toll of all of us, my wonder is not that the radio lectures were not in all respects what they might have been, but that any of them came to be delivered at all.

Actually, not just the preparation but the entire mechanics of rehearsal and delivery of these weekly talks proved to be more of a strain and exertion than I had supposed. Together with the effort of preparation, and the need for some rest between times, they would in fact themselves have been a full-time job, and should never have been mingled with other responsibilities and pursuits. Every Saturday, I would have to go up to London to edit and rehearse the one to be delivered the following day. The text would be tried out for time; we would listen to the recording; and then, with Anna's skillful and tactful help, the work of editing — sometimes just changes in phraseology, sometimes replacement of longer portions or the entire talk — would begin. She taught me in this way a number of valuable lessons, including notably the omission of introductory passages and the avoidance of unusual words (so that the listener would never have to say: "How's that again?") which added materially, I am sure, to the effectiveness of radio delivery. On Sunday evening, then, I would drive into London once more and appear at the BBC studios, on Great Portland Street, for the real event. Frantically scratching corrections and insertions on my text to the very last moment, I would be ushered, just before nine o'clock, into a large, glass-lined room, devoid of furniture other than two chairs, one large table between them with a microphone, a large wall clock, and a radio receiver. Through double glass windows at the end of the room one could observe the pantomime activities of the technicians, as they supervised the transmission and worked at their turntables.

Just before nine o'clock the announcer would appear, and then the nine o'clock news would begin to come in on the receiver. The announcer, seldom the same one two times running, would be as impersonal and anonymous in the flesh as were, proverbially, the voices of BBC announcers as heard over the air. Together, in silence, the two of us would sit through the news program, both of us keeping a watchful eye on the clock, I still scratching feverishly at my prepared text in the unquenchable conviction that there must be something I could do to it at this last moment that would rescue it from woeful failure and transform it into relative success.

As the hand of the clock approached the 9:15 deadline, its movement took on a dread inexorability, as though the approaching moment was to be that of my own execution. Relentlessly and with what seemed to be a perverse acceleration, the final seconds would tick away. As the last of them passed, there would be a stern wave of the hand from the technician on the other side of the glass, to indicate that we were on the air; and the announcer would swing into his introduction, concluding with the final terrifying and merciless: "Mr. Kennan," after which he would tiptoe silently out of the room. I knew, then, that for twenty-eight and a half minutes into the future I would be left alone — alone as I had never been before — alone as I had never hoped to be — alone to acquit or disgrace myself, as my capacities might determine — but alone beyond the power of any other human being to help me. Anna Kallin had now done all that anyone could do for me. For these twenty-eight and a half minutes, I would have to keep on talking — saying something, somehow; and even an inadvertent sneeze or a blowing of the nose, not to mention a moment of panic or forgetfulness or a confusion in the order of my pages, could produce catastrophe.

Had these talks received no more than what might be called normal attention and publicity — had they been accepted by the public as a courtesy extended to a prominent visiting scholar in England, listened to by a reasonable number of professionally interested people and polite acquaintances, and acknowledged with an occasional and respectful mention in the press — all of this, while strenuous and difficult in view of the overburdening of time and energy, would have been bearable. But what actually occurred was something none of us had anticipated, or even dreamed of, and something which, even to this day, I find it hard to describe without creating misunderstanding, lest I sound as though I were boasting, whereas actually I look back on the entire experience with chagrin and remorse.

The first strong hint I had of the effect the talks were producing came during the rehearsal, on a Saturday morning, of one of the early ones. I happened to glance through the glass and saw one of the technicians, a wiry, little Cockney woman who I later learned was the wife of a London bobby, pounding the table vehemently with her fist in enthusiasm and approval.

This was only a foretaste of what was impending. I am obliged to conclude, almost with a sense of guilt, that the talks, broadcast not only live in England but later from recordings over all of Canada and over one of the major American networks as well and published in a large number of languages, were certainly one of the most (if not *the* most) widely listened to series of political talks ever delivered anywhere. To make this bold recognition and to observe that the talks provoked an unprecedented volume of discussion in England and elsewhere is still not to recapture the entire extraordinariness of what took place. Perhaps it will be best if I simply take, at random, some of the observations of others, as they flow from the enormous pile of press clippings that lies on my desk.

The *Daily Telegraph*, London: "For the past six weeks the British public have been offered each Sunday night the magisterial advice and exhortation of Mr. George Kennan. . . . Like the Hound of Heaven, he has chased us, with 'unperturbed pace, deliberate speed, majestic instancy . . . down the labyrinthine ways of his own mind' in the search of a true assessment and solution of the free world's predicament. It has been one of the most widely followed intellectual hunts in broadcasting history."

Life magazine: "The unofficial words of a retired U.S. diplomat have become a major political issue throughout the Western world. . . . The Reith Lectures are always an event in Britain, but Kennan's were a sensation in most of Western Europe as well. Kennan's views will continue to reverberate in political argument for weeks to come."

Ernst Friedlaender, on the North German Radio: "One may well say: scarcely ever before has any political lecture series anywhere in the world aroused such interest. . . . Every politically interested person is today talking of Kennan. Even the man in the street, so often charged with being politically uninterested, is pricking up his ears. . . . And this without any propaganda and certainly without any official support."

Max Ascoli, in the *Reporter*: "The thoughts of a lonely man who is not very much at home in his own land made top news in every country irrespective of its political order; his thoughts were translated and commented on in every language men use to communicate to each other their anguish about the survival of this earth."

Max Freedman, in the *Washington Post and Times Herald*: "at no time in the history of the British Broadcasting Corporation, have any lectures received the world attention which has honored the six lectures . . . delivered in London recently by George F. Kennan. They have been studied in governments and debated in many lands."

Joseph Alsop, in the *Chicago Sun-Times*: "What Kennan had to say about the Soviet Union and its relations with the West attracted vastly more interest and stimulated vastly more controversy in Britain, France and Western Germany than anything either President Eisenhower or Secretary of State John Foster Dulles has said in recent memory. . . . Altogether, Kennan has received enough attention to delight most castoff policymakers. But Kennan, quite characteristically, has only been made miserable by it all."

Forum (Western Germany): "Two absent people: N. A. Bulganin and George F. Kennan, have influenced the Paris NATO Conference more than all the assembled statesmen and politicians."

The *New Republic:* "No recent event — probably not even the launching of the two Soviet sputniks or the failure of the American space-rocket — has had greater impact on thinking Germans than the statements made by . . . George Kennan."

To these various assessments of the impact of the lectures one ought perhaps to add the observation that the truly enormous reaction they produced was, curiously enough, not at all one of agreement. On the contrary, scarcely anyone who responded in print or over the air waves professed himself in accord with all that was said, and most critics, including a number of very important ones, objected most violently to many parts of it. Yet — and this embarrassed me more than anything else — the criticisms, almost without exception, were cast in terms respectful of myself as a person and designed to spare, if possible, my own feelings. However remarkable may have been this reaction in other respects, never, surely, has anyone been so widely and generously forgiven as a person for what were, in the eyes of his critics, such grievous errors as a thinker.

How is one to explain such a reaction?

In attempting to answer that question, I must leave aside the whole question of effectiveness of delivery and the impact of personality in the radio voice. Others could speak to that more suitably than I can. Taking into consideration only the content of the lectures as delivered and later published, I believe that the explanation for the reaction has to be sought in the relation of subject matter to the happenings and atmosphere of the day.

Of the six lectures, four — the first two and the last two — were unexceptional, in the sense that they were, generally speaking, favorably received but did not arouse great controversy.

In the first of the talks, I dealt with the recent evidences of substantial Russian economic progress and sought to dispose of some of the more exaggerated and alarmist of the Western reactions to this phenomenon. In the second, I talked about the state of mind of the Soviet leaders, as the factor that lay at the heart of our difficulties with them; and inveighed against the tendency in the West to believe that this situation could be suddenly and usefully altered — either by meetings at the summit or by war.

The fifth lecture was devoted to the question of the mutual relations of Russia and the West to the Third World. It was an attempt to put into perspective the phenomenon of Russian interest and activity in the underdeveloped countries. I warned against regarding this as something abnormal and menacing, and urged that when people threatened that if they didn't get from us the aid they wanted they would "go Communist," our answer should be: "Then go."

The last of the talks, dealing with the NATO alliance, was an appeal not to let the pursuit of a posture of strength within the framework of that alliance come to constitute a barrier to any and every sort of negotiation with the Russians. This last lecture, too, I may say, probably grated to some extent on many ears; but it aroused relatively little controversy.

The explosive substance was in the third and fourth talks. The third had to do with the German problem and the question of trying to remove the division of both Germany and Europe. The fourth was addressed to the nuclear arms race and the military problems of Europe.

Before recalling the substance of those talks one should note, I think, the background of events against which they were delivered.

It was now two years since Western Germany, to my own intense unhappiness, had been taken into the NATO alliance. Since that time, the development of Western Germany as a military power had been energetically pressed. Something between a quarter and a third of the accepted program of German rearmament, designed to produce in the end twelve ground force divisions in addition to certain air and naval units, had by this time been carried to completion. The question now loomed before the NATO command and (in view of its great importance) before the Western governments themselves, as to whether the armed forces of the Continental NATO members, including Germany, should be based on nuclear weapons — on the so-called "tactical" nuclear weapons, that is — or whether the possession and use of such weapons, and the training necessary to their employment, should be restricted, as it had been up to that point, to the forces of the two members of the alliance that already possessed nuclear armaments: the United States and Britain. During the summer and autumn of 1957 this question was actively under discussion among the NATO planners, with the trend of opinion running strongly in favor of the introduction of nuclear weapons into the Continental armaments. In December, there was to be held in Paris a summit meeting of the NATO powers, scheduled — as it happened — to begin on the day following the last of the Reith Lectures, at which a final decision would be taken on precisely this question. If anything useful was to be said about it, it would, obviously, have to be said before that date.

It seemed evident to me, and I assumed it to be evident to everyone else, that if it should be decided that the armed forces of the Continental NATO members should be based on, and geared to, the use of nuclear weapons, then any eventual negotiations with the Russians over the problems of both nuclear disarmament and European security would become much more complicated, and the chances for their success greatly reduced. In the absence of such a step, the problems of nuclear disarmament could still conceivably be discussed among three powers — the US, UK, and the Soviet Union, alone. Once the step in question had been taken, the interests of several Continental NATO members would also be intimately involved, and they, too, would have to appear at the negotiating table. But everyone knew that in multilateral international negotiations the difficulty of reaching agreement increased with the square of the number of parties present at the table.

Beyond this, a decision to introduce nuclear weapons into the arsenals of the Continental NATO members would mean that there could now be no solution of the political problems of Germany and Central and Eastern Europe that did not presuppose a prior or simultaneous agreement in the whole great field of nuclear disarmament. The two problems would become inextricably linked, to the detriment of the possibility for the solution of either of them.

This prospect was, as I saw it at the time, particularly disheartening because there was every evidence that if something was not done at a very early date to halt the competition in the development of nuclear weapons and their carriers, this competition would soon move into a much more expensive and dangerous phase. On August 26, 1957, the Russians had announced the successful testing of their first intercontinental ballistic missile. On October 4, just before the Reith Lectures began, they had startled the world by launching the first earth satellite — the so-called Sputnik. This had captured people's imaginations everywhere. It presaged the early perfection by the Russians of the ICBM. It suggested a Russian superiority over the West in the development of such missiles. It caused Western alarmists, such as my friend Joe Alsop, to demand the immediate subordination of all other national interests to the launching of immensely expensive crash programs to outdo the Russians in this competition. It gave effective arguments to the various enthusiasts for nuclear armament in the American military-industrial complex. That the dangerousness and expensiveness of this competition should be raised to a new and higher order just at the time when the prospects for negotiation in this field were being worsened by the introduction of nuclear weapons into the armed forces of the Continental NATO powers was a development that brought alarm and dismay to many people besides myself.

Finally, there seemed also, at that point, to be a special urgency in the search for a solution of the German problem. The division of Europe, it was clear, could not be removed without the removal of the division of Germany. But the abortive Hungarian rebellion of the previous year had brought home to many people the bitterness of the agony which a continuation of this division, meaning as it did the continuation of Soviet domination, spelled for the Eastern European peoples, and the dangers it could present for the stability of the Continent.

At the same time, a number of statements had recently been made on the Communist side which hinted at the readiness to arrive at some sort of agreement on military disengagement if only one would desist from developing Western Germany into a nuclear power. Khrushchev, speaking before the East German parliament on August 8, 1957, had said: "The Soviet Union has repeatedly called [for] . . . an agreed gradual withdrawal of troops from Germany. Furthermore, the Soviet Union has repeatedly declared its readiness to withdraw all its troops not only from the German Democratic Republic, but also from Poland, Hungary and Rumania, if the U.S.A. and other NATO countries would withdraw their troops from Western Germany, France, Britain, etc." * The Polish Foreign Minister, Adam Rapacki, had proposed, on October 2, at the United Nations, the creation of an atom-free zone, to comprise both Germanys as well as Poland. None of these proposals or suggestions was acceptable as it stood; but all suggested that there was a strong interest on the Soviet side in preventing the nuclear armament of Western Germany — an interest strong enough to suggest a willingness to pay a certain price for the achievement of this objective. And the attractiveness of the idea of a military and political neutralization of further portions of Europe had been enhanced by the successful examples of Yugoslavia, now effectively neutralized by virtue of its own resolute action, and Austria, which had been politically neutralized and from which Soviet and Western forces had been finally withdrawn, by agreement among the great powers, in the course of the preceding two years.

If, in short, the prospects for a simple continuation of present

---

* Keesing's *Contemporary Archives*, 1957, September 10–28.

policies, marked by the further pursuit of the nuclear weapons race and the maintenance for an indefinite time into the future of the division of Europe and Germany, never looked blacker than they did in that autumn of 1957, there were also several reasons for regarding the possibility of some sort of disengagement of the Soviet Union and the United States from their position in the heart of the European continent as not entirely beyond the limits of possibility.

Now turn to the content of those two crucial Reith Lectures. Pointing to the instability (from the standpoint of developments within Eastern Europe) of a continued division of the Continent, and the dependence of this arrangement on the similar division of Germany, I urged a review of the Western position with relation to the German problem, and particularly of our insistence that a reunified Germany should be free to become a member of NATO. I pointed to the irreality of that position, which in effect demanded a unilateral withdrawal of the Soviet Union from its positions in Central Europe without any compensation at all.* I then pointed to the disadvantages of trying to base Europe's security indefinitely on the presence of American forces in the Western portion of a divided Germany. This concept, I said,

expects too much, and for too long a time, of the United States, which is not a European power. It does less than justice to the strength and the abilities of the Europeans themselves. It leaves unsolved the extremely precarious and unsound arrangements which now govern the status of Berlin — the least disturbance of which could easily produce a new world crisis. It takes no account of the present dangerous situation in

---

* Lecturing, as I was then doing at Oxford, on the policies of the Western powers in World War I, I could not help reflecting on the similarity of this present Western position in the German problem to the "unconditional surrender" policy pursued by the Western side in two world wars; and I sometimes felt, as I delivered these talks on the eve of the fateful Paris NATO conference — the point of no return — as I thought Lord Lansdowne must have felt when, in 1917, he published his famous (and equally unsuccessful) plea against the continuation of the World War, in the name of unconditional surrender, for another terrible year. This experience, and this parallel, confirmed my doubts that a coalition of democratic powers is ever capable of negotiation with a hostile power on any other basis than unconditional surrender.

the satellite area. It renders permanent what was meant to be temporary. It assigns half of Europe, by implication, to the Russians.

I recognized that Moscow had recently shown no enthusiasm for German unification, and conceded that perhaps the Soviet leaders did not want it on any terms. But I pointed out that their position had never been realistically tested by negotiation. How much of their lack of enthusiasm was resignation in the face of our own un-realistic position, we could not know. "Until we stop pushing the Kremlin against a closed door," I said, "we shall never learn whether it would be prepared to go through an open one." There was a question, furthermore, whether, if we were to offer an Amer-ican withdrawal from Germany on terms more acceptable to Rus-sian interests, the Russians could afford to reject the offer. The Eastern European satellite leaders would, I pointed out, be effec-tively our allies in the effort to arrive at such a solution.

I urged, therefore, that we drop our insistence that an eventual all-German government should be free to join NATO, and declare ourselves instead the partisans of a neutralized and largely disarmed unified Germany. And I argued against the assumption that any mutual withdrawal of Western and Soviet forces from that country would necessarily operate to our disadvantage. I could not spell out, I said, the details of any plan of disengagement; this had to be left to the military planners. I could only say that on principle it seemed to me "far more desirable to get the Soviet forces out of Central and Eastern Europe than to cultivate a new German army for the purpose of opposing them while they remain there."

My plea, I said in conclusion,

is not that we delude ourselves that we can have a German settlement tomorrow; and it is not that we make frivolous and one-sided conces-sions to obtain one. My plea is only that we remember that we have a problem here, which must sooner or later be solved, and better sooner than later; and that we do our best to see that the positions we adopt with relation to it are at all times as hopeful and constructive as they can be made.

In the second of the two lectures, dealing with the military problems, I emphasized both the dangers and the illusory nature of the race in the cultivation of nuclear weapons. I accepted our retention of such weapons as a deterrent, but as that only. I opposed the basing of our defense posture upon them (which was exactly what was then being done) and denied the reality of much of the thinking on which our cultivation of them was based. I wholly distrusted, I said, the calculations that were involved. I did not think anyone really knew what would be the effects of the actual use of such weapons. And I shuddered at the likely consequences of a continuation of the competition in their cultivation. To what sort of life, I asked, did this competition condemn us?

Are we to flee like haunted creatures from one defensive device to another, each more costly and humiliating than the one before, cowering underground one day, breaking up our cities the next, attempting to surround ourselves with elaborate electronic shields on the third, concerned only to prolong the length of our lives while sacrificing all the values for which it might be worth while to live at all? If I thought this was the best the future held for us, I should be tempted to join those who say, "Let us divest ourselves of this weapon altogether; let us stake our safety on God's grace and our own good consciences and on that measure of common sense and humanity which even our adversaries possess; but then let us at least walk like men, with our heads up, so long as we are permitted to walk at all."

We had to recognize, I said, that the weapon of mass destruction was, in any form, sterile and useless. It might serve for a time as an answer to itself, as a shield against utter cataclysm. But it could not serve the purposes of a constructive and hopeful foreign policy.

The true end of political action is, after all, to affect the deeper convictions of men; this the atomic bomb cannot do. The suicidal nature of this weapon renders it unsuitable both as a sanction of diplomacy and as the basis of an alliance. Such a weapon is simply not one with which one can usefully support political desiderata; nor is it one with which one readily springs to the defense of one's friends. . . . A defense posture built around a weapon suicidal in its implications can serve in the long run only to paralyze national policy, to undermine alliances, and to drive everyone deeper and deeper into the hopeless exertions of the weapons race.

I then warned particularly against the development of a reliance on the so-called "tactical" nuclear weapon. Even this, I pointed out, was "destructive to a degree that sickens the imagination." What would be the use of a war fought in Europe with weapons of this nature? It was time we stopped judging warfare just in terms of formal victory or defeat. Modern war, I said,

is not just an instrument of policy. It is an experience in itself. It does things to him who practices it, irrespective of whether he wins or loses. Can we really suppose that poor old Europe, so deeply and insidiously weakened by the ulterior effects of the two previous wars of this century, could stand another and even more horrible ordeal of this nature? Let us by all means think for once not just in the mathematics of destruction — not just in these grisly equations of probable military casualties — let us rather think of people as they are: of the limits of their strength, their hope, their capacity for suffering, their capacity for believing in the future. And let us ask ourselves in all seriousness how much worth saving is going to be saved if war now rages for the third time in half a century over the face of Europe.

The reader will note that I did not, in these lectures, ask for a unilateral abandonment of the nuclear weapon as a deterrent. I only pleaded that we not base our defense posture upon it, not place it at the disposal of others, and not encourage others to come to rely on it for their own defense or that of NATO as a whole. Implicit, if not explicit, in these observations, was my own long-standing opposition to the principle of first use — to the assumption, that is,

that we would resort to the use of these weapons in any major encounter, whether or not they were first used against us. I felt that to
make our entire defense posture dependent, in this way, on nuclear
weaponry was not only to leave ourselves no options, in case of
serious jeopardy to our national security, between the extremes of
global catastrophe or utter helplessness, but also to place the stamp
of obvious hypocrisy on any part we might take in the discussion of
the possibilities for abolishing or controlling such weapons.

On the condition that the principle of first use should be abandoned and the spread of nuclear weapons into other hands avoided,
then I was reluctantly prepared to accept, as I indicated in the 1957
lectures, the retention of these weapons by ourselves as a deterrent
until such time as we could come to an agreement with the other
two nuclear powers on the abolition of these and all other weapons
of mass destruction. But these lectures were given, as we have seen,
on the eve of the decision of the NATO powers to build such
weapons into the defenses of the Continental countries; this was
bound to mean their general proliferation. And I heard no retrac-
tion from Secretary of State Dulles or from President Eisenhower
of the Dulles doctrine of "massive retaliation," which was only another expression for the principle of first use. A year or two later,
the Kennedy administration would inaugurate policies designed to
reduce our dependence on nuclear weapons and to give us other
and less apocalyptic options; but this time had not yet come. That
meant that the conditions in which I could accept the retention of
these weapons by ourselves as a deterrent were swept away on the
very morrow of the day the Reith Lectures were completed, and
that a situation was then created to which what was said in those
lectures on the subject of nuclear weaponry was no longer relevant.
I had warned, in the lectures, of the way in which, in such circumstances, my view would have to change, saying that if this (indefinite competition in the cultivation of these weapons and their general proliferation) was the best the future held for us, I would be

tempted to say: "Let us divest ourselves of this weapon altogether."

Well — in another lecture, delivered a year after these others, over the same facilities of the BBC, I spoke about these matters with much greater frankness. Taking issue emphatically with the view that NATO could not defend itself, if it wanted to, in a world where only conventional weapons existed, I turned to the question of the environmental effects of the development and possible use of nuclear weaponry. These weapons threatened, I said, the very intactness of the natural environment in which, and in which alone, civilization would have a future. To risk this seemed to me to be "simply wrong,"

. . . wrong in the good old-fashioned meaning of the term. It involves an egocentricity on our part that has no foundation either in religious faith or in political philosophy. It accords poorly with the view we like to take of ourselves as people whose lives are founded on a system of spiritual and ethical values. We of this generation did not create the civilization of which we are a part and, only too obviously, it is not we who are destined to complete it. We are not the owners of the planet we inhabit; we are only its custodians. There are limitations on the extent to which we should be permitted to devastate or pollute it. Our own safety and convenience is not the ultimate of what is at stake in the judgement of these problems. People did not struggle and sacrifice and endure over the course of several thousand years to produce this civilization merely in order to make it possible for us, the contemporaries of 1959, to make an end to it or to place it in jeopardy at our pleasure for the sake of our personal safety. Our deepest obligation . . . [relates] not to ourselves alone but to the past and to the future.

I add these passages from a later lecture because they give a more complete picture of my own view on nuclear weaponry than was given in the few passages which it was possible to devote to this subject within the restricted framework of the 1957 lectures.

It was against this background that I brought forward, in that fourth Reith Lecture, my arguments against basing the armaments of the Continental countries on nuclear weapons. But this, of course, raised the question of the alternative. If these countries were not to have nuclear weapons, and if American forces were to be withdrawn, what sort of defenses should they — and a unified Germany in particular — then have? I could not hold a brief for conventional forces of the old pattern. "They were designed," I said, "to meet only the least likely of the possible dangers: that of an outright Soviet attack, and then to meet it in the most unpromising manner, which is by attempting to hold it along some specific territorial line." This was futile. We had to get over the idea that the principal danger was a Russian "yearning to attack and occupy Western Europe." The Soviet threat was a combined military and political one, with the accent on the political. What, then, was the answer?

It was here that I made, unquestionably, the greatest mistake of the entire lecture series. I did so by advancing, in the closing minutes of a lecture severely limited in time, an idea which, if it had anything in it at all (and I am inclined to think, even today, that it did), was of so unusual and exploratory a nature, so far removed from, if not in advance of, the thinking of nine hundred and ninety-nine out of a thousand of the people who might be listening to me, and so easily subject to misinterpretation and even ridicule, that it could never have been adequately explained and presented in the five minutes of broadcasting time that then remained. The problem of defense of the Continental nations, I said, was primarily one of the health and discipline of their societies. What they would need, in the event of a military disengagement that would bring about the removal of American forces from their territories, would be a strategic doctrine addressed to this reality.

Under such a doctrine, armed forces would indeed be needed; but I would suggest that they . . . might better be paramilitary ones, of a territorial-militia type, somewhat on the Swiss example, rather than regular military units on the World War II pattern. Their function should be primarily internal rather than external. It is on the front of police realities, not on regular military battlefields, that the threat of Russian communism must primarily be met. The training of such forces ought to be such as to prepare them not only to offer whatever overt resistance might be possible to a foreign invader but also to constitute the core of a civil resistance movement on any territory . . . overrun by the enemy. . . . For this reason they need not, and should not, be burdened with heavy equipment or elaborate supply requirements.

I tried to surround this suggestion with caveats. It was, I said, only suggested as a general rule; there would be exceptions. Some countries would require other forms of defense as well.

But the fat was now in the fire. Having said a number of things that a great many people understood very well indeed but which ran strongly counter to the policies of their governments, I had now compounded confusion by saying something that no one (except perhaps a few people in Asia) understood at all.

My punishment was not long in coming. I had, after all, offended all the leading NATO statesmen now in power, and even some who were not.

Mr. John Foster Dulles had only recently stressed, in his public statements, the great importance of the rearmament of Western Germany; and Mr. Acheson regarded himself, with pride, as the very author of this effort. I had proposed to sacrifice it. Both Republicans and Democrats were thereby aroused against me.

Chancellor Adenauer had specifically stated, at the NATO Council meeting in Bonn in May of 1957, that unification could not be obtained by the neutralization of Germany; that this would not reduce tensions; that a neutral zone would serve no purpose. I, ignoring his great authority, had spoken in favor of neutralization.

The British Foreign Secretary, Mr. Selwyn Lloyd, had said (at the same NATO Council meeting): "We are right to base our whole defense on the nuclear deterrent." I had said exactly the opposite.

What, in those circumstances, could one expect?

Mr. Acheson at once put out an indignant statement, saying that I had "never grasped the realities of power relationships" but instead took a "rather mystical attitude toward them," and ridiculing me for my remarks about the problems of Continental defense. The German Foreign Minister, Herr Brentano, was quoted as saying, in some confidential inner-German meeting, "Whoever says such things [as I had said] is no friend of the German people." Mr. Dulles, pressed by newsmen to say whether he and his colleagues had heard my views, replied sourly that it would have been very difficult for them not to hear them. In New York, eleven "experts on Germany," including such of my good friends as James Conant, Carl Friedrich, Hans Kohn, Louis Lochner, Samuel Reber and Arnold Wolfers, put out a sharp collective statement in which they said that much as they respected my past services, they deeply regretted that I had taken these positions.

In the journalistic world, the most important attacks came, on the American side, from *Life* magazine (whose editorial attack was also the most superficial and least impressive), and on the European side, to my great surprise, from the esteemed *Neue Zürcher Zeitung,* an organ which I had long admired and considered (I still do) to be one of the two or three greatest newspapers in the world. I had not realized how close this paper was to the Adenauer regime.*

Day after day, in the first weeks of 1958, this paper lambasted me, either editorially or by gibes in its news columns or by reprinting of other attacks. There was a special irony about this, for in the course of a Christmas visit to the Continent, shortly after completion of the lectures, I turned out to be so exhausted and run-down from the

---

* One of the ironies attending the reception of these lectures was the fact that the most bitter reproaches I had to endure for advocating a neutralization of Germany came from the two ostensibly neutral countries of Sweden and Switzerland.

strains of the autumn that I ended up in the great Kantonsspital in
Zurich with a combination of duodenal ulcers and acute sinus infection. But there, lying in bed in the clinic, I was served daily with
copies of this paper, and I was thus treated, day after day, to the
longest and most bitter series of criticisms of myself and my views
that I could have found anywhere in the world. My critics in the
offices of the great Zurich paper had, of course, no idea that I was
present in their city. I responded to these attacks finally, in my desperation, with a long letter to the editors which they published, and
to which they replied (in late February 1958) with two successive
front-page articles.

In addition to these criticisms from prominent sources there
were, of course, hundreds of critical observations made in other articles and reviews, particularly after the appearance of the lectures
in book form.

Many of these criticisms, including some of those that came from
very prominent sources, rested on misunderstandings or distortions
of what I had said. I was charged with having advanced a "plan"
for disengagement. I had advanced no such plan; on the contrary, I
had said that only governmental planners were competent to draw
one up. Time after time, my views were discussed as though I had
proposed a unilateral American withdrawal from the Continent. I
had never spoken in any terms other than those of a mutual action.
I was charged with advocating the dismantling of NATO. I had
never suggested such a thing. I was charged with urging that we
"trust" the Russians. For years, I had argued against the very use of
the word "trust" in international relations. Etc., etc.

I was widely ridiculed for my suggestions about the paramilitary
militia forces. Scarcely one of the critics failed to ring this bell.
Even my friend Carlo Schmidt, professor of political science at
Frankfurt and Vice President of the German Bundestag, said, in
defending me on the floor of the Bundestag: "Why, after all,
should so prominent (*bedeutender*) a man [as Kennan] not have

for once a scurrilous thought?" To which Kurt Kiesinger, the future German Chancellor, objected: "But on so decisive a point?" "No," answered Schmidt, "this is no decisive point. Perhaps he was thinking of old times at West Point. Perhaps his American ancestry reaches back into the days that we know from the Leatherstocking tales. I don't know. Atavistic factors also sometimes play a part."

Altogether, what between the distortions, the misunderstandings and the ridicule, I felt very much put upon.

On the other hand, almost all the criticisms (even that which came from the eleven German experts) were, as noted above, friendly and respectful, and some of them were of very high quality indeed — so much so that one might almost say that whatever the deficiencies of my Reith Lectures, they were worth delivering if only for the excellence of a portion of the response that they evoked.

The most impressive of the reactions came from precisely those two men — one an American, the other a European — to whom one might have looked for this sort of response: Walter Lippmann and Raymond Aron.

Aron's criticism was first advanced at a round-table discussion held in Paris, under the auspices of the Congress of Cultural Freedom, in January 1958, and addressed to the content of my Reith Lectures. I was to have attended this meeting, but to my own great unhappiness was unable to do so, for reasons of health. The discussion group included, in addition to Aron, such formidable friends and figures as Denis Healey, the future British Minister of Defence; Joseph Alsop; Sidney Hook; Richard Lowenthal (for my money, the greatest authority on international communism then and since); Carlo Schmidt; Denis de Rougemont, the impassioned prophet of European unification; and several others of like prominence. Aron, who had returned only the previous day from a visit to Russia, spoke informally. Sweeping away, like Lippmann, the less vital errors and questionable passages of the lectures and moving right to the main point, which was the subject of disengagement, he struck at once to the very heart of my thesis: which was my opinion that the existing division of Europe was unsound, intolerable, and had to be changed. He did not himself say that this thesis was necessarily wrong, but he said that it was unrealistic, because this was a situation that nobody in authority anywhere wanted to change. In both Washington and Moscow "the present partition of Europe has been held to be less dangerous than any other solution. Why? Because if we try to change it, we have to restore the fluidity to the European situation."

This was, he explained, a paradox.

The present situation of Europe is abnormal, or absurd. But it is a clearcut one and everybody knows where the demarcation line is and nobody is very much afraid of what could happen. If something happens on the other side of the Iron Curtain — and we have the experience of a year ago — nothing happens on this side. So a clear partition of Europe is considered, rightly or wrongly, to be less dangerous than any other arrangement.

An *equivocal* situation, Aron went on to say, was more dangerous than an abnormal one. We had to take care not to exchange a small danger for a greater one. It was a matter of evaluating risks; his evaluation was not the same as mine; he was "for once, by accident and with deep regret, on the side of the statesmen."

This, the fact that no one in authority in Europe or America really wanted to see the division of Europe removed — that the pious lip service to the cause of German unification on the part of all the Western statesmen from Adenauer down was the sheerest hypocrisy — was the point that Lippmann was to make, with even more powerful effect, in his articles of a year hence. And it was, of course, vital to the entire argumentation of my lectures. I have often thought that we might all have been spared a lot of trouble if someone in authority had come to me before these lectures were given and had said: "Look here, George, the decision to leave Europe divided — and divided for an indefinite time to come — has already been taken, even if it hasn't been announced; the talk about German unification is all eyewash; and there isn't the faintest thing to be gained by your attempting to change this situation." But then, I am afraid, there couldn't have been any lectures at all by me on that subject.

Aron had a second point: which was that there would be little value in a mutual disengagement, because the Russians, if faced with internal developments disagreeable to their political purposes in any of the satellite countries from which their troops might have been removed, would simply send their troops back into that country again, on the pattern of the recent Hungarian intervention, and reassert their authority. I was not much impressed with this point, as an argument against my lectures, because I personally would not have considered acceptable any agreement on disengagement which did not provide assurances with relation to just this sort of development and sanctions against it. But I must now, in retrospect, give Aron credit for a most remarkable prophetic insight, because in making this point he offered, ten years in advance of the event, a classic formulation of the so-called Brezhnev doctrine, the public pronouncement of which would be evoked from Mr. Brezhnev by the stresses of the Czechoslovak crisis of 1968. The Russians, Aron said, "have formulated a new doctrine of what I call *la Sainte Alliance.* It is the right of 'disinterested help' to any Communist government threatened by 'counterrevolution.' "

Considering our previous public differences, I was much moved by the generous and understanding nature of Lippmann's reaction. Writing in the *Atlantic* (April 1958), he first softened his remarks by observing that Kennan had spoken "gently and quietly, as it is in his nature to do." He, too, then took me to task for the passage about the guerrilla forces, and said that there were, in the lectures,

"other highly debatable *obiter dicta* . . . as for example, his advice
to continental Western Europe to renounce all nuclear weapons,
and his assertion that rich nations, like the United States, need not
feel any responsibility for the underdeveloped nations." But these
"dicta," he went on to say, were "beside the main point. . . . As
compared with the central issue of occupation vs. disengagement,
to make much of the other dicta is, as the saying goes, to pick fleas
out of the mane of a lion."

Walter Lippmann's most telling and penetrating comment on the
matters discussed in my Reith Lectures appeared, actually, not at
that time but in a series of articles published more than a year later
(April 6, 7, 8, and 9, 1959) in the *New York Herald Tribune*,
under the title of "The Two Germanys and Berlin." Here, in his
own calm and impersonal way, without ever mentioning myself, he
tore to pieces by implication the assumptions concerning the division
of Germany on which my own lectures had been based — largely
on the same grounds as those already advanced by Aron.

The reception evoked by these Reith Lectures — the torrents of
publicity, the hundreds of comments, the unjust attacks, the telling
criticisms — all this came to constitute for me, in the most literal
sense of the term, a traumatic experience. I was utterly appalled and
unsettled by the turmoil I had unleashed. Whether what I had done
was admirable or horrible, I was unable to judge; but that I had
done something quite different from what I had meant to do was
clear. By the time the lectures came to an end, I was too shocked to
be able to read even the most important of the critical reactions
they were provoking. After delivery of the last of the lectures, on
December 15, I spent the night at the home of friends, in Chelsea.
In the course of a solitary early-morning walk, the next day, I went
into Victoria Station and dutifully bought the morning papers with
all the stories and comments about the last lecture. But I then dis-

covered that I could not bring myself to read them. I thrust them
into my overcoat pocket, and carried them about there for days,
unwilling to look at them. I don't think I ever read them.

This was the state I was in; and while I did indeed write two or
three things in reply to critics — the letter to the *Neue Zürcher
Zeitung*, an article for *Foreign Affairs* in reply to Dean Acheson's
criticisms, etc., — I could never face, in those years, the task of attempting to assess, or reply to, the criticism in general. I cringed at
the sight of it. It was painful to me. I never wanted to hear of it
again. Even now, it is only with a neurotic distaste that I can bring
myself to look at the great stacks of critical comment that have
survived from that time. But memoirs are a commitment; and it
seems to me that I have no choice but to sit briefly in judgment, as
so many other people then did, over the George Kennan of that
day and to attempt to put into a proper perspective the things that
he was bold enough or rash enough to say in those radio lectures.

I have already offered my *mea culpa* for the observations about
the paramilitary forces and the concept of defense in depth against
foreign occupation rather than defense by conventional forces at
the frontier. Even to this day, I am not convinced that those observations did not reflect certain insights which deserved a more respectful examination than they received. What I outlined there was
almost precisely the concept on which the Chinese Communist
armed forces are today based; and nobody laughs at Comrade Mao
for his adherence to this concept. This is the concept by which, by
and large, the Vietcong have been inspired; and I think that most
Americans have learned not to laugh at the Vietcong. I was somewhat bitterly amused, furthermore, to read, in April 1971, statements by the Austrian Chancellor, Herr Kreisky, concerning the
problem of Austria's defense, which sounded not greatly different
from the passages in question of the Reith Lectures.* I am free to

---

* The Paris *Le Monde*, of April 24, 1971, had this to say about Herr Kreisky's
views:
"For an army insufficiently equipped and incapable of fulfilling its mission,

admit, however, that I was very foolish to say these things. Either they were wholly misconceived and had no value, in which case the statement of them was the expression of some real intellectual failure on my part, or they were so much ahead of their time as to be unintelligible. In either case, they should not have been said. One of the things I have had to learn in life is that in political matters truth prematurely uttered is of scarcely greater value than error.

This point aside, I can see that the difference between myself and my critics, as reflected by this episode, rested primarily on three points of interpretation.

I, in the first place, attached a much greater importance than did the Western statesmen and Western opinion generally to the possibility of a military evacuation by the Russians of Eastern Germany, Poland and Hungary. My critics professed to see the greatest danger for Europe in the inordinate size of the Soviet conventional forces, particularly the ground forces. I was much less impressed with this factor. I suspected, in the first place, that current Western estimates of the size of these forces were exaggerated (this was later shown to be quite true).* But in addition to this I was aware, from what I knew of Russian history, that it was nothing unusual for Russian governments to maintain ground forces much greater numerically than those of any other European power. They had done this throughout the nineteenth century. They had done it in the 1920s and 1930s. Yet in those days no one had insisted on the presence of American forces in Europe. I, too, saw the Soviet ground

---

Chancellor Kreisky would like to substitute 'a force of rapid intervention,' suitable for engagement in a limited local conflict or, in case of invasion, for mounting simultaneous actions at a number of territorial points. 'The defense of the country is not possible without the support of the workers' is the view of the head of the government. His views were echoed by an official of the Ministry who said: 'In 1950, the workers saved Austria from an attempted Communist *putsch*. We have to be in a position to defend each river and each bridge.' "

* People talked at that time in terms of 175 divisions. Today, that figure seems to have been quietly reduced to something more like 85. And it is significant that this reduction has not had the slightest effect on the opinions about disengagement held by the very people who once bandied the larger figure.

forces as a danger to Western Europe, but not primarily because of their numbers — rather because they now had, in contrast to the situation existing in earlier decades, an area of deployment — namely, the Eastern zone of Germany — in the heart of Europe. And for this reason, to me, in contrast to my opponents, the main problem was to get them back where they belonged — behind the Pripet Marshes. Once they had been thus removed from the heart of Europe, one would no longer need, to oppose them, the elaborate security measures then being pursued in NATO. Nothing irritated me more, in the criticisms to which my Reith Lectures were subjected, than the tendency of the critics to ignore this point and to speak as though the modifications in the Western defense posture that I had suggested related to a situation in which Soviet forces were still stationed some sixty miles from the North Sea.

Secondly, I rated much higher than did others the possibility of just such a Soviet retirement. The others, I thought, greatly underrated the price the Soviet leaders would be willing to pay to get the Americans out of Germany. And I was impressed with the fact that in the effort to achieve this result, the satellite leaders, quite obviously, would be our covert allies. Gomulka had only recently stressed publicly that it was the presence of American troops in Germany, not Soviet pressure, that caused the Poles to accept Soviet garrisons on their territory. The day the Americans left Germany, he had said, he would take up with Moscow the question of the retirement of Soviet forces in Poland. In the weeks just prior to the delivery of my talks, the Russians had concluded new military assistance agreements with Poland, Hungary and Rumania; and in each of these agreements, obviously at the insistence of the satellite governments, the temporary nature of the stationing of Soviet troops on the soil of these countries had been stressed. In addition to this, one had the repeated public statements of Khrushchev and Bulganin, offering such withdrawal as part of a mutual disengagement.

I also had much less confidence than did my critics in the only alternative to some form of disengagement, which was a continuation of the existing division of the Continent. I could see, in these circumstances, no solution of the Berlin problem. Five years of residence in that city had given me an admiration for its people, and a sense of its importance to Germany and to Europe, much higher than anything experienced by those who criticized me. I did not believe (and circumstances, I think, have borne me out in this skepticism) that the city could retain indefinitely its vitality within the framework of a divided Germany; and to accept the permanency of that framework appeared to me to be to condemn it to a slow death.

I was equally disinclined to settle for a European policy which left no room, even in concept, for the Eastern European peoples, which would have had no place for them even should they be able to liberate themselves, which offered them no alternatives to Soviet domination but an attempt at a reversal of alliances and association with a military grouping which the Soviet leaders regarded as directed against themselves. By holding out to them no other possibility than this, one was — it seemed to me — actually making oneself the ally of Moscow in the preservation of Soviet domination in that area.

Finally, I had no confidence in our ability to play indefinitely the part which a continuation of existing policies seemed to demand of us. I have already cited my warning that the United States was not a European power and could not be expected to keep forces in Europe indefinitely. I feared, therefore, that the real alternative to the effort to arrive at some sort of compromise with the Russians over Central Europe would be eventually a unilateral withdrawal on our part, for reasons of our own, for which we would receive no compensation whatsoever. I often had occasion to recall those anxieties when, in later years, I read of Senator Mansfield's repeated urgings that we withdraw our troops unilaterally for financial reasons.

Looking back on the controversy today, I cannot hold myself seriously at fault for entertaining these views. My error was in the supposition that they were likely to be shared by anyone else, no matter how eloquently I argued them. I quite failed to realize, when I undertook the drafting of these lectures, the intensity of the fear that the specter of a reunited Germany aroused in Western countries, the depth of attachment there to the programs already evolved for uniting Western Germany economically with the rest of Western Europe and militarily with the Atlantic Community, and the widespread horror of any sort of development, be it even German unification and the removal of the division of Europe, which might jeopardize the progress now being made in that direction. I was obliged to recognize for the first time, in the reaction to the lectures, a state of mind in Western opinion and Western statesmanship in which something close to an absolute value was attached to the prospect for integrating a part of Germany into a part of Europe. This was a project that assumed the continuation of a divided Continent; and for this reason any views, such as my own, that envisaged even the possibility of a removal of the division were bound to appear dangerous and heretical. I was dealing here, in my critics and in the offended statesmen, with people who would not have considered the withdrawal of a single American battalion from Western Germany even if the Russians had been willing to evacuate all of Eastern Germany and Poland by way of compensation. But it took the reaction to the lectures to make this apparent to me.

The trouble with the Reith Lectures was not that all that I said was wrong, but that the time for saying much of it had long since passed. Two years earlier these observations might have been useful; now, their usefulness was questionable. Here, as on other occasions, the error was in the timing; and here, again, it was the timing that was decisive. It was the timing that had caused the "X-article," ten years earlier, to be praised beyond its deserts and to be effective

beyond the hopes that lay behind it. It was timing now that caused
the Reith Lectures to fall on such stony and resistant, if strongly
echoing, soil. If in some respects the lectures were ahead of their
time, in others they were behind it.

I do not know, today, whether I performed a useful function, or
a pernicious one (as many then thought) by delivering these talks. I
am inclined now to regret that I did so; because the task, added to
the strains of the Oxford lecturing, was beyond my strength; and I
was not able to give to it the best that I had. On the other hand the
lectures may have helped, through the discussion they unleashed, to
clarify and sharpen Western thinking on the issues of the cold war.

However that may be, it is clear to me now that the experience
marked, for better or for worse, the end of what possibilities I
might have had for useful and constructive contribution to thinking about the problems of Western policy with relation to Russia in
this era. If the talks were, from the standpoint of attention and
publicity, a startling success, they were a failure from the standpoint of the response to the ideas advanced. Aware of that failure, I
came away from them in a state which I can only describe as one of
intellectual brokenheartedness. The Western powers were now
embarked on a path for which I had no stomach. In the effort to
solve the problems of Europe by perpetuating its division, and the
effort to remove the danger of nuclear weapons by an all-out competition with the Russians in their development, I could not be an
effective guide; I had no confidence in either undertaking.

There would be temptations, in the coming years, to sound off
further on current problems of European and military policy.
Sometimes, the temptations would be yielded to. These yieldings,
as I see today, might better have been omitted. I had had my say.
The pursuit of history, the common refuge of those who find
themselves helpless in the face of the present, would have made —
did make, in fact, at times — a better occupation.

I cannot leave this subject of the Reith Lectures without a brief word about the place, in my life and thoughts, of the great and unique country in which those lectures were delivered. I had spent two or three months in London during the war. I had traveled in the British Isles on a number of occasions. This was the first opportunity I had had (it would not be the last) to live in England for some length of time.

When it came to the experiences of daily life in Oxford, in 1957–1958, I can describe my reactions only as a love-hate complex. Oxford, as many people know, contrives to combine in one small area some of the most exquisite features of England's past and some of the least attractive ones of her present. The gray flood of motor-cyclists that swept up the High Street on weekday mornings used to fill my soul with desolation: hundreds on hundreds of drab figures, sexless and inhuman behind their goggles and overalls, hunched grimly over their handlebars as they pressed their way from one of the great industrial suburbs to another. I loathed the overcrowded stores on the Cornmarket, with their shoddy, standardized inventories and their bored, indifferent shopgirls, just as I loathed the traffic-choked thoroughfares before them, with their lines of traffic — stalled buses panting, coughing and blowing their diesel fumes into your face. There was, it seemed to me, a peculiar bleakness about English parks and streets on the long, dull weekends, with everything closed down — an emptiness so trying to the soul that I could picture no conceivable antidote to it other than becoming young again and falling wildly in love. I can remember one desperate Sunday afternoon in what we were told was spring, when I drove the two little children out to a damp, deserted playground on the edge of town; there, there was a merry-go-round and a swing on it, and there the children swung, with the complacent, indomitable fortitude of such small creatures, while a short distance away white sails, actually belonging to boats being piloted by intrepid English enthusiasts on an invisible Thames, appeared to float over the sodden fields — among the snow flurries. England, on such Sunday afternoons, could try men's souls.

The flat, too, was awkward. We were lucky, I know, to have it. It was spacious and centrally located. I am not without gratitude to our Balliol hosts for making it available. But it was a place meant, like so many other Oxford premises, to be inhabited only with the help of servants; and of these, of course, there were none. The place was up a total of fifty-seven steps. Every room, except the hallway-landing, had to be separately heated. All the fuel for the coal grates had to be carried up the stairways, and all the ashes, together with the "swill," back down again, and this by none other than the master of the house who also occasionally, between lectures, swept the back stairs, since no one else did it.

All this, of course, was good for me, and presented problems only because of my folly in overburdening my time with other things. But the English, particularly outside London, have a way of trying the American patience with a maddening casualness and impracticality in material matters — a studied persistence in doing them, if at all possible, the hard way, just as we irritate them with bizarre habits of our own; and to this species of stress I was no more immune than any other American who undertakes to share their life.

This was one side of Oxford; but how richly it was balanced on the opposite pole! Within sight of our windows, across the street, were the noble walls of Merton College, the first secular institution of higher learning in the Western Christian world; and over its portal we could admire, when we wished, the stone lintel with the fine mediaeval bas-relief of John the Baptist. A few steps in any direction from the door of our house took you to scenes of comparable beauty and rarity. I could work, when I wished (or better, when I could find time) in the long reading room of the Codrington Library, at All Souls, surely among the most serene and beautiful of the world's library premises. I was never unaware of the fact, and never unappreciative of it, that all about me in the colleges, values were being cultivated, traditions pursued, and ancient customs — sound, symbolic, significant customs — perpetuated, in all of which I — a conservative person, a natural-born antiquarian, a firm believer in the need for continuity across the generations in form and ceremony — could take only comfort and delight. In addition to which there was the generously extended hospitality of a host of kind and exquisitely civilized people, who did all in their power to make our stay there a pleasant one.

I rebelled inwardly against Oxford, I sometimes felt, less as an American than as a Scot. The lush, wealthy, elegant Southwest of England whose spirit Oxford reflected and whose traditions it perpetuated was not my part of the British Isles. I would have fitted better into the landscape, I suppose, several hundred miles to the northeast. I can recall exposing to my friend Isaiah Berlin, at the time of my arrival, the fear that I would never fit into an Oxford common room: people there would be too urbane, too witty, too quick in repartee; I was only a gloomy Scot. He tried to reassure me. "Think nothing of it," he said. "Balliol's full of gloomy Scots."

Perhaps it was. Although Balliol was officially my academic home in Oxford, I seldom had time to go there, and that was no one's fault but my own. Yet there was something in what I had said; and as time went on, I became aware that in those moments when I rebelled against Oxford, I was rebelling against it not primarily as an American but increasingly as an Anglo-American and almost as a Britisher himself: applying the same standards, grumbling about the same things, assuming in fact the same right to grumble as did any Britisher. Britain, in other words, was quietly thrusting into me the tentacles of its great absorbent power. I knew that I would never be an Englishman, but I would never again, I also knew, be a stranger in England. And I can recall reflecting, towards the end of my stay in Oxford, that if I were suddenly to be told that I was fated to spend the rest of my days as a scholar in that city, I might have begun at once to worry about where I was to find a place to live, but I would not have found it in any way out of the ordinary, and would have shed no tear.

England as a whole I viewed, in those days, with a mixture of apprehension and solicitude. I was appalled at the overpopulation of the southern part of the island, and at the complacency of the British public in the face of that fact. I felt, from my limited vantage point, a greater liking for older people there than for younger ones, and a greater admiration for the old upper class than for the lower middle class which had so largely replaced it in political power, although this last was balanced, I must admit, by memories of the magnificent qualities exhibited by the common people of London during the war. I recognized the necessity of much of the great social change that had come over Britain in recent decades; but I felt that this change had been much too rapid and abrupt for anyone's good, and above all wasteful, in a way Britain could not really afford — wasteful particularly of the talents and goodwill of the old upper classes, who had been so recklessly thrust aside. I resented, more perhaps than most Britishers, the headlong Americanization of so much of the country's life. The things I hated in my own country I hated even worse in England, because they did not seem to belong there. I reflected, in sadness, that if California was only the rest of America but sooner and more extreme, America as a whole bore the same relationship to Britain. And for this I blamed exclusively the British themselves. No one forced them to be like us. The decision was their own.

I took note, with detached skepticism, of the endless argument, then only gathering strength but destined one day to culminate in entry into the Common Market, about the possibilities for overcoming Britain's industrial backwardness, her chronic exchange difficulties, her persistent economic stagnation. Increased industrial efficiency might, of course, help, as a palliative of sorts. But Britain was not to be saved, it seemed to me, by further industrialization, further modernization, further integration into, and dependence upon, a world market. The only line of development I could have viewed as hopeful would have been a drastic reduction of population, with a view to bringing it into a more acceptable relationship to domestic food supply, and the cultivation of a higher degree of economic autarchy and a reduced dependence on imports and on international exchanges generally. Perhaps it was a mere nostalgia for things irreparably past; perhaps it was that I loved what I saw of the older England more than many Englishmen appeared to do; the fact remains that I could develop little enthusiasm for the prospect of Britain's advancing into the modern age. I was more concerned to speculate on the means by which she might contrive to preserve some of the precious and unique features of her own past. The question of the Common Market lay, at that time, far in the future, and this is not the place to comment on it; but I must confess that when I read, at that time, the early discussions of the schemes for connecting England with the Continent by means of some sort of railway or highway tunnel under the Channel, I was staggered and horrified: I could view them only as the expression of some sort of death urge. How anyone could wish to sacrifice that precious insularity of which Shakespeare had once taken such eloquent note may have been comprehensible to many Englishmen. It remained incomprehensible to at least one American.

11

Yugoslavia—The Background

IN January 1961, the month in which the administration of John F. Kennedy came into office, I was completing the teaching of a one-semester graduate seminar at Yale University. On the twenty-third of that month, just three days after the change of administration, I happened to look in at the office of Branford College, where I was living as a visiting fellow, to see whether there was any mail for me. It was noon hour; the regular office staff was out to lunch. An undergraduate was minding the telephone. He was holding the receiver to his ear when I came in, and I could see that he looked agitated. Seeing me, he jumped up in relief and said: "Mr. Kennan, the President of the United States wants to talk to you."

It was indeed the new President. His purpose in calling was to ask me whether I would be prepared to accept an appointment as ambassador either in Poland or in Yugoslavia. I expressed appreciation and asked time to think it over. Later in the day I called him back, accepted, and said I would prefer Yugoslavia.

While this particular suggestion came as a surprise to me, it was not the first communication I had had with Jack Kennedy in the period of his campaign and election. He had written me, in February 1958, a kind and thoughtful letter about the Reith Lectures, which he had read in full.* Nearly a year later, he read an article I

---

* He was kind enough to say, in this letter (February 13, 1958) that while he did

had written for *Foreign Affairs* entitled "Disengagement Revisited," in which I had expanded on what I had said in the Reith Lectures on this subject and had replied to the criticisms advanced by Dean Acheson and others. He thought, he said, that I had "disposed of the extreme rigidity of Mr. Acheson's position with great effectiveness and without the kind of *ad hominem* irrelevancies in which Mr. Acheson unfortunately indulged last year."

A year later, only a few days before he took office as President, at a time when the pressures on him must have been simply tremendous, I received a third note, one written this time in longhand from Jamaica, where he was snatching a few days of rest before entering on the duties of the presidency. He had read, he said, the talk I gave over the BBC just a year after delivery of my Reith Lectures. "It impressed me," he wrote, "as does everything you say, with its dispassionate good sense." This observation was followed by one which has, in the light of what the ensuing decade was to bring in our relations with Southeast Asia, a certain historical significance. "I was especially interested," he wrote, "in your thoughts on our considering not merely limitations in testing but the abrogation of the weapon itself. I wonder if we could expect to check the sweep south of the Chinese with their endless armies with conventional forces? In any case, we shall all be discussing this two or three years after the moment of opportunity has passed."

In accepting the President's offer of appointment, I was quite aware that the differences of view that divided me from the official establishment in Washington, as reflected in the Reith Lectures and their reception, disqualified me as an advisor to this or any other President on the major problems of the cold war. If I now went

---

not agree with all the points made in the lectures (particularly not the passages dealing with our relations with the underdeveloped countries), he thought the contents of the lectures had been twisted and misrepresented in many of the criticisms, and he was glad to know "that there is at least one member of the 'opposition' who is not only performing his critical duty but also providing a carefully formulated, comprehensive and brilliantly written set of alternative proposals and perspectives."

abroad as a diplomatic representative, I went as someone prepared to accept established policy in the major problems of Europe and the cold war and to do the best I could within that framework. But relations with Yugoslavia constituted an area in which these great problems were not immediately and acutely involved. And I was pleased to be asked to serve once more. I had naturally never been happy about the manner in which I had parted from the governmental service in 1953. I welcomed an opportunity to perform 'one more tour of duty, if only at a modest post, and then to retire all over again — as I hoped — in full honor and good standing. Finally, Jack Kennedy struck me as a man who deserved, at that point in his life, whatever help you could give him.

Again, therefore, just as nine years earlier in the assignment to Russia, academic life was at once disrupted; winter and early spring were given over to preparations for departure. And again, it was early May when, having proceeded to Europe by the civilized means — i.e., the ocean liner — then still available, we arrived late one evening at the Belgrade railway station — myself, my wife, the two youngest children, and a dog which worried us all mightily because it had insisted on repressing all its natural functions ever since Venice and we feared complications for the red carpet of the welcoming committee when it finally emerged from the confinement of the train.

I mentioned the uncomfortable, bursting dog. I do not wish to burden this account with the personal. We all have our human ups and downs, and mine were no more remarkable than anybody else's. But I cannot refrain from making it clear that this tour of service in Yugoslavia constituted for me one of the richest, most pleasant, and most rewarding of the personal experiences of a Foreign Service life. That this should have been so lay partly in the nature of the country and partly in the relatively happy conditions surrounding (at least at the Belgrade end; the tie to Washington is another story) the conditions in which my work was performed.

There is surely no more varied country, none more replete with contrasts of scene and atmosphere, and none whose geographical position is more central to the great historical problems of the Danube basin and southeastern Europe generally, than Yugoslavia. It is, actually, not one country but an aggregate of six widely varying countries. The most ancient, enduring and significant of Europe's cultural borders — the line, substantially unchanged over the centuries, which separated Byzantium from Rome, Eastern Christianity from Western Christianity, and finally the Turkish Empire from the Austro-Hungarian one — runs today through the very center of the country. Its marks on both people and landscape are still visible at a glance. Yet what lies to either side of it is also significantly divided, each side in its own way. The Byzantine–Turkish–Eastern Orthodox side, thrusting northeastward in a great salient to embrace the extended massif that runs up the middle of the western side of the Balkan peninsula, has its Serbian, Montenegrin, Albanian-Moslem and Macedonian components, not to mention the provinces of Bosnia and Herzegovina with their Serbian-speaking Moslem population, their great natural beauty, and their weird, cruel past. The Roman-Austrian-Catholic side, covering the plains and coastal areas surrounding this massif from the east, north and west, is divided into parts that have been exposed to Hungarian, Austrian and Italian influences (Croats, Slovenes, and Istrian-Dalmatians) respectively. This variegated cultural and religious pattern is matched, or nearly matched, by the variety of climate and landscape — so much so that I often think of Yugoslavia as including within its relatively small area (about the size of Wyoming) almost all the geographic regions of the United States. It has its Great Plains, its Appalachians and Rockies, its Mississippi, its California and Florida, its tropics and snowbound winters — everything, indeed, except an Eastern seaboard.

Belgrade is situated almost at the center of this welter of cultures, climates, tongues, and traditions. From its ancient hilltop fortress, poised on what was then a northeastern outpost of the Turkish salient, the members of the Turkish garrison could once look down, across the broad confluence of the Danube and the Sava, onto lands that were under Austrian authority, and thus a part of Western Europe. Leaving Belgrade by car, even over the inferior roads that still existed in my own time there, you could be within an hour or two on the great fertile plains of the Banat, with their extensive state farms, once German estates; or on the broad straight main street of one of the erstwhile Hungarian villages of the Vojvodina, with its muddy cobbles, its wandering flocks of geese, and its brightly painted house facades joined one to the other by high board fences; or in the great provincial cathedral church where the famous Croatian Bishop Strossmayer once conducted his services; or in one of the vineyards of the Serbian Šumadija, a region as beautiful in the flesh as in its lovely name; or in the dim recesses of one of the remote Byzantine monastery churches of the Middle Ages, with its naïve but sorrowfully impressive and intensely beautiful frescoes. An easy day's drive, if time allowed, would place you in one of the magnificent mountain valleys of southern Serbia; or in the Bosnian capital of Sarajevo, where the footprint of the 1914 assassin has been perpetuated in the asphalt of the street; or in the unique atmosphere of the Croatian Zagreb, a city of music, art and the theater, about which there is something that always made me feel it was destined to be one of the great cities of the future; or in the small architectural gem of a baroque-Alpine culture: the Slovene capital of Ljubljana, with its lovely spires, its intense cultural life, and its incomparable surroundings of hill, field and forest, all scrupulously pruned and intensely beautiful. All this, and more, was easily accessible from Belgrade; and the access to it was facilitated and enriched by the great kindliness, sweetness, and hospitality of common people, everywhere, to the itinerant foreigner — particularly, I think, to the American. Travel in that country was a never-ending feast of places, faces, and atmospheres; and for me particularly, whose sensitivity to atmosphere is of such quivering, helpless acuteness, and so difficult to convey to others that it often reminds me of the water-diviner's twig, the impact was overwhelming and unforgettable.

One was never unaware, of course, of the long, and even recent, unhappy past of this region. One knew that only thirty years earlier its inhabitants, or their parents, now so generous and engaging in their response to the traveling foreigner, had been carving each other up by the hundreds of thousands with the utmost ferocity. One had to believe that under all this charm and hospitality there lay a relatively low threshold of potential brutality. Still, one could not help but like these people and respond to them. They were, for the most part, strong, simple people, proud but dignified, initially suspicious but always responsive to the courteous approach. One readily believed that even in their brutalities they were passionate, courageous and sincere — not cynical or cowardly or sneaky.

It is, therefore, mostly pleasant experiences that remain in memory. And they are hard to describe, for they return to consciousness only in vivid but disjointed, almost symbolic, flashes of memory — scenes, episodes, moments of experience. Should I name some of them as examples? I must warn that they form no unity. I can think, offhand

— of the little shepherd child, ragged and barefoot, who suddenly appeared out of the dry brush of a mountainside in Montenegro, while we were waiting for a punctured tire to be changed, shyly presented my wife with a handful of wild flowers she had picked for the purpose, and scurried back into the bushes, to rejoin her goats;

— of the peasant girl to whom I once gave a lift, on a dusty country road in western Croatia, who, when she reached her destination, dived into her little shopping bag, produced from its depths a single orange, and insisted that I take it because it would not be right for her to accept the ride without paying me;

— of the impoverished nuns at a remote Byzantine church, far back in the forest, who would not let us depart before they had produced a meal for us from the pathetic produce of their little kitchen garden;

— of the young priest's wife who, when we once picnicked in a hillside churchyard in central Serbia, suddenly appeared with a platter of hot cheese cakes which she offered to us with quiet dignity "because you are strangers near my house," after which she leaned against a tree, crossed her brown bare feet, and surveyed us, long and pleasantly, with a placid, unselfconscious curiosity;

— of the elderly gentleman with steel teeth and an old-fashioned frock coat who, as we were inspecting a church in a small town of central Serbia, advanced grandly towards us down the churchyard path, extended a hand and presented himself as "eighteen years mayor of this place," said he observed that we were strangers, informed us that he had his home in the town, and asked us whether we would like to come there and drink raspberry juice with him, which we did;

— of the contrast that presented itself to you when, on completion of the four-hundred-mile drive from Belgrade to Trieste, you passed the Italian border point on the plateau above Trieste and then suddenly came out on the brink of the escarpment and saw, falling dramatically away beneath you, the great vista of the city and the western Adriatic and the teeming expanses of Western Europe beyond;

— of the road winding along the upper reaches of the deep Neretva valley, in Herzegovina, past the place where the Yugoslav partisans, bravely carrying their hundreds of wounded with them, crossed the river under the guns of the Germans, with such heavy loss of life, in 1943, and made their way up into the wilder mountains on the other side;

— of my beautiful and conscientious Serbian teacher, and of the excursion I once made with her and her husband to the mediaeval church at Žiča, I driving my own car and attempting to concentrate on avoiding the endless potholes of the gravel highway, she, however, holding me sternly to the use of the Serbian language and relentlessly correcting, hour after hour, my distracted abuses of it, until the music of it literally rang in my head;

— of the young man, standing with a group of peasants by a roadside fountain, who, when I said "good day" to him in Serbian and asked him whether anyone would mind if we walked up into the vineyards above us, replied, looking me firmly, but not without kindliness, in the eye: "If you say 'good day' to them up there the way you said it to us, no one will mind."

Such, by way of example alone, are the things that remain in memory. They represent one side of diplomatic life. And the totality of it cannot be pictured without them.

I might mention also the conditions in which my work, in Yugoslavia, proceeded.

This was, first and foremost, a matter of my own embassy staff, and particularly the regular diplomatic officers and the officials of the United States Information Service with whom, since they all came under my authority, I had to work in special intimacy. These were men of a different generation than my own. They had come up in a different sort of bureaucratic environment: less human, less personal, vaster, more inscrutable, less reassuring. Some of them tended initially, I thought, to be wary, correct, faithfully pedantic, but withdrawn and in a sense masked. The studied absence of color, in personality and in uttered thought, had become a protective camouflage. But of course they were real people underneath, and in most instances very valuable and intelligent ones, in some instances highly competent and even talented. And rightly or wrongly (an ambassador, separated from his subordinates by that treacherous curtain of deference they dangle before him, can never really know what they think of him) — rightly or wrongly, I felt that I could be useful to them; that I, the relic of an age when diplomacy was considered an art rather than a skill, had things to teach them; that I was able to give greater meaning and interest to their work than it would otherwise have held. The things I had to teach them were matters of the style rather than the substance of diplomatic work; but to us of the older generation of diplomatists, style was of the essence, and I had no shame for this limitation. They viewed me, I suspect, with a certain amused astonishment, enjoyed the rhetorical melodrama of my numerous telegraphic conflicts with the Department of State, were intrigued by my unorthodox reactions to the work they performed and the experiences they reported to me, and were aware — as I like to think — of the genuine respect and affection in which I came to hold them. For me, in any case, the Belgrade experience would have been worth it for the association with them alone.

On the other side were the Yugoslav officials with whom we had to deal. Let me speak first of those of lower and middle rank. What a contrast they were to our Russian counterparts of earlier days! Generally approachable, competent and courteous, they were always willing not only to listen but also to respond. It was possible to meet them socially, outside their offices, without self-consciousness or strain. Many of them, met in this way, were good company: cheerful, relaxed, helpful. They were, for the most part, intelligent, buoyant people, full of an easy informal charm. They made, for anyone familiar with Russian conditions, an almost startling impression of frankness and openness. To an extent, this was what it seemed to be; but we soon learned that there were strict and well-established limits. These were, almost without exception, people who had fought in the partisan war against the Germans under Tito's leadership. This experience had bred an abiding sense of comradeship and a disciplined structure of loyalties. It was evident, when one came to know them better, that words and actions on their part were governed by some unseen but very effective coordinating and disciplining bond. They, too, like their Soviet counterparts, were to a certain extent a conspiracy in the face of outsiders but, so far as we were concerned, not a hostile one — just wary. This wariness was the product partly of their Communist past, but partly also of a certain disbelief that anyone not born and bred in Yugoslavia would ever be able to understand the complexities of that curious assemblage of nationalities, and finally of a healthy appreciation for the fact that in diplomacy, as in other walks of life, no one looks after your interests unless you do so yourself.

In Yugoslavia, as opposed to the Communist countries farther east, one could easily come to know most of the leading political figures and to have pleasant, cordial and sometimes even informal relations with them. There were exceptions. The leaders of some of the outlying republics (Bosnia and Macedonia, in particular) were not always friendly or forthcoming. But these exceptions tended generally to prove the rule. My wife and I were personal guests of President Tito and Mrs. Broz on a number of occasions. The President of the Croatian Assembly once gave us a delightful day with himself and his family on his yacht, in the Adriatic, off the island of Hvar. In Belgrade, other higher officials had us to their homes on a number of occasions. I could continue this list. There was no compulsion on these people to extend these kindnesses; and my wife and I, accustomed to other and less agreeable customs, deeply appreciated them.

The dominant personality, throughout the period of my stay there and indeed ever since, was of course Josip Broz Tito. I had met him, and had come to respect him for his accomplishments, even before I went to Belgrade as ambassador. This respect grew, then, with our official acquaintance. He was a man of simple origins. His higher education had been confined very largely to the indoctrination he had received, just after the Russian Revolution, as a prisoner of war in Russia. The rest of what he knew had been learned in the hard school of life as a Communist revolutionary and, eventually, a partisan political and military leader. He considered himself by outlook and conviction a good Marxian Communist, and never encouraged anyone to suppose that he was anything else. He was not incapable of ruthless severity where he felt it to be essential to the protection of the cause. Nor was he incapable, when the situation called for it, of guile and dissimulation — of the ruse of war, in short — in his dealings with any political force that he considered hostile or untrustworthy. As a seasoned political leader, he knew when to speak and when to hold his peace. But he was not cruel; nor was he, like Stalin, oversuspicious. He showed, on the contrary, loyalty and sometimes much patience towards those who had served him faithfully. After the break with Moscow in 1948, only two of his associates — both men revealed, I suspect, to have been serving clandestinely as Soviet agents while occupying high positions in his intimate entourage — paid with their lives for their betrayal.* He conducted, thereafter, no extensive purges in his own party, and punished people only when he considered (and this went for Djilas, too) that their offenses were flagrant, persistent, and malicious.

Nor was he tricky. I was always aware that there were things he thought it better not to discuss with me; and this I understood. The quiet discipline of his party applied to him as to the others. But what he did say, I could depend on. I do not have the impression that he ever tried to deceive me or mislead me. On at least one occasion he gave me friendly, useful and sensible advice.

I do not mean to give the impression that Tito was never a problem for the American ambassador. Nothing could be farther from

---

* Neither was executed. One was shot trying to cross the border. The other committed suicide.

the truth. I think he liked me personally; but as every professional diplomat knows, personal likes and dislikes have very little to do with the serious aspects of diplomacy. I have said that he always considered himself a good Marxian Communist. As such, he cared more, in the last analysis, for the opinions of people in the international Communist movement than he did for ours. He had taken a bold and heavy responsibility upon himself by breaking with Stalin in 1948. He felt that he had had good reason to do it. He could not forget, however, that this had been challenged with greatest vehemence, over the course of several years, in Moscow and elsewhere in the Communist bloc — that the break had long been viewed there, in fact, as a sort of betrayal of the movement. He was anxious, without sacrificing the independence of his position, to vindicate his action of 1948, to force the Soviet leaders to recognize its correctness, to treat him with respect, to take account of the interests of his regime. In the years since Stalin's death, he had played his cards, skillfully and consistently, with a view to bringing all this about. Sensitive to the charge of having betrayed the cause and gone over to the imperialists, he had often shaped his public statements on world issues in such a way as to depict himself as a good Communist and to appeal to the outlooks of people in the Communist part of the world even at the cost of offending people in the West. He did this, even while trying to maintain, at the same time, correct and normal relations with the Western countries. There was a certain conflict here, of which I am sure he was well aware. He would have liked good relations with both sides. From us, this was in fact all that he did want. But from the other side there was something more he wanted, too; and this was recognition of himself as a good Communist, and vindication of his action in defying Stalin. If, to obtain these things, he had to take on occasions a Communist line more emphatic and more offensive to the West than would otherwise have been the case, he was prepared to do it. His position was that of a prodigal son of the Soviet-dominated Communist movement. He was determined that any reconciliation with the family should take place on his terms, not on its. But it remained for him, through all vicissitudes, his proper family; and it was *its* opinion of him, not ours, that really counted. Here, on this one point, we could not compete.

It was my misfortune that these efforts on Tito's part to win forgiveness and approval in Moscow without sacrificing his highly prized independence reached the peak of their intensity, and were finally crowned with success, precisely during the period of my service in Belgrade. Only four months after my arrival, there took place the notable Belgrade Conference of "nonaligned" nations, at which some twenty-six heads of state from nations that answered this description met in the Yugoslav capital. I thought I knew what it was that Tito was endeavoring to achieve by acting as host to this elaborate and, for the Yugoslavs themselves, expensive gathering. Three years earlier, when there had been a new and sharp disagreement between the Yugoslav and Soviet Party leaders over the question of the new constitution of the Yugoslav Communist Party, Khrushchev had said publicly (and said in Eastern Germany, of all places) that the way to deal with Tito was to ignore him. "Let him go his way; pay no attention to him," was the gist of Khrushchev's statement. "Left alone, he will not amount to much." Well, now, the Belgrade Conference, presenting to Moscow the spectacle of some twenty-six heads of state, leaders of countries with which Moscow would particularly have liked to have close relations, assembled in the Yugoslav capital under Tito's chairmanship, was Tito's response to this bitterly resented remark. Tito would show Khrushchev who, only three years later, was isolated.

And it worked. A year and three months later, in December 1962, Tito would pay a visit to Moscow on the invitation of the Soviet government, would be permitted to address the Supreme

Soviet, and would receive an ovation from the members of that well-disciplined body. What a triumph, for a man in his position! What American ambassador could ever compete with this?

It is not surprising in these circumstances that several times during the period of my incumbency as ambassador, American-Yugoslav relations were disturbed by statements on Tito's part, eagerly picked up and relayed to the West by the world press, that sounded, especially to uncritical and unschooled listeners, as though he was, as the saying went, "taking the Moscow line" and realigning himself with the Soviet-Communist bloc. At the Belgrade Conference itself, for example, he made things very difficult indeed for me by inserting into his major speech, at the last moment and just after a hasty conference with the Soviet ambassador, a statement, obviously not originally contemplated, to the effect that he "understood" the reasons why the Russians had just violated (as they had — unilaterally and without warning) the nuclear test ban agreement. After his return from Moscow, furthermore, he even stopped referring to Yugoslavia as "nonaligned," and dropped for a time his disapproving references to the two opposing military "blocs." These changes, plus repeated public discussions by him of Yugoslav internal problems in terms that seemed designed to appeal to Soviet prejudices, made it difficult for me on occasions to oppose the anti-Yugoslav tendencies that were making themselves felt with particular vehemence on the American side of the water — tendencies that came to constitute for me an even greater problem than Tito's determination to appear, in the eyes of people to the east of him, as a good Communist.

In turning to this subject of American opinion and policy with relation to Yugoslavia, I am going to place a special demand on the attention and patience of the reader by asking him to note, and to bear in mind as I pursue this account further, certain aspects of the relationship between Yugoslavia and the United States as they prevailed at the time of my service in Belgrade. I do this because without this background, the difficulties that arose for the performance of my mission there cannot be understood; yet these difficulties were so revealing and illustrative with relation to the workings of the American governmental and political system in the conduct of diplomacy that the examination of them in detail seems to me to be well worth the effort.

Yugoslavia, it will be recalled, had broken dramatically from the Soviet bloc in 1948, even at the risk of a military confrontation. Since that time, and down to the moment of my arrival there (as indeed ever since), it had led an independent existence. It was not, as I found it (or, again, at any other time), a member of the Warsaw Pact. Its military policy was an independent one. It was not collaborating militarily, and had not been so collaborating for the past thirteen years, with the Soviet Union or any other member of the Warsaw Pact. It was not buying arms or accepting military instructors from the East. It was not a member of the Eastern European economic organizations — the Soviet-dominated COMECON. It did not even have observer status in that organization. It did, on the other hand, have observer or associate status in more than one of the Western organs of international economic collaboration.

As a result of Yugoslavia's independent position, supported by the Trieste settlement and by Albania's break with Moscow, the Soviet Union, which fifteen years earlier had had easy naval access to a number of places on the eastern shore of the Adriatic Sea, now had no positions on that sea at all; and the Yugoslav Army, the third largest military force in Europe, stood as a highly useful barrier between the southern European NATO forces and the forces of the Soviet bloc. Needless to say, this was a situation greatly to the advantage of European peace. It constituted a vast improvement on the situation that had prevailed in that region prior to Yugoslavia's break with Moscow. The Western powers had, therefore, an important stake in its preservation.

This was not all. Yugoslavia's internal institutions, while formally those of a "socialist" state, differed in many significant respects from those of the Soviet Union and its satellites. They were not ideologically acceptable to Moscow. At the time of my service there, these differences were being sealed, for a long time to come, by the provisions of a new Yugoslav constitution, the final drafts of which were being completed at the time of my arrival. There was no evidence in the terms of this new constitution of any tendency to try to realign Yugoslav institutions in such a way as to bring them closer to those of the Soviet bloc.

There prevailed, finally, in the case of Yugoslavia, nothing even resembling the Iron Curtain that divided Soviet society from the outside world. Travel was liberally permitted — in both directions. There was no ban on listening to foreign broadcasts. The Voice of America was broadcasting daily, without protest on the Yugoslav side, to a Yugoslav audience estimated at more than a million listeners. The United States Information Service was operating libraries and reading rooms in three of the larger Yugoslav cities. These were extensively visited by the Yugoslav public. They lent American books, and American documentary films, liberally to private Yugoslav parties. Yugoslavs were not punished for taking advantage of these facilities.

In all questions of normal bilateral relations between the two countries we had, so far as I can recall, nothing to complain about in Yugoslav behavior. We might dislike some of Tito's statements about other matters. They might cause us anxiety for their effect on our American opinion. But he had a right to his own views. The statements of *our* governmental leaders did not always please *him*, either. And in its practical dealings with us, we continued to find the Yugoslav government fair and reasonable.

In these circumstances we had of course every reason to pursue our efforts to bring about a better understanding in Yugoslavia for ourselves and our country. We had reason to continue to try to correct what we believed to be certain distortions in the official Yugoslav view of world affairs. But we had no reason to try to upset in any major way the situation that then prevailed. Least of all did we have reason to do things that would tend to discourage the Yugoslavs over the prospects for development of their relations with ourselves or to push them back into a more intimate association with the Soviet Union and the other countries of the East. On the contrary, there were many reasons going beyond just our own relationship with Yugoslavia why such a policy would be foolish and injurious to our own interests. The other Eastern Europeans were watching, with greatest interest, the progress and outcome of Yugoslavia's effort to lead an independent political existence. The conclusions they would draw would obviously have an important effect on their own attitudes and policies. If Yugoslavia prospered by her independent policy, it would suggest that they, too, might someday have an alternative to a one-sided and exclusive orientation towards the Soviet Union. If Yugoslavia failed in this effort, they would see no choice for themselves but a continued total dependence on the Soviet Union. As an illustration of what was involved here, I may mention my own conviction that the independent policies later developed by Rumania were importantly influenced by awareness on the part of the Rumanian leaders of the example provided by the neighboring, and in the physical sense very similar, Yugoslavia.

It should be noted that the relatively normal and constructive state of our bilateral relations with Yugoslavia was not, at that time, in any important sense a function of any programs of American aid. We were in fact, at the time of my service there, giving scarcely any aid to the Yugoslavs at all. We *had* given such aid in the past. Food and raw materials had gone forward to them in considerable quantities in the 1950s. There had also been at one time a military aid program; but this had been terminated at Yugoslav request in 1957, four years before I went there. Since that time, the Yugoslavs had been paying dollar cash for military items purchased in the United States.

We had, in the late 1950s, made developmental loans to Yugoslavia for specific industrial and transportation projects, to a total amount of $120 million, some for repayment in their own currency, some for repayment in dollars, some mixed. The last of these loans had been made two years before I went there. The Yugoslavs were faithfully meeting the scheduled payments for interest and amortization on these loans.

We had also been operating, for some years, an extensive program of technical assistance, a program under which some thirty-five hundred to four thousand Yugoslavs had been brought to Western countries for technical training, in addition to which a number of Americans had been sent to Yugoslavia for instructional purposes. I personally felt that this program, while useful in its time, had served its purpose. With my concurrence, and indeed in accordance with my recommendations, it was in process of liquidation during most of my period as ambassador there. The Yugoslavs were not pressing, or even asking, for its continuation.

Finally, we had made with the Yugoslav government, and were continuing to make, annual contracts for the sale to Yugoslavia of surplus wheat and other agricultural products under the relatively favorable terms of Public Law 480 — i.e., the so-called "Food for Peace" program.

This was the situation prevailing at the time of my service there. It meant that with the final liquidation of the technical assistance program and the gradual repayment of the developmental loans, Yugoslavia would soon be receiving from us virtually no governmental aid at all, with the exception of the purchase of surplus wheat on relatively easy terms. Aid to Yugoslavia, in other words, was at that time largely a matter of the past.

It will be agreed, I think, that this was a relatively happy and promising state of affairs to be existing in the relations between the United States and a country that still considered itself, if the words of its leaders were to be believed, a Communist one; and one might have thought that a diplomatic mission, namely, the American embassy at Belgrade, which had had a good deal to do with bringing this state of affairs into existence, would have enjoyed a certain amount of credit, and been given a certain latitude of further action, by the American Congress. This, however, was not to be; and the reason it was not to be, as I soon had occasion to learn, was primarily the unshakable impression that still existed on the part of many members of Congress (a) that Yugoslavia was just like any other Communist country (after all, had not President Tito said things that sounded just like Moscow?), and (b) that a starry-eyed State Department was insisting on giving aid, including military aid, to the Yugoslav Communists in large amounts.

As to the first of these points — the misimpression concerning Yugoslavia's status and character: this was the result of innocent, if scarcely excusable, ignorance on the part of some of our legislators, and of unwillingness on the part of others, for domestic political reasons, to recognize, or to admit to recognizing, the true state of affairs.

The unfeigned ignorance was appalling. One distinguished member of the House of Representatives from a Middle Western state, on being apprised by me of the startling fact that Yugoslavia was not a member of the Warsaw Pact, expressed incredulity ("Aw, go on" was the response). When I assured him that this was true — that the Yugoslavs had broken with Moscow fourteen years before — his response was an angry "Well, why in the hell doesn't the State Department ever tell us anything?"

The pretended ignorance and the sheer anti-Yugoslav prejudice with which it was associated was even more disturbing. I find it hard, to this day, to give a wholly adequate explanation for the prevalence and virulence in Congress of this state of mind. It seemed on the face of it extraordinary that the feeling against a country which did not belong to the Communist bloc, which followed a neutral policy, and which treated us with comparably greater liberality and friendliness in bilateral relations than did any of the Moscow-controlled Communist countries, should be faced with greater hostility in the Congress than were the Moscow-controlled countries themselves. Yet this is the way it was.

A portion of this anomaly could be attributed to the influence in various parts of the country of Croatian and Serbian immigrant elements. It is a common and long-standing phenomenon of American political life, as noted above in the chapter on "Russia and the Cold War," that ethnic groups of this nature, representing compact voting groups in large cities, are often able to bring to bear on individual legislators, and through them on the United States government, an influence far greater than an equivalent group of native citizens would be able to exert.

The American Croatians in particular were, in this respect, no exception; on the contrary, they were an outstanding example. Particularly great, to all appearances, was the influence they exerted through certain elements in the hierarchy of the Roman Catholic Church.* They were, in any case, by reason of their own long-standing feud with the Serbs in their country of origin, violently opposed to the existing Yugoslav government, which (like its pre–World War II predecessor) they regarded as controlled primarily by heretical Serbs; and they carried over without hesitation into American political life this bitter, bloody and long-standing confessional feud — not without effect on their representatives in

---

* I once, during the initial phase of my Yugoslav experience, offered in conversation with Robert Kennedy, then Attorney General, to go on the road in the southwestern part of our country, to talk with those members of the Catholic clergy who I thought had the poorest understanding of Yugoslav problems, and see whether I could not straighten them out. He discouraged me. I had better wait, he said, until some other issue came up which interested them more and took their minds off Yugoslavia; then one would be able to talk with them.

Congress. In doing so, they were not slow to wrap their demands, to suit the Washington-congressional taste, in the relatively respectable mantle of a militant anticommunism, denying the Yugoslav independence vis-à-vis Moscow, denying the unique qualities of Yugoslavia as a Marxist-Socialist state, and doing all in their power to establish the thesis that Yugoslavia was, to all intents and purposes, no different from the Soviet Union. They were opposed to the maintenance by the United States government of relations with Yugoslavia; they would happily have seen us become involved in a war against that country. This being so, they never failed to oppose any move to better American-Yugoslav relations or to take advantage of any opportunity to make trouble between the two countries. And this they succeeded, with monotonous regularity, in doing.*

These circumstances provide a partial explanation for the bitterness of anti-Yugoslav sentiment in the Congress, but they do not explain it entirely. There was something else there which I find it hard to put my finger on. Ever since the McCarthy days (this was, in fact, part of the legacy of McCarthyism) American political life had continued to be extensively dominated by what I might call the "anti-Communist stance." The profession of a high-minded, bristling anticommunism had become a ritualistic observance in the deportment of a great many American politicians — a standard fea-

---

* An example of what we were up against here can be seen from the charge, put to me many times informally by Yugoslavs, that the former Minister of Internal Affairs of the Fascist regime set up in Croatia by the Axis powers during World War II, a man by the name of Andrija Artuković who, if the charge was correct, must have had on his conscience an appalling multiplicity of executions and atrocities, was living peacefully in this country in California, having entered the United States illegally under an alias; but that it had proven impossible to get him deported. For the truth of these charges, I cannot vouch, never having had either occasion or facilities to establish the facts; but the State Department never denied it, and I assume there was something in it. I don't think the Yugoslavs really wanted Artuković back; a war crimes trial such as they would have had to conduct if he had been returned would only have stirred up old animosities and disturbed the peacefulness of Yugoslav life. But every time they had difficulties with us over other matters, they hauled out the Artuković case as a club with which to beat me over the head.

ture of the chauvinistic rhetoric with which one demonstrated to the folks back home, on any and all occasions, that one was a one hundred percent American, devoted to genuine American values, and not, like the State Department, a spineless dupe of the enemy outside the gate. But now, with the development of a Soviet long-range nuclear potential and with the general recognition in American opinion of the delicacy and complexity of Soviet-American relations, one had to be careful how one talked about the Soviet Union. One did not, after all, want to place oneself in the stance of the reckless warmonger. Yugoslavia, on the other hand, was attractive as a target precisely because of its relative helplessness. It was a target off which you could bounce your anti-Communist utterances with complete impunity, knowing that few people cared enough or knew enough about it to call you on the fine points. The Yugoslav government, after all, had no strong body of supporters in the United States who could make trouble for you. And no one could conceive of, or react apprehensively to, the possibility of a Yugoslav-American war.

Added to this was the reaction of irritation produced in many people when they were asked to muster the subtlety of understanding to recognize that Yugoslavia might be "Communist" and still be essentially different from the Soviet Union and the other Eastern European satellites. In the simplistic vision of the American mass mind, evil, as I have had occasion to point out before, is always in the singular, never in the plural. People become both resentful and suspicious when asked to believe that evil is complex rather than unitary. So it was in this instance. If Yugoslavia had to be accepted as "different," then the question arose as to what else might also be "different." You had to ask this question then with relation to every other Communist country — China included. But what remained, in this case, of the whole theory of a deadly bipolar antagonism on which so much of American policy was based? Was this — the suggestion that Yugoslavia was different — was this not just another insidious trick of those effete, overintellectual compromisers with evil known to inhabit the State Department?

Things were not made easier, of course, by the fact that the Yugoslav leadership continued to employ the word "Communist" as a description of itself and of Yugoslav institutions. This, coupled with the tendency of Americans to let themselves be guided by semantic symbols, positive or negative, rather than by the realities behind them (and perhaps not Americans alone: "Mankind," said Gibbon, "is governed by names"), made it more difficult than it would otherwise have been to argue with the people who cast their opinions in terms of "Communist Yugoslavia" or "Red Yugoslavia."

As for the stubborn endurance of the impression that we were still giving massive aid to the Yugoslavs; this was, I think, the result of several causes: partly real ignorance, partly a subconscious unwillingness to recognize the facts (the misimpression made too good a whip with which to belabor the State Department), partly real misunderstandings, and partly confusion as to the difference between aid and trade.

Certain of the elements of this last misunderstanding were amusing as well as illustrative. We had, prior to my arrival in Belgrade, sold to the Yugoslavs, rather reluctantly and with warnings of their inadequacy, some obsolete, surplus and no longer classified fighter planes, of a type which we had not used since the Korean War. The alternative was to scrap them and get nothing for them at all. The Yugoslavs, not receiving from us any military aid and not wishing to receive it, paid dollar cash for them on the barrelhead. But then complications ensued. After the planes themselves had been delivered, but before shipment of the electronic components necessary to make them operable, Senator John G. Tower of Texas discovered that we were (not unnaturally, in the circumstances) training a few Yugoslav pilots in Texas in the use of the planes. An angry cry at once went up in the halls of Congress and elsewhere;

scoldings and threats were at once thundered out to the various echelons of the executive branch of the government most intimately concerned; and it soon developed that we were unable to persuade anyone in Washington to take the responsibility of shipping the electronic components. I was indignant. We had sold the Yugoslavs the planes, and taken money for them. The planes were useless to them without the remaining equipment. This was inexcusable behavior. We were not, after all, as I complained to the State Department, crooks.

I did everything conceivable to break this deadlock. I went home and saw the President and even got his oral approval to delivery of the components. I still could not spring the components from Washington's jealous clutch. Whether they were ever delivered or not, I do not know; if they were, it was not in my time. But in the course of trying to find out what was holding things up, I stumbled on a situation about which I could only shake my head in wonder. In one of the many discussions of this problem in my office at Belgrade, I was told by my associates that it would be impossible to arrange shipment of the components until the military aid bill for that year was passed by the Congress, because the shipment would have to be made under the authority of that legislation. "What do you mean — military aid bill?" I asked. "This is not aid. The Yugoslavs have paid cash for these items." This might be so, I was told, but when the Pentagon sold anything to anyone, the item was formally processed there as military aid, and whatever payment was made in return was paid directly into the Treasury. In the eyes of the Pentagon, therefore, and so far as it officially knew, this was military aid; and it was in this guise, evidently, that it came before the Congress.

It took some time to get this into my head. When I did grasp it, I could picture it, as I told my associates, only this way: "You and I agree that I shall sell you my watch, but on these terms: I deliver the watch to you; you then put the money into my back pocket while I am not looking; and we both pretend that the watch was a gift. I, then, shall never permit you to forget my generosity, and you will take care to be everlastingly appreciative." Obviously, in the face of such bureaucratic procedures, confusion between trade and aid could hardly be avoided.

And a second source of confusion, which afforded me scarcely less surprise, existed precisely in the fact that many people in Congress seemed unable to recognize the distinction between these two concepts — trade and aid — at all. In their view, trade with us, even on terms acceptable to us and even if we got dollar for dollar in value out of it, was to be regarded as a favor extended by us to the other party, and to be appreciated accordingly, rather as though they had been permitted to kiss our hand. The basis for this curious view always mystified me; it could just as well, when one stopped to think of it, have been argued the other way around. But the outlook had then, and has I believe to this day, considerable currency among American legislators. It is a view explicable only by the belief that there is something so wonderful about us that to be permitted to buy anything from us or to sell us anything is a species of grace conferred by us on the trading partner, to be valued and reciprocated accordingly.

12

Yugoslavia—The Conflict

THIS, then, was the background against which my duties in Belgrade had to be performed; and the resulting complications were not long in making their appearance.

The first of these — only a mild harbinger of what was to come — concerned neither trade nor aid. It concerned that miserable product of legislative hysteria mentioned in Chapter 5, above: the Captive Nations Resolution, adopted by Congress in 1959. Among the twenty-two nations, some real, some imaginary, to the liberation of which this resolution committed us, Yugoslavia figured along with the members of the Communist bloc. To the extent this measure was taken seriously and sponsored by the executive branch of the government, all of us — the State Department, the President, and I as the President's personal representative — were morally committed to the overthrow of the Yugoslav government.

The Captive Nations Resolution called upon the President to declare each year something called "Captive Nations Week." It was clear that by doing so he would be associating himself with the spirit and sense of the resolution itself. During the previous Republican administration, President Eisenhower, faithful to the Dulles policy of "liberation" in words if not in deed, had regularly taken this step. The event normally occurred, as I recall it, in the month of June. As I prepared to leave to take up my duties in Yugoslavia, in May 1961, the question was therefore imminent: Would the new Democratic administration do likewise?

It seemed to me somewhat illogical to go out as ambassador professing to wish to promote good relations with a regime which, at the same time, I was committed to overthrowing. I therefore took the matter up with Mr. McGeorge Bundy, in the White House, before leaving for my post, and urged that President Kennedy omit this confusing and offensive gesture. Soon after arrival at Belgrade, I received word that the President had agreed to omit it. In the initial stages of my service in Belgrade, I therefore took the liberty of predicting, to the Yugoslavs, that they need have no worry: things had changed, in this particular year no declaration of Captive Nations Week would be made.

One can, then, imagine my feelings when I received, one day in June, a telegram informing me cryptically that the President's intention had been reversed and that Captive Nations Week would be declared that very day. Who it was who had twisted the President's arm, I never learned; but it was clear that here, right at the start of my mission, domestic policy had triumphed clearly and dramatically over foreign policy. I should of course have recognized the obvious implications of this decision and have modified my hopes for the success of my mission. But this was only one of many problems; and in the complex fabric of diplomacy, as elsewhere in life, "hope springs eternal."

The real crisis began a year later, in June 1962, when the Foreign Aid Bill and the Trade Expansion Bill for that year came, respectively, before the Senate and the House of Representatives. On or about the seventh of June I was staggered to be informed by the State Department that Senator William Proxmire, of Wisconsin, had introduced, on June 6, an amendment to the Foreign Aid Bill barring the extension of any and all aid to Yugoslavia. So far as I know, no one in the Foreign Aid administration or in the State Department had received any forewarning of this action, or any opportunity to discuss it with the Senator, before it was taken. The amendment was watered down, within a day or so, at the instance of senators who had the interests of the farm states at heart; and as it finally entered the bill, an exception was made for the sales of surplus wheat. But even these shipments under PL 480 might go forward, it was stipulated, only if there were a formal finding by the President that the shipment was in the interests of national security, that the recipient country was "not participating directly or indirectly in any policy or programs for the Communist conquest of the world" and that this same recipient "was not controlled by any country promoting the Communist conquest of the world."

This was not all. Within a week after the receipt of this unpleasant news, another blow fell. The Ways and Means Committee of the House of Representatives, acting with the obvious blessing if not at the initiative of its chairman, Mr. Wilbur D. Mills, Democrat, of Arkansas, had introduced into the Trade Expansion Bill, then before the House, a clause requiring the executive branch of the government to cancel the extension of most-favored-nation customs treatment to Yugoslavia and Poland.

Let me attempt to explain what these amendments meant for Yugoslav-American relations.

The first of them barred, as stated, all forms of "aid" to Yugoslavia except, in certain circumstances, surplus food sales. It was perfectly clear to anyone having even the most minimal knowledge of the situation that a measure of this nature was neither necessary nor desirable. It was unnecessary, because the aid programs were, as we have seen, with very minor exceptions already in process of liquidation, and the Yugoslavs were not asking either for their continuation or for new ones to replace them. It was undesirable, because in these circumstances it could not fail to be offensive. It was hard to interpret it otherwise than as a gratuitous and studied slap at a smaller government against which, in our bilateral relations, we had no serious grievance. It was further undesirable because, while there was at the moment no thought of giving more aid to Yugoslavia, no one could be sure that circumstances would not arise in which we would want to give it. I myself, for example, while approving the liquidation of the aid programs generally, would in certain circumstances — if, for example, the schedules of payment on the existing developmental loans had been faithfully met and if there were to be a request from the Yugoslavs that we support some new and promising project — have given favorable consideration to a request for a new loan. I thought it undesirable that Yugoslavia should be left entirely dependent on Moscow for this sort of assistance. The fact that it was not desirable at the moment to give aid did not mean that it was desirable not *to be able to give it,* in any circumstances. Unforeseen contingencies could easily arise. But a clause such as this one would deprive us of all flexibility in these matters. It would place us in a position where we could not do anything for the Yugoslavs even if we found it in the national interest to do it.

The attempt to deny to the Yugoslavs the most-favored-nation customs treatment which that country had enjoyed, by treaty, for some eighty years, was even worse. This of course was a measure designed to restrict trade, not aid. There seemed to be an impression in some quarters that this term meant that Yugoslavia, enjoying such treatment, was *the* most favored of all foreign nations in the treatment its goods received at the hands of the American customs authorities. This was of course wholly erroneous. The term means, and meant, merely that the treatment given shall be not less favorable than that given to the most favored of other nations. Since such assurance is given to most of the countries of the world, what the term really signifies is simply that the country in question is assured of normal treatment under our tariff laws and will not become the object of unfavorable discrimination at the hands of the American customs authorities.

The Yugoslavs had the right to such treatment on the basis of the old US-Serbian commercial treaty of 1881. (What the amendment called for was, in effect, the denunciation by our government of this venerable treaty.) They had enjoyed such treatment even at the time when they were faithful followers of Stalin and when their country formed part of the Soviet bloc. To deprive them of it now was, for many reasons, a bitter blow. Their trade with us was small, and in our favor. It meant little to us; it meant a great deal to them. They owed us money; and they were faithfully endeavoring, through the cultivation of this trade, to earn the dollars with which to pay these debts. The denial of most-favored-nation treatment would, it was clear, hit some of their exports very severely. It would render these exports subject to the provisions of the old Smoot-Hawley Tariff of 1930, the rates of which were, on an average, some 300 percent higher than the most-favored-nation rates. There were instances in which duties would have been raised as much as 700 percent on individual Yugoslav items. The Yugoslavs were already concerned, furthermore, about the effects upon themselves of the development of the European Common Market, to which they did not belong. Denial of most-favored-nation treatment by us would mean that any advantages granted by us to the Common Market countries would not automatically be extended to them, thus placing them at an added disadvantage with relation to this powerful European grouping.

Nor were the injuries confined to what might happen when the legislation took effect. The mere announcement that such a clause had been included in the bill affected Yugoslav commercial interests adversely in a number of ways. The anti-Yugoslav elements in various parts of our country leaped at the chance to make trouble. Orders for Yugoslav goods were canceled; boycotts were organized; demonstrations took place. In some instances Yugoslav goods — at one place, little baskets, the products of peasant handicraft — were taken into the streets and burned before the supermarkets that had been selling them. And the worst of it all was the Yugoslavs had done, to my knowledge, absolutely nothing that could possibly have warranted such treatment at our hands. There was simply no way I could explain it or justify it to them. It was sheer spitefulness.

I must digress here for a moment to point out that these attempts to bind the hands of the administration in its relations with Yugoslavia raised an interesting question of theory with respect to the conduct of diplomacy generally. In the harsh realities of international life, a government influences another government through the dialectical interaction, in its own conduct, of measures favorable to the interests of that other government and measures that affect its interests adversely. Let us call these measures, for want of better description, favors and injuries, respectively. Both are, at one point or another, necessary ingredients of any effective policy: the favors in order that one may encourage and reciprocate policies on the other country's part that show a due responsibility to the interests of world peace and due consideration for the national interests of others; the injuries in order that one may be in a position to retaliate for hostile or inconsiderate policies on the other side. But if these instruments of diplomacy are to be of any value, then whoever conducts policy must be in a position to manipulate them currently, fluidly, and at will, as the situation may require. If his freedom of action is publicly restricted — if his hands are bound by rigid restrictions which mean that for a long time to come he can neither reward a friendly disposition on the other side nor chastise an unfriendly one — then these instruments are of course drained of all effectiveness. A favor which, to the certain knowledge of the other party, cannot be retracted, comes soon to be taken for granted and ceases to be regarded as a favor. An injury or hardship which, to the similar knowledge of the other party, cannot be removed, ceases to have any punitive effect; for the other party knows that whatever concessions he might make to achieve its removal would be devoid of result. It is useless, in other words, to be able to extend aid unless you also have it in your power to withdraw it; and it is useless, similarly, to deny aid unless you also have it in your power to extend it again, if circumstances change. For this reason, legislative clauses such as these, rigidly committing our government's behavior for many months into the future, could serve on principle no useful purpose. They could only irritate the other party, without offering any prospect of improving his behavior.

But beyond this: such actions were pernicious in their effect on American foreign relations because they tended to separate the ability to *act* in a sensitive question of foreign policy from the ability to *discuss* that action with a foreign government. The Department of State and the ambassador at Belgrade were there to serve as channels of communication between the Yugoslav government and our own about the problems of our mutual relations. But if we were to have no influence over the shaping of policy in such a matter, of what use was it to the Yugoslav government to be able to discuss it with us? In each of these cases the congressional action came as a complete surprise, and even shock, to the Department of State, not to mention myself. No effort had been made to consult our opinions, to explain to us the rationale of the action, to give us a chance to clear away possible misunderstandings. The Department of State, given its bureaucratic elephantiasis and the wild fragmentation of authority within its own walls, and given also its tendency to confront congressional committees either with senior figures who were ignorant or with junior ones who were cagey, guarded, and unconvincing, was admittedly not always successful in its liaison with Congress. Still, in a sensitive matter where its own ignorance could scarcely have been greater, Congress would have been better advised to leave the conduct of foreign policy in the hands of those who had been constitutionally charged with it; because external interference of this nature, separating the power to shape policy from the power to discuss it with a foreign government, could only paralyze the process of diplomacy; it could scarcely improve it.

The remainder of the tale can be told in few words.

The White House was, I believe, as shocked as I was at these congressional actions. On the day that Senator Proxmire's amendment was introduced, McGeorge Bundy addressed a letter to Senator Mike Mansfield (June 6) protesting strongly and eloquently against the insertion of the clause. "The proposed amendment," he wrote,

deprives the President . . . of the discretion necessary for the effective conduct of foreign policy. The President has not abused that discretion and would not do so in the future. . . . The President has closely limited the forms of assistance [to Yugoslavia] which he will allow. The law as it stands permits this kind of flexible and immediate response to favorable or unfavorable developments. The amendment would remove all opportunity for calculated responses, and would freeze us out of any ability to affect affairs in these countries.*

I myself returned to this country on July 1 and at once visited the President and the appropriate people in the Department of State, to see what I could do to help. I was told that plans were afoot for inducing the House of Representatives, by private discussions, to drop the most-favored-nation amendment; so I should not bring up that subject myself. As for the aid bill: the President was disinclined, for the moment, to do more than he had already done (he had pressing reasons to wish to see the bill as a whole go through, and did not wish it to be held up in a fight over this particular item); but he encouraged me to talk to individual legislators in both houses of Congress, and he facilitated, so far as he could, my contacts with them. In addition to that, he urged me to take my case to the public.

In response to the first of these suggestions, I spent an entire week tramping the halls of the buildings on Capitol Hill and arguing with various congressional figures. The experience was an instructive one, inasmuch as it showed me, as nothing else ever had,

* *New York Times,* June 7, 1962, p. 16.

the enormous gap in understanding and outlook that separated a person like myself from the likes of those I was talking with. Time after time, it seems to me, I thought I had explained to my listeners that what was at stake in the matter of the fighter planes (they all seemed to have this on their minds), was not really "aid," that the miserable airplanes were not gifts but items sold and duly paid for. Then there would be a moment of puzzled silence, after which the skeptical legislator would say something like this: "Well, Mr. Ambassador, you may be right; but I still can't see why we have to go on giving aid to a lot of damned Communists."

I also took my case to the press. The President had already released to the press, to my own surprise and consternation, portions of one of my confidential telegrams from Belgrade. It was a message written by way of reaction to the news of the two amendments. It was intended only for the eyes of my superiors in Washington, and not for those of the Yugoslavs. It could, however, scarcely have come as a surprise to them. In these excerpts, as printed by the *New York Times* on June 15, I had described the introduction of the amendments as "little short of tragic." All this had come, I pointed out,

at a time when years of untiring effort by the devoted people at this post [the Belgrade embassy] were beginning to bear fruit, when basic forces had begun to move in our direction, when recent demonstrations of anti-Western tendencies had begun to create visible strains in Yugoslav officialdom, and when continuing restraint, patience and subtlety of approach might have led to results of significance.

Senator Proxmire, stung — I suspect — by this and other criticisms of his action, then wrote to the editor of the *New York Times* a letter which appeared in that journal on June 22. Citing, as proof of Tito's subservience to Moscow, a pro-Soviet statement the latter was said to have made in 1956, the Senator went on to charge

him with "serving international communism by proselytizing
newly emerging countries in Asia and Africa to what Tito calls
'international proletarianism.' " In doing this, Tito, it was said, was
seeking "to align these countries with the Soviet bloc against the
United States and the free world." (These words evidently had reference to the Belgrade Conference.)

Bearing in mind the President's encouragement to take my case
to the public, I replied to Senator Proxmire's letter with one of my
own, published by the same paper on July 2. Taking issue with the
Senator's suggestion that the Yugoslavs had attempted to persuade
the other neutrals to associate themselves politically and militarily
with the Soviet bloc, I went on to say:

If Yugoslav influence on other neutrals has been unsatisfactory from
our standpoint, there is no reason to suppose that it has been any more
satisfactory from the standpoint of the Moscow-Peiping leaders. The
latter will be both amazed and amused, I am sure, to hear it alleged that
Yugoslavia's efforts in its relations with other neutrals have been exerted
on their behalf.

Even if what Senator Proxmire wrote about Yugoslav policies had
been accurate, this would not have affected my view of the amendment
he introduced in the Senate. The issue is not . . . that of aid or no aid
to Yugoslavia. The issue is whether the Executive Branch of the Government is to be allowed sufficient latitude to handle intelligently and
effectively a delicate problem of international affairs, and one which
has the widest implications for our approach to the problem of world
communism generally.

In the study we have devoted to Yugoslav affairs in recent months we
have overlooked, so far as I am aware, not the slightest detail of what is
known about the relations between Yugoslavia and the countries to the
east. These matters have been given most careful thought and have been
scrupulously taken into account in every recommendation that has gone
forward. . . .

. . . It is my considered judgment that no conceivable interest of our
Government will be furthered by dramatic and vindictive measures

which amount only to a self-imposed limitation on the possibilities open to us, and serve only to cut us off from any conceivable constructive approach in a vitally important area of our international relations.

In addition to this reply to Senator Proxmire, I then took the initiative in writing a much longer article for the *Washington Post and Times Herald* (published by that journal on July 8). Here, after describing the situation of Yugoslavia much as I have described it above, I termed it essential that the Yugoslavs should

move into the coming period with the confidence that if their own policies are ones which show reasonable respect for Western interests, they can have the advantages of a normal and mutually profitable political and economic relationship with the West.

This confidence, I went on to say, was precisely what the two amendments would deprive them of. Together, they would have the effect

of confronting the Yugoslavs with a closed and locked door on the Western side precisely at a time when it is imperative that it be clear to them that this door is open. Never has it been more important that the choices by which they are confronted should be fair ones, and not ones slanted, as the amendments could cause them to be, in favor of a pro-Soviet orientation. None of us can deal with the Yugoslavs successfully . . . if we have only a closed door behind us to point to.

I did not believe, I wrote, that even these amendments would have the effect of forcing Yugoslavia back into the Soviet bloc. The leaders of that country would continue to make every effort to maintain its independence whether or not our Congress showed sympathy for that effort. But it would be impossible for any of us to explain to them why we should wish to make it harder for them to do this than it already was. It was difficult to believe, I said,

that any member of Congress who knew the facts, and had reflected on their true meaning, could wish to share responsibility for the grievous narrowing of the possibilities of American statesmanship which amendments of this nature would impose.

These arguments, together with the other efforts put forward by the White House, the State Department and myself in this direction, had at least the effect of shaking the Senate on the question of the aid limitation; and the language of the bill was eventually modified in such a way as to permit us to continue with an orderly liquidation of the aid programs.

But there still remained the question of the most-favored-nation clause. This was much more serious. The Yugoslavs were not asking for aid, and did not regard it as anything to which they were rightfully entitled within the framework of normal bilateral relations. But trade was another thing. And most-favored-nation treatment was a matter of trade.

Relying on the assurances given to me in Washington in July that arrangements would probably be made in private discussions to bring about the elimination of most-favored-nation denial, provided only the matter was not pressed publicly, I, after return to Yugoslavia at the end of July, lived peacefully at my post through August and most of September, naïvely assuming, in the absence of further word from Washington, that this problem, too, was being solved. I could not have been more wrong. On the late afternoon of September 27, the bomb fell. I had already returned to my home from the office when the phone rang — a long distance call from Washington. It was Mr. Frederick G. Dutton, Assistant Secretary of State for Congressional Relations, who was calling. He had, he said, some very bad news for me. To the department's great surprise, the House-Senate conferees, just then engaged in reconciling the views of the two houses on the Trade Expansion Act, had decided to retain the clause denying most-favored-nation treatment to the Yugoslavs. The bills would now go before the two houses for final approval, and this clause, if nothing further was done to prevent it, would certainly be adopted. There was, he said, only one possibility of averting this action; and this was for me to appeal immediately and personally to the President and request his personal intervention.

Whether Mr. Dutton meant by this approach to put me on the spot or whether this was the result of his previous lack of experience with diplomatic affairs, I cannot say; but this was certainly the effect of what he had done. The call had come over the open international telephone lines. It had certainly been monitored by the Yugoslav government, as all such calls to a foreign diplomatic mission normally are anywhere in the world. The Yugoslavs, then, had heard this message as clearly as I had. If I did nothing, they would know that the last possibility of preventing this blow had not been explored, and that it had not been explored because I personally had failed to explore it. I had told them many times how averse I was to this clause; my good faith was now at stake.

I therefore summoned our old Russian butler, Alexander — the usual intermediary with the telephone central — and told him, to his startled amazement, to pick up the phone and order an immediate call, person-to-person, to the President of the United States. This he did, and, to my own amazement, the President came at once on the line. I stated my case to him in the strongest terms I could find. It was scarcely necessary for me to do this, for he knew very well how I felt. His response was: "I think that the person you should talk to is Mr. Wilbur Mills, and I will have the call transferred, if I can, to his office." This he did, and to my further surprise, I at once got Mr. Mills on the line.

Anticipating something of this sort, I had put in writing the burden of what I had to say, and in speaking to Mr. Mills, I read from this piece of paper.* I still have it, fortunately, and it gives me a faithful and exact record of the words I used. "Mr. Mills," I said,

* After making this statement to Mr. Mills, I phoned the Department of State, dictated the wording of it, and asked them to put it in writing and send it to him at once.

speaking in my official capacity as ambassador in Belgrade and against the background of thirty-five years of experience with the affairs of Eastern Europe, I must give it to you as my considered judgment that such an amendment, coming at the present time and in present circumstances, would be unnecessary, uncalled for, and injurious to United States interests. It would be taken, not only in Yugoslavia but throughout this part of the world, as evidence of a petty and vindictive spirit, unworthy of a country of our stature and responsibility. This judgment has the concurrence of every officer in the mission. If the amendment is adopted, it will be in disregard of the most earnest and serious advice we are capable of giving.

I cannot remember the exact terms of Mr. Mills's response; I can remember only that it was cursory, negative, and offered no hope whatsoever for a reversal of the action. A few days later, on October 4, the bill, still containing the offensive clause, became law. And the President, at the signing of it, joined in the paeans of praise that had been heaped upon Mr. Mills, in the Congress and elsewhere, for the great statesmanship he was held to have shown in piloting the bill to completion.

For the next ten days, I pondered the implications of this incident for myself. On October 14, my diary tells me, I took a long lonely walk of many miles through the suburbs of Belgrade, trying to come finally to terms with what had happened. Try as I might, I could not get over the logic of the essential facts. I was now fifty-eight years old. I had given most of an active lifetime to the Foreign Service. I had had, as I had pointed out to Mr. Mills, some thirty-five years of experience with the affairs of Eastern Europe. He, so far as I knew (and I find this confirmed in an article about him that appeared in the *New York Times Magazine* on February 25, 1968) had never been outside the United States. Yet in an important matter of foreign policy, affecting most intimately not only the Eastern European post at which I was stationed, but also the attitudes of surrounding countries, the elected representatives of my country had supported his judgment over my own. They had made their choice. Mr. Mills had been given a vote of confidence. I had been disavowed. And this disavowal had been dramatically exhibited to the Yugoslav government, to which I was accredited.

It would have been useless for me to remain in Yugoslavia in these circumstances. An ambassador can have usefulness only when it is believed that he has some influence at home. But no ambassador, I think, had ever had his lack of such influence more eloquently demonstrated before the government to which he was accredited than was mine in the course of this single phone call. I might, from that time on, remain *bien vu*, as an individual, by the Yugoslav leaders. They might continue to regard me with personal respect and even with a certain sympathizing commiseration. But it would have been quixotic to suppose that my influence with them, from here on out, could be any greater than my influence with Washington had been shown to be.

One could try to accept this fact without bitterness or recrimination. But one could not get around it. It took the heart out of any further belief in the possible usefulness of a diplomatic career. And the potential personal enjoyments of such a career, great as they were, in Yugoslavia, particularly, were not great enough to compensate for the formidable drawbacks — the dreary diplomatic receptions, the many hours wasted in empty formality, and above all, the limitations on the ability to study and to write for publication — which this way of life has always involved.

I decided not to act abruptly. Only three months later did I apprise the Department of State of my desire to resume my life in Princeton at the beginning of the next academic year. But the decision had been taken, in the roads and streets of the Belgrade suburbs, on that unhappy morning.

Two months after the most-favored-nation incident, Tito made his triumphal visit to Moscow. I had nothing to say against this publicly. I had always taken the position, vis-à-vis the press, that we wished for Yugoslavia good and pleasant relations with all countries. We had no desire that good relations with us on their part should proceed at the cost of their good relations with anyone else. I also had no great fears about it privately. I knew that Tito, however gratifying might be the reception he received in Moscow, would not be disposed to sacrifice or to compromise in any way, if he could help it, the independence he had won at the cost of so much danger and difficulty. It would simply have been nice, I thought, had I been able to fortify him, as he made that journey to Moscow, with the assurance that in resisting Soviet pressures for a reassociation of Yugoslavia with the Soviet bloc he could always be confident of an alternative, in the form of friendly, reliable and mutually profitable relations — above all, economic relations — with the United States.

I was, however, now disarmed, and could only remain silent and passive. The Yugoslavs would now have to fight their own battles as though we did not exist.

It was summer — the summer of 1963 — before I finally left Belgrade. The intervening months were, by and large, pleasant ones.

Not that official relations were untroubled — God knows. The American longshoremen's unions refused to load or unload Yugoslav ships in American ports; the Yugoslav consulate in Chicago was bombed; Congress occupied itself with retaliatory measures against countries, including Yugoslavia, whose ships visited Cuba; in short, the sterling quality of American anticommunism continued to be demonstrated daily in a dozen unpleasant ways.

But my own relationship to all this was now a detached one; and by virtue of this fact my personal relations with the Yugoslav leaders were now placed on a different and in many ways more pleasant footing. They knew, now, the full measure of my helplessness. They did not hold it against me. They knew that to a limited extent, and for political reasons as compelling to them as were President Kennedy's reasons to him, they had even contributed to this helplessness. But recognizing its existence, they were now at liberty to treat me as an individual and as a personal friend — a friend who, they knew, understood their situation and had done what he could, albeit unsuccessfully, to assure them of fair treatment on the other side of the Atlantic and elsewhere in the West. I met them now, therefore, on a new and more relaxed basis. They did not bother to bring to me their complaints about the harassments to which their ships and officials were exposed in the United States; and it would have been idle for me to grumble any more about the tenor of Tito's public statements or the unfair treatment in the Yugoslav press of our position vis-à-vis the underdeveloped nations — or Vietnam. They knew that even if they were to desist from these statements and practices, I, personally, would not be able to assure them any better treatment in Washington than they were now receiving.

So we now enjoyed each other's company as individuals. On at least three occasions, in those remaining months, I had long, relaxed, and frank talks with Tito. On March 14, 1963, in particular, I visited him at his retreat at Brioni. This time, instead of receiving me in the formal mansion on the main island, he had me ferried over to his own personal hideout on a small adjacent one. There he showed me his personal carpenter's workshop, after which we settled down to a pleasant hour or two over a bottle of wine. Now that it was clearly understood all around that I represented nobody and was talking only as a species of disembodied spirit, I outlined to him what I thought might, in happier circumstances, be the basis of a tacit mutual understanding between our two countries — a basis which, if accepted, would give us both a greater degree of confidence and security in our dealings with each other. I cast it in terms not of anything that either of us would be asked formally to agree to, but rather of mutual expectations — of what each of us would permit himself to expect, whether he liked it or not, of the other. I have the notes of this scheme, as I jotted them down at breakfast that day, before our talk; and I reproduce them here, for they summarize whatever wisdom I was able to gain from these two years of struggle with the problems of American-Yugoslav relations.

We Americans would expect, I suggested:

(a) that Yugoslavia would remain a Socialist state in the Marxist-Leninist sense, and would continue to emphasize that quality publicly;

(b) that Yugoslavia would continue to manifest a high degree of solidarity with other Socialist countries on world problems;

(c) that Yugoslavia's internal institutions, social and political, would remain substantially as defined in the new constitution, and would in any case not be deliberately altered to fit Soviet patterns.

(d) that Yugoslavia would not join the Warsaw Pact nor would she enter into any special arrangements of military collaboration with the USSR, such as coordination of military plans, acceptance of Soviet military installations or units on Yugoslav territory, etc.; and

(e) that Yugoslavia would continue to refrain from any and all efforts, either independent or in association with members of the Communist bloc, to subvert non-Communist states, particularly those of the Western Hemisphere.

Yugoslavia, on the other hand, would expect of us:

(a) that the United States would not, as a rule, extend to Yugoslavia any special economic assistance, although it would, when warranted by special circumstances, continue to do what it could, within the framework of existing legislation, to provide liberal credit terms for the purchase, against dollar repayment, of wheat and other surplus agricultural commodities in the United States;

(b) that the United States would extend to Yugoslavia, on the other hand, all normal facilities for commercial intercourse, including most-favored-nation treatment;

(c) that the executive branch of the United States government would

exert its influence to create and maintain an atmosphere of public opinion in the United States favorable to the maintenance of friendly and
correct mutual relations;

(d) that the United States would assure to Yugoslavia the possibility
of the purchase, against dollar repayment, of spare parts for military
equipment already purchased; and

(e) that the United States would continue to use its influence to promote a favorable development of Yugoslavia's economic relations with
Western European countries (i.e., the Common Market).

I suggested that so long as neither side found itself seriously disappointed in these expectations, both governments should endeavor
to keep relations normal and pleasant: cultural relations would be
cultivated as heretofore; the treatment accorded to each other's citizens in matters of residence, travel, activity, etc., would not be
worsened over what it then was; economic relations would be encouraged and promoted. And efforts would be made to support this
pattern of relations, ultimately, with a suitable sequence of official
courtesy visits.

I took no detailed notes on the actual course of this conversation,
and it is not for me to attempt to formulate President Tito's reactions. No one, obviously, could expect him to commit himself on
the spur of the moment to a set of propositions which represented
only the musing reflections of an individual who had no power to
speak for his own government in such matters, and which only too
plainly would have found no support at the moment in the halls of
that government. But I remain today of the opinion that if governments took greater pains to clarify, in this manner, exactly what
they might reasonably expect of one another, and spent less time
protesting over things they had every reason to expect, or trying to
get the other party to sign up to formal written undertakings to do
this or that or to refrain from this or that, then the course of international relations might in many cases be eased. I thought it then

not unreasonable to suppose that if the Yugoslavs were to find themselves justified in the expectations I had defined above, Americans would not be disappointed in addressing to them the reciprocal expectations also there set forth. In a way, I think this is the way things eventually worked out, in subsequent years. But I was at the time, as I say, a disembodied spirit.

We left Belgrade — Mrs. Kennan, the two youngest children, and myself — on July 27, 1963, on the air attaché's old C-47, for a final farewell visit to Brioni, and then to the West.

It is not without emotion that I read, today, the cryptic entries of my pocket diary from those last two or three days of our Yugoslav experience. The years in that country had, for all the official disappointments, been a wonderful time, full of color, discovery, and warm, rich personal associations. And these last days were full — fuller than usual, I think, because of the nature of the country and its people — of those tugs of the heart that attend, for me, all partings, reminding me that each of them, in its way, constitutes a small fragment of the phenomenon of death. The Skoplje earthquake had taken place only on the day before our departure. The tragedy of it had struck us with particular force because we had visited Skoplje less than a fortnight before. I had gone down at once, when I heard the news, and given blood at one of the great popular blood-collection centers that had already been established in Belgrade. The remainder of that last day had been taken up, between good-bye ceremonies, visits, and presentation of gifts, with telegrams to Washington about the earthquake, and efforts to arrange for the immediate dispatch of an emergency field hospital from our military establishment in Germany. (The efforts were successful, and I was immensely proud of the speed and efficiency with which this unit arrived, moved into Skoplje, and went to work.)

I shall let the diary tell, in all its weary terseness, of the last hours.

July 27, 1963

Baggage was packed on truck and removed. Out to airport. Said our goodbyes. Everybody depressed and horrified at the dimensions of Skoplje earthquake.

Proceeded, in Air Attaché's plane, under command of Colonel White, to Brioni. Arrived there (on the mainland) at 12:30 P.M. Were met by Kljun (the President's personal aide) at the airport, and by Soldatić (the Presidential Chief of Protocol) at the dock on the other side. The others went swimming while I slept. Then, in late afternoon, we all went for a walk to the ruins of the Roman Villa and prowled around them.

Dinner — very informal, on account of the Skoplje disaster — at the hotel, with Koča (Koča Popović, famous military leader of the Partisan War, then just terminating years of service as Yugoslav Foreign Minister) and Madame Popović, and Lekić (Yugoslav diplomat, about to assume the duties of Ambassador to the United Nations) and his wife. All very much anticlimax. Koča, tanned and a little physically tired from his strenuous vacationing, obviously dragooned into attendance.

July 28

I stayed in the hotel most of the morning, telephoning to Belgrade. Learned, to my delight, of the arrival of the field hospital, during the night, at the Surčin hospital. At 12:25, we were driven — all of us — to the President's house on Brioni, where we were given a semiformal luncheon. Present, in addition to the President and Madame Broz, were Kardelj (Vice President) and his wife, Gošnjak (Minister of Defense) and wife, Lekić and wife, and Soldatić. The children sat at table, and were very good. Tito made a graceful little farewell toast, referring to me as a "naučnik" (a scholar). I replied very badly. The catastrophe threw a pall over the entire event, and tended to monopolize the discussion.

At 3:30 we were already over on the mainland and at the airport again. Much talk about whether Christopher (13 years old) should or should not discard his turtle; but he contrived to hang on to it.

By 4:30 we were at Venice.

Thus ended — somewhat anticlimactically, with many confused tearings at the heart, but in good time, I believe — the last of many diplomatic assignments.

There was a small sequel to this experience. Just as I was leaving Belgrade, I heard of plans in the Department of State to invite President Tito to visit the United States. This was no doing of mine. I had envisaged eventual high-level visits when and if relations between the two countries were placed on a sound basis. At the moment, with the cancellation of the old commercial treaty and the denial of most-favored-nation treatment presumably looming before us, I did not consider this to be the case. I doubted — rightly, as it turned out — that we were even in a position to give the Yugoslav chief of state a dignified and suitable reception in our country. The initiative for the visit came, I must assume, from the Department of State, the workings of whose mind in such matters I was unable to decipher even after some thirty-five years of acquaintance with it. The Secretary of State, Mr. Dean Rusk, had visited Belgrade in the spring of the year, for purposes no less obscure to me than the invitation to Tito to visit the United States; perhaps the idea was his initiative. The State Department of that day viewed visits, so far as I could observe, as a substitute for statesmanship.

In any case, Tito, accompanied by Madame Broz and his usual official retinue, arrived in the United States some time in mid October 1963. No new ambassador having as yet been appointed, the President asked Mrs. Kennan and myself to go down to Williamsburg, where the party was to be received and initially accommodated, to welcome them on his behalf, and to accompany them on their visit to Washington. This we did. Tito and his party treated us as old friends; we enjoyed their company; and Colonial Williamsburg, in the capacity of their first local hosts in this country, did well by them.

But the visit had a strong undercurrent, and sometimes more than an undercurrent, of anxiety and unpleasantness. The members of the Yugoslav party were all well aware that the reason why they were housed at Williamsburg was that our government was unable, or unwilling, to protect them from hostile demonstration, insult, and possibly even worse, in Washington. For the meeting with the President, the following day, it was necessary to fly them by helicopter directly from Williamsburg to the White House grounds. Even then the hostile demonstrators, including some in full Nazi uniform, were assembled in droves across the street from the White House; and their savage screams and chants were audible even over the strains of the two national anthems, as the ceremony of welcome proceeded. The Yugoslav guests were unable to understand then, as am I to this day, why people in the uniform of our late enemies should have been permitted thus to demonstrate, within a few yards of the White House, against the head of a state that had been associated with us in the struggle against that enemy.

I did not accompany the Yugoslav party to New York; but I was told that there things were much worse. The party was housed, if my memory is correct, in the Waldorf Towers. The street outside was never free of hostile demonstrators, many of whom, one suspects, were not even American citizens; it proved impossible for the women of the Yugoslav party even to eat in the hotel's coffee shop: demonstrators were permitted into the shop, where they stood on the chairs and hurled insults and imprecations, even including the epithet "prostitutes," at these diplomatic guests — this with the evident tolerance and sympathy of the New York police. This was all the more painful because the guests in question, as anyone who knew them could testify, were women of great quality and spirit, most of whom had fought in the ranks of the partisan army in the struggle against the Germans. They were decidedly unaccustomed to such treatment, and would not easily be made to forget it.

One must remember, in this connection, that I myself had only recently traveled thousands of miles in Yugoslavia, often in most intimate contact with the population, and had never once met with anything other than kindness and courtesy.

There was, fortunately, at least one pleasant day for our unhappy visitors. It was the day they spent at Princeton, as guests of the University. Once again, Mrs. Kennan and I found ourselves automatically in their entourage, and accompanied them on their comings and goings. The East Coast autumn was at its golden best; the abundant Princeton foliage was in color; the University was a relaxed and genial host; people smiled at the cavalcade from the streets; there were no clenched fists or imprecations. I was pleased at the thought that these Yugoslav friends could return to their country with the knowledge that there was at least one place in the United States where they could be decently received.

But I was still mystified, and remain so now, as to the rationale of the whole procedure. I find it hard to believe that Yugoslav-American relations were bettered by it. And I puzzle, too, over the question of what is wrong with the outlooks and habits of a great country which professes itself unable to assure to the personal guest of its own President, so long as that guest is on its territory, immunity from the most disgusting sort of insult and harassment. You don't have to invite a guest; but when you invite him and he comes, you owe it to yourself to see that he receives a guest's treatment. Here in this small instance, as in many larger ones, I have been tempted to ask whether a country that cannot do better than this should not recognize certain limitations on its ability to play a major active role in international affairs.

I was impressed, on the day when I escorted President Tito to the White House, with the political sensitivity and skill with which President Kennedy edited and improved the luncheon speech I had drafted for him, and the tactful courtesy with which he treated this unusual guest. I could not suspect, of course, that this was the last time I would ever see him.

Our personal relations, the most-favored-nation hassle notwithstanding, had remained good. I had always been grateful to him for his patient attention to the things I had written. During the period of my service in Belgrade, he had given orders that all my messages of substance were to be sent to the White House, and he had evidently read them quite faithfully. I had also seen him on a number of occasions, and had never failed to admire the quiet youthful gallantry with which, as it seemed to me, he bore the strains of his high office. He had always treated me, an older person, with a mixture of courtesy and respectful curiosity.

I bore him no ill will for his failure to help me in the rougher passages of Yugoslav-American relations. I could imagine what his political problems were. I thought I knew the sort of advice he was getting from other people — notably from his domestic political advisors. I was sure that it was not with happy feelings that he had seen himself obliged to lay my diplomatic career on Mr. Mills's altar. Having always tried to dissuade him and others from addressing unrealistic expectations to the Yugoslavs, I was not in a good position to address similar expectations to him.

Some three years later, I was interviewed about these experiences, in Princeton, by my good friend, the late Louis Fischer, for the Oral History Project of the John F. Kennedy Library. I was asked by Louis on that occasion whether I had not found Kennedy, despite "the brilliance and precision of his mind and the beautiful style, the beautiful figure and his achievements as President" (these were Louis's words), to be "cold." My reply, the transcript tells me, was this:

Louis, not exactly cold. I didn't feel this. I felt that he had a certain real warmth, but that he was, in a sense, shy and somewhat set apart by his family background in a way that members of large and very solid families sometimes are. In other words, a man who has had such an overpowering family intimacy as I felt he had had often finds this, I think, almost enough in life, and it is not so easy for him to seek real friendships outside of it. This was my feeling: that no outsider could ever enter into his intimate circle at this stage of his life. . . . He had, of course, the sort of politician-actor's countenance. What Freud called the "persona" — the outer personality, that is, as distinct from the "ego"

— was very highly developed with him. As in the case of most people who are on the political stage, he was acting his part in a way most of the time. But he always treated me, and others that I could see in his presence . . . in a kindly fashion — and not really coldly. One didn't have the feeling that there was any underlying contempt or callousness or cruelty.

Shortly after the Tito visit, on October 22, to be exact, precisely one month before the President's assassination, I had occasion to write to him, giving him my impression of the visit. But thinking of him as I last saw him there in the White House, stumbling with this ineffable gallantry through the dark forest of pressures so cruel and choices so hard, I was moved to add a brief personal note and to enclose it with the official letter. The note read as follows:

Dear Mr. President:

You get many brickbats, and of those who say approving and encouraging things not all are pure of motive. I am now fully retired and a candidate for neither elective nor appointive office. I think, therefore, that my sincerity may be credited if I take this means to speak a word of encouragement. I am full of admiration, both as a historian and as a person with diplomatic experience, for the manner in which you have addressed yourself to the problems of foreign policy with which I am familiar. I don't think we have seen a better standard of statesmanship in the White House in the present century. I hope you will continue to be of good heart and allow yourself to be discouraged neither by the appalling pressures of your office nor by the obtuseness and obstruction you encounter in another branch of the government. Please know that I and many others are deeply grateful for the courage and patience and perception with which you carry on.

Very sincerely yours

He replied, on October 28, addressing me for the first time as "Dear George." "Your handwritten note of October 22," he wrote, is a letter I will keep nearby for reference and reinforcement on hard days. It is a great encouragement to have the support of a diplomat and historian of your quality, and it was uncommonly thoughtful for you to write me in this personal way.

The receipt of this personal note, from a man who had less than four weeks to live, redeemed in large degree the disappointments of this generally enjoyable assignment.

Epilogue

THIS completes the account of the major episodes of an official and public career. The assignment in Yugoslavia was to be the last of them. With its completion, nothing remained but further years of the normal life of what might be called a semi-public figure in and outside the United States: the letter-writing, visitor-receiving, speech-giving, and conference-attending existence, of which the Almighty may be able to measure the usefulness; the subject certainly cannot do so.

I see, on looking over these pages, that the account of these various episodes lends itself, in major outlines, to a depressing interpretation. I would like, before ending the tale, to do what I can to correct this effect, particularly as concerns the life of the Foreign Service Officer.

It is true that the function of American career diplomacy is marked by a certain tragic contradiction. The Foreign Service Officer is taught and encouraged to believe that he is serving the *national* interest — the interest, that is, of the country as a whole — in its external relations. He finds himself working, nevertheless, for people to whom this is not the main concern. Their main concern is domestic politics; and the interests they find themselves pursuing in this field of activity are not only often but usually in conflict with the requirements of a sensible national diplomacy. Such is the degree of egocentricity of the participants in the American domestic-political struggle that the possibility of taking action — or, more commonly, making statements — in the field of external relations presents itself to them primarily as a means of producing this or that effect on the political scene. The result is that American diplomacy is seldom conducted solely for what appear to be its ostensible ends. It is often so conducted when the questions at issue are ones in which no strong domestic-political issue is visible. It is also so conducted, within reasonable limits, in time of war or great national danger. But for the remainder, official Washington is inclined to view whatever happens in its own internal relationships as much more important than whatever is happening elsewhere in the world, or indeed in its relations with the rest of the world. The result is that the objectives of American diplomacy, as the career diplomatist is trained to see them, tend to be different ones than those frequently reflected in the instructions he receives from his government. And since he is helpless to achieve what he considers to be his objectives without governmental support, these objectives are often not possible of achievement at all.

It would not be so bad, perhaps, if this incongruity could be admitted. But it is the very essence of the exercise that it must never be. The exploitation of external relationships in the interest of internal political competition is a procedure dependent for its success precisely on the denial of its own nature. To be politically effective at home, the domestically inspired foreign policy ploy must masquerade with reasonable plausibility as a genuine measure of foreign policy. Even if the apparatus of diplomacy were to be staffed exclusively by political aides and supporters of leading Washington officials, bent only on promoting the political fortunes of the latter, their activity would still have to be disguised as the promotion of national interest.

The period from 1945 to 1949 was one of those rare times (I am not sure, in fact, that there were actually any others except briefly after World War I) when the conduct of America's peacetime diplomacy may be said to have had its own integrity as purely an exercise in foreign policy. This was partly, no doubt, a carry-over from the atmosphere of dedicated public service that had marked, together with all its mistakes, the diplomacy of the war. The continued presence, or in some cases the spirit, of such men as General George Marshall, Henry Stimson, James Forrestal, Robert Lovett and John J. McCloy — all in a sense voluntary and nonpolitical laborers in the governmental vineyard — still dominated the Washington scene. And the challenge posed by Stalinist communism, in the face of the severe dislocations and general instability of the post-hostilities period, was still strong enough to impose on Washington generally a sense of the primacy of foreign policy. But all this changed with the election of Harry Truman to the presidency in his own right, in 1948. With this development, the vultures of domestic politics swarmed back onto the scene, insisting that the external relations of the country were no longer important enough to be permitted to interfere with the struggle for internal political power, clamoring to be given the due of which they had so long been deprived. Normality took over.

The experiences recounted in this volume all took place in the ensuing years. They all reflected, inevitably, the contradiction described above. And the reflection was all the more harrowing in my own case because of a tendency on my own part (it may well be a weakness) to a total disregard for the American domestic-political process. Others were able to discern in its turgid stirrings momentous issues — issues of such worldwide significance as to deserve precedence over immediate questions of foreign relations. The outside world, too, these others felt, had a vital stake in the triumph of this or that cause in American political life. They were therefore able to view with resignation, if not with understanding, the primacy accorded to these causes in the underlying motivation of American diplomacy.

Not so I. A stricter sense of administrative logic; a greater fastidi-
ousness about the allotment of tasks and responsibilities; the sense of
need for a neat and precise delimitation of functions; a preference
for hierarchy and authority over compromise and manipulation;
and a distaste amounting almost to horror for the chaotic disorder
of the American political process: all these affected my view of political Washington. I did not question the necessity of this dreary
confusion. I did not blame the people who took part in it for doing
what they did. Someone had to do it. It was a matter of temperament. For some of them I even had high respect. But I saw it as a
regrettable, if unavoidable, concession to the frailties of human
nature; and thought one should not deceive oneself about what it
was, or expect it to be more. Where others saw a stage on which
momentous issues were being dramatically resolved, I saw only a
sordid, never-ending Donnybrook among pampered and inflated
egos; and I could never bring myself even to dare to hope that anything very constructive or worthwhile might come out of it. This
being the case, I reacted painfully and without resilience to its
frequent intrusions into foreign policy.

Our function, the function of career diplomacy, was, as it appeared to me, a pure one: a matter of duty, dedication, reason and
integrity. Despite my distaste for the nature of the domestic-
political process, I never doubted, in those years, the basic decency
of our national purpose, the desirability of our gaining the respect
and understanding of others, the possibility of our playing a useful
and constructive role in the world, and the propriety of our effort
to do so. I was wholly prepared to accept the thesis that the cause
of peace and of world progress depended very importantly, if not
exclusively, on the soundness of concept and quality of leadership
we might be able to bring to our conduct as a world power. I was
never cynical, therefore, about the significance of our role in world
affairs; nor did I ever doubt, even when in sharpest disagreement

with individual elements of policy, that we could and should be a force for the good in world affairs; that the general thrust of our diplomacy had positive, rather than negative, significance; that to serve the improvement and cultivation of our relations with other countries was to serve a good cause. This last seemed to me to represent, in fact, a responsibility of the utmost solemnity, beyond comparison more important than any of the personal ambitions or party interests which found expression in domestic-political life. When, therefore, these latter factors insinuated themselves into the diplomatic process, as they so often did, this struck me as an intolerable corruption of its essential integrity. I felt as I can imagine the surgeon might feel if told to deflect the knife and make the cut in a different and unsuitable place because he might look better, so doing, to people in the seats of the theater.

If, then, my efforts and undertakings in diplomacy seemed generally to end in failure, the failures must be judged in the light of these idiosyncrasies. And their gravity, as personal disappointments, must not be overrated. They were not all there was. Diplomacy, as a career, is tragic only in its results, not normally in its experiences. There were thousands of mornings, in the thirty-odd years of that life, when the journey to the office was marked by the joy of living and the delight in foreign scenes; when amusement as well as exasperation was derived from the ineptness of the telegrams from the Department of State found lying on the desk; when a sense of triumph was derived from the surmounting, by sheer ingenuity, of official incomprehension at home; when minor tasks were challenging and enjoyable; and when, above all, one warmed oneself, and found meaning for life, in the friendship and companionship of colleagues, not to mention the sympathy and loyalty received at home in a profession where man and wife share problems, triumphs and disappointments as in few others. It was a rich life in detail, if awkward and confused in the broader pattern. More than that, it was educational, as few other careers can be, and seldom without value as a preparation for the life of a scholar that was later to come.

Recognizing the inability of the individual to survey with any degree of objectivity and clarity the usefulness of his own strivings — recognizing, to use the words of our forefathers, that God's purposes, even if they were visible to us, which they are not, would not be likely to be identical with our own — I am disinclined to attempt to assess, even in my own mind, the usefulness of this career. Like any life, of any older person, seen in retrospect by an older person, it contains many individual episodes I wish could have been otherwise: things said — left unsaid; things omitted — done; things done — done otherwise or not done at all. But viewing it as a whole, I find no regrets for it, and consider myself no less fulfilled than most others.

A French writer once wrote, with that marvelous pithiness to which the French language sometimes lends itself: "Dans les choses humaines rarement peut on tout; on peut un peu. C'est toute une vie que de realiser ce peu." * These memoirs are the account, in my case, of that "peu." I hope the reader will not expect them to be more.

* Paul Marin, *Français et Russes vis à vis la Triple Alliance*. Paris, 1890.

Postscript

The Moving Finger writes; and, having writ,
Moves on: nor all your Piety nor Wit
Shall lure it back to cancel half a Line,
Nor all your Tears wash out a Word of it.

Edward Fitzgerald, *Rubáiyát of Omar Khayyám*

TWENTY years have now passed since the last of the episodes treated in these memoirs, and fifteen since the memoirs themselves were completed. These latter are of course not exactly what they would have been had they been written today; for the perspective is never the same at any two periods in a man's life. For this same reason I view the book with greater detachment today than I did when the first of these epilogues was written. I see it, in fact, as the reflection of two quite different efforts. The first of these was the struggle of a single man, as described in the book, to come to terms with his epoch and with himself. The second was the effort of that same man to stand off, at a later period of his life, and to view that struggle with the maximum of detachment (total detachment is of course never possible) and to assess its value with a reasonable measure of honesty, objectivity, and fairness all around.

Well, it is not the part of the man seventy-nine years of age to set himself up in judgment over the man of sixty-five and to pronounce upon the success or failure of those efforts. Others have done that. Others will presumably continue to do it. What can most usefully be done at this moment is to invite attention to the great changes in external environment that have taken place since the last of the events described in these volumes took place, and to ask how these relate to the life described in the memoirs and to the author's critical judgment of that life.

It is one of the most ominous marks of our own time that the moving finger now not only writes but writes with a gathering, and indeed terrifying, swiftness. These memoirs were ones concerned primarily with American foreign policy and particularly with the relationship between the United States and the Soviet Union. If one could measure graphically the pace of change in these areas over the past twenty years what would emerge would be, I suspect, an exponential curve — one of accelerating speed, as in an explosion. Consider only what has happened in these two decades: Vietnam; the Nixon-Kissinger effort at a balanced policy towards the great Communist powers, conducted under the somewhat misleading name of "détente"; the 1973 war in the Near East; Watergate and the disintegration of the Nixon-Kissinger initiatives; the Iranian hostage crisis; the events in Afghanistan and Poland; the final deterioration of the Soviet-American relationship under the Reagan administration; and the great polarization of Western opinion on the subject of nuclear weaponry, as unleashed by the question (in itself of inferior importance) of the stationing of intermediate-range weapons on, or directed against, the territory of Western and Central Europe.

In normal circumstances an author can derive satisfaction from the pleasing fancy that his views and insights, as set forth long ago in an autobiographical work of this sort, have been vindicated by the passage of time. There are passages in these memoirs, I suppose, if one cared to look for them, which would lend themselves to this sort of interpretation; for where the material itself fails fully to justify it, the self-esteem of the author easily supplies whatever is missing.

But this present moment is not conducive to any such self-indulgence; and I must confess to having no heart for it. Whether or not some of the insights brought forward in these volumes were prophetic — whether or not some of the views were vindicated by the intervening events — all this, seen through the growing darkness of the nuclear shadow now lengthening upon us, is of supreme unimportance.

The author has tried, in more recent writings (particularly *The Nuclear Delusion*, Pantheon Books, 1982), to bring out something of the true significance of this shadow; and, because the shadow is so largely self-engendered, he has tried to suggest ways in which we ourselves might move to dispel it. But it is a shadow that has been forty years in the gathering; and hence no single view of its gravity or of the possibilities for its removal can be fully explained without reference to the lifetime experience out of which that view was formed.

The reappearance of these memoirs comes at a time when this entire subject, and sometimes even the author's own small contribution to the discussion of it, are increasingly preoccupying public attention. This is the author's justification for hoping that their appearance will serve to give greater depth to what he himself has written; will bring out more clearly the origins of what is unquestionably the greatest problem of our time, if not for any time; and will finally, by revealing some of the places where we may have gone off the track, suggest some of the places where, with greater courage and with sober reflection, we might get back onto it again.

George Kennan
Princeton, 1983

Annex

FOREIGN SERVICE DISPATCH 116, of September 8, 1952
FROM AMERICAN EMBASSY, MOSCOW
TO DEPARTMENT OF STATE, WASHINGTON
SUBJECT: The Soviet Union and the Atlantic Pact

IN view of what appears to be the increasing importance of the problems revolving around the impact of NATO policies and activities on the Soviet Union, and of the probability that these problems may soon have to be the object of a careful examination within our government, I thought that it might be useful for me to set forth at this time certain general considerations concerning the place which the North Atlantic Pact has had in Soviet thinking and the effect it has had on Soviet policy.

When World War II came to an end, the leaders of the Soviet Union had no desire to face another major foreign war for a long, long time to come. Within the Soviet Union, the war had left great exhaustion and physical damage in its train. In addition to this, it had meant a setback of approximately a decade in the effort of the Soviet leaders to make out of the traditional Russian territory a powerful military-industrial center. It was plain that even when recovery from the damages and fatigues of the war had been effected, Russia would still be a country with a crude and unbalanced industrial foundation, lacking an adequate energetics basis and a modern transportation system. Finally, in the newly won satellite area, the Kremlin faced a formidable problem in the task of consolidation of its power, involving the liquidation of the older influential classes and political groups, the training of a new administrative class, the formation of new police and military forces, etc. All of these things were bound to take time. The building of a modern transportation system in the Soviet Union, in the absence of major aid from capitalist sources, would alone represent at least a ten- to fifteen year operation. Another major military involvement, striking into the heart of the programs for the completion of these tasks, would obviously have most disruptive and undesirable effects, in part even dangerous to the security of Soviet power. For all of these specific domestic reasons the Kremlin leaders had no desire, at the close of World War II, to become involved in another major foreign war for the foreseeable future, and this — in terms of Soviet policy determination — meant anything up to fifteen or twenty years.

Nor, we may safely conclude, did the Soviet leaders think it likely in the years 1945–1946 that any such war would be forced upon them in the immediately forthcoming period. The Western democracies were also exhausted from the long exertion. The United States was demobilizing with great rapidity. In Japan, although the Soviet Union had been excluded from any direct voice in the control, the occupying forces were for various reasons following a policy little different in many respects from that which Moscow would have urged, involving in particular complete demilitarization and the rapid dismantlement of the military-industrial potential of the country. Above all, Germany, most important of all countries from the standpoint of Soviet security, lay prostrate: occupied, dismembered, and divided — a considerable portion of her territory and military potential actually ceded to the Soviet Union or to Soviet satellites and a further proportion under Soviet occupation. In these circumstances, the formation of a foreign military coalition which could threaten the Soviet Union did not loom as a likely eventuality on the Soviet horizon. The men in the Kremlin could hope that it would be many years, at any rate, before they would have reason to fear that a war might be forced upon them by foreign initiative.

Before we leave this question of the outlook of the Kremlin on the problems of war or peace at the conclusion of World War II, let us hasten to recognize two things that this outlook did *not* mean.

In the first place, it did *not* mean a relinquishment on the part of the Kremlin of the hope of further expanding its power in the coming period. We must remember here that the Bolshevik leaders had never been taught to view an outright military attack by the Soviet Union on the capitalist world as a promising or correct approach, much less the only possible approach, to the task of expanding Communist power. This was not for reasons of moral scruple, but for a number of other reasons: among them the congenital caution of the land-power-minded and semi-Oriental Russian statesman; the specific calculation, prevalent up to that time, that communism was still weaker than the main forces of capitalism and must avoid an open and all-out contest with them as a matter of common prudence; and finally, the belief that the capitalist world was itself afflicted with incurable weaknesses, divisions and diseases which would operate with inexorable logic to weaken its unity and its power, even in the absence of a major military conflict between the forces of "socialism" and "capitalism."

In these circumstances, ever since the beginning of the revolution it had been orthodox Communist strategy not to seek an open and general military confrontation with capitalist power, but rather precisely to avoid such confrontation and to conduct the attack on the capitalist world in a much more cautious manner, representing what Lenin termed a "state of partial war," and involving the elastic and opportunistic use of a wide variety of tactics including outstandingly such things as deception, concealed penetration and subversion, psychological warfare, and above all the adroit exploitation of every conceivable form of division in capitalist society, whether on the international scale or within the domestic framework of capitalist states. By such means, it was considered, the Soviet Union could avoid the danger of annihilation that had always to be considered to reside in a general war between communism and capitalism, and yet make the most of those weaknesses, divisions and diseases to which the capitalist world was held to be a prey.

Actually, the conditions that existed as World War II came to an end seemed to offer high promise for the success of such tactics. The effects of Nazi rule on the social fabric of the occupied countries, as well as of Germany herself, had weakened the traditional institutions of those countries, and had in fact performed a good deal of the work which the Communists would in any case have wished to carry out in order to soften these countries up for seizure of power by Communist minorities. The postwar exhaustion and bewilderment of peoples everywhere heightened vulnerability to Communist pressures and deceits. The positions gained in Eastern Europe by the advance of the Red Army in the final phases of the war, plus the Soviet right, on the basis of Yalta and Potsdam, to a prominent voice in the determination of the future of Germany, protected by the veto power in the Council of Foreign Ministers, made it seem to Moscow implausible that vigor and hope and economic strength could ever be returned to the Western European area otherwise than on Moscow's terms; and these terms, in the Kremlin's mind, would be built around a set of conditions in which the triumph of Soviet-controlled forces would be assured. In France and Italy, furthermore, the Communists had succeeded in exploiting both the resistance to the Germans and ultimately the liberation from them, for purposes of infiltration into every possible point of political, military and economic control, and had thereby reached positions of influence from which it seemed most unlikely that they could be dislodged without chaos and civil war. In these circumstances the Kremlin had good reason to hope that a relatively brief period — let us say three to five years — would see Communist power, or at least Communist domination, extended to the Western European area in general, even in the absence of any further military effort by the Soviet Union. By virtue of such a development, as Moscow saw it, the preponderance of military-industrial strength in the world would be assembled under Soviet control. England would represent at best an isolated industrial slum, extensively dependent on the Communist-controlled Continent across the channel. Taken together with the possibilities for Communist success in China, where the immediately desired phase of "expelling the imperialists" seemed to be progressing almost unbelievably well with no effort at all on Moscow's part, all this meant that prospects were not bad for the rapid advance of the Kremlin to a dominant and almost unchallengeable position in world affairs. Thus the lack of desire or expectancy for a new major foreign war did not mean that Moscow had no hope for the expansion of Bolshevik power in the postwar period.

The second thing that was *not* implied in this Soviet view about war, at the termination of the great military struggle with the Germans, was the necessity for any drastic demobilization of Soviet military strength, comparable to the demobilization which was taking place in the West. While a considerable demobilization was actually carried out in the Soviet Union, an armed establishment was retained which far outclassed, in numbers and power of ground forces in particular, anything that existed in the non-Communist sector of the world.

There were a number of reasons for this. The Soviet naval and air forces were regarded at the end of the war as so inferior to the comparable Western contingents that no policy was conceivable in Moscow except one of the most vigorous continued expansion of these arms. As for the rest — the maintenance in peacetime of ground forces of forbidding and, to all outward appearances, quite excessive strength was traditional not only to the Soviet government but to Russian governments generally. The annals of the nineteenth century are replete with complaints of other powers over just this sort of policy on the part of the Tsar's government. It was practiced again in the Twenties and Thirties of the present century. At that time Soviet ground forces were generally far superior numerically to any other force in Europe, and remained so until completion of German rearmament in the late 1930s. The prompt reversion to this pattern after World War II represented, therefore, the resumption of a practice which seemed quite normal to Soviet leaders.

If one looks at the psychological basis of this practice one finds a welter of considerations and explanations. For various reasons, Russian forces have generally appeared — have often, in fact, been deliberately caused to appear — more formidable to outsiders, particularly from the standpoint of possible offensive employment, than they appeared to their masters within Russia. Russian political leaders have usually operated against a background of uncertainty and anxiety with respect to domestic political and economic conditions which heightened their congenital sense of insecurity and caused them to wish for a larger margin of numerical safety in armed strength than would be thought necessary elsewhere. The maintenance of land armies in Russia has generally been cheap financially, and has had certain domestic political advantages insofar as it kept a good portion of the young male population in a regimented and controlled status. Finally, the Soviet leaders, interested in extending their real power by measures short of general war, have not been oblivious to the possibilities of such things as threats and intimidation — the possibilities of the use of the shadow of armed strength rather than its substance — as a means of influencing the political behavior of peoples elsewhere. In the wake of World War II, the maintenance of large land forces (with the number of divisions somewhat inflated by their relatively small size) served this purpose excellently, particularly in the face of the extreme nervousness of the war-shocked and terrorized populations of Western Europe.

If, then, we may summarize the Soviet position with respect to the prospects of major war and peace in the postwar period, as this position existed, let us say, in the beginning of the year 1946, it would be somewhat as follows: A third major war was not desirable, and was not likely to occur for many years. During this period the Soviets would continue the "partial war" against Western society with undiminished vigor and with very good chances of success. For traditional reasons, and as a useful contribution to the political struggle, the Kremlin would continue to maintain a large Soviet armed force and to supplement it as rapidly as possible with Communist-dominated and Communist-inspired forces in the satellite countries.

The year 1947 and the first months of 1948 produced a number of phenomena which from the Soviet point of view were both surprising and displeasing. In the first place the Western powers, although they had agreed to peace treaties with the satellites which left the structure of Soviet power in those countries undamaged, refused to agree to treaties for Germany and Austria which would sanction the permanent establishment of Soviet power or influence in those countries. And in each case they contrived to bypass the Soviet veto in the Council of Foreign Ministers by setting about independently to re-create life and hope in their own zones of control. This was the first great blow to Soviet hopes in the political war. Then, in the spring of 1947, a serious and ominous challenge to further Soviet political expansion in Europe was presented by United States acceptance of responsibility for assistance to Greece. This was followed shortly by the shattering impact of General Marshall's Harvard speech and the launching of the Marshall Plan project. These events led directly to the crisis of the spring of 1948, marked by the final passage of the first regular ERP legislation by the Congress of the United States, the arrival in Europe of the first large shipments of interim aid, the failure of the Communist-inspired wave of strikes and the challenge to the civil order in France, and the failure of the Italian Communists in the elections of that spring.

Both the imposition of the Berlin blockade and the Soviet crackdown in Czechoslovakia were reactions to these reverses for Moscow in the cold war. Of these, the development in Czechoslovakia was particularly important from the standpoint of Western reaction. Ever since the return of the Beneš regime in 1945 the situation in Czechoslovakia had been in reality completely in Moscow's control. The Kremlin had seen fit to let the Czechoslovak Communists take things easy in 1946–1947 and had permitted a certain amount of outward freedom in Czechoslovakia up to that time, partly because things were going its way in large degree behind the scenes, partly in the hope of misleading Western European intellectuals into believing that Communist domination in a given country did not necessarily mean extreme and immediate sovietization, but rather represented something "liberal" people could safely contemplate or accept. Such a policy of relative moderation and liberality gave promise of success, and could be followed with relative impunity, as long as Moscow was on the political offensive in Western Europe. It was needed, as indicated above, to deceive and render complacent elements in the Western European public whose tolerance or co-operation were required for the completion of the Communist plans. And while it involved certain dangers and disadvantages, it was clear that these would easily be taken in the Communist stride *if* further successes could be had farther afield. But once the Communist forces in Western Europe were thrown on the defensive, as indeed they were by the launching of the Marshall Plan project in the summer of 1947, it became dangerous for Moscow to continue to tolerate this relatively high degree of outward freedom and liberality in Czechoslovakia. When on the political offensive, one could afford to ignore large pockets of enemy forces behind one's lines; when one was on the defensive, such pockets became intolerable. Czechoslovakia and the Western sectors of Berlin were both such pockets. The Soviet crackdown on Czechoslovakia in 1948 therefore flowed logically from the inauguration of the Marshall Plan program, and was confidently predicted by United States government observers six months in advance of the event.

It is clear from the above that the sudden consolidation of Communist power in Czechoslovakia in 1948 was not a sign of any "new Soviet aggressiveness" and had nothing to do with any Soviet decision to launch its military forces against the West. Nevertheless, it was the spring of 1948, and particularly the period on the heels of the Czech developments, that saw the rise of a strong wave of military anxiety throughout the Western countries, and even a species of "war scare," supported particularly by reports from Western observers in Berlin. To date there has never been any evidence that would tend to confirm that Moscow had any thought at that time of launching its armed forces against the West or that its views on this subject were in any way different from those described above. Nevertheless, a firm opinion crystallized in Western circles that there was danger of a Soviet attack; and with this opinion came a feeling that rather than, or at least together with, consolidating the political gains that had been achieved in the past year and proceeding to the crushing of the Western European Communist parties in conjunction with the restoration of decent economic conditions in the countries concerned, the thing to do was to proceed to the formation of a Western military alliance against the Soviet Union. As will be recalled, the negotiations in this direction, namely the negotiations for the Atlantic Pact, were begun in June 1948 and concluded in December of that year.

I do not mean to say that there was no justification for the conclusion of the Atlantic Pact. Large numbers of people, both in Western Europe and in the United States, were incapable of understanding the Russian technique of penetration and "partial war" or of thinking in terms of this technique. They were capable of thinking about international developments only in the old-fashioned terms of full-fledged war or full-fledged peace. It was inconceivable to them that there could be real and serious threats to the independence of their countries that did not come to them in the form of foreign armies marching across frontiers; and it was natural that in undertaking to combat what they conceived to be a foreign threat they should have turned to the old-fashioned and familiar expedient of military alliance. They had understood that there was a threat; but they had not understood the nature of that threat, and were hardly capable of doing so.

Nor was it possible for anyone to argue that this outlook was wholly wrong. In the first place, the use of violence had never been ruled out of the Soviet bag of tricks; violence occupied, in fact, a prominent place in that collection. One could not even say that international violence — that is, war — had been fully ruled out. The Soviet outlook still allowed for the use of violence on the international scale in certain circumstances. Its lack of plans for instigating major warfare at that particular time rested primarily on the peculiarities of a given situation which rendered such an idea unpromising and inexpedient. Were the Western world to fall into a state of military weakness that constituted a direct invitation to cheap and easy aggression, it was quite possible that Soviet thinking might change. Or again, were the political war to progress favorably enough from the Soviet standpoint, it was always possible that a decision might be taken to use the Red Army in the wake of successful political operations, for purposes of giving the decisive push or conducting the mopping-up operations at minor cost. Any drastic alteration in the terms and course of the cold war, either to Soviet advantage or disadvantage, might in fact have operated to alter the Soviet attitude on war.

Furthermore, it was clear that any marked disparity between the armed strength of the Communist and non-Communist world, to the disadvantage of the latter, would be mercilessly if subtly exploited by the Kremlin for purposes of intimidating Western European peoples and inflicting them with uncertainty and lack of confidence in resisting Communist political pressures. In fact, the mere existence of such a disparity would have this effect even in the absence of any deliberate, overt Soviet effort to exploit it. There was thus a clear, legitimate and undeniable need for strong military strength in the West. And this, in terms of modern armament, meant arrangements for pooling in many ways the military resources and territorial facilities necessary for the conduct of modern war on the grand scale by the Western powers as a group.

It was impossible, therefore, for anyone to argue that war had no place at all in Soviet thinking, or that there was no need of a strong military posture on the other side. Yet in the manner in which the Atlantic Pact concept was put forward and received in Western society, there was unquestionably a certain misplacement of emphasis and lack of balance. The crucial fact was simply that, despite the good and sound reasons for Western rearmament and alliance, in the given situation an attack on Western Europe was not likely. Such an attack did not constitute the device by which at that time the Soviets hoped or expected to expand their power in Western Europe. In the threat that unquestionably hovered over the peoples of Western Europe, and of which they had now become extensively conscious, the accent simply did not lie on the prospect of open aggression by the Red Army: it lay on the continuation of sharp political pressure by a variety of much more subtle and insidious devices. And these devices were of such a nature that they would not be fully or decisively answered by a decision of the Western powers to unite together for purposes of military defense. The only important immediate effect which such a decision would have upon them lay in the degree to which it might deprive the Kremlin of the weapon of military intimidation. This weapon constituted an important part of the Kremlin's strength in the "partial war," but it was by no means the only part or even the main one. Yet these things were never adequately explained to the world public in the original advancement of the Atlantic Pact project.

For all these reasons, I believe that the men in the Kremlin were somewhat amazed and puzzled by the manner in which the Western powers proceeded, in the year 1948, to the conclusion of a military alliance — a manner bound to interfere to some extent with the economic aid program which was only then being undertaken by the United States and which, in its initial stages, had been attended by such striking political success. It seemed implausible to the Soviet leaders, knowing as they did the nature of their own approach to the military problem, and assuming that the Western powers must have known it too, that defensive considerations alone could have impelled the Western governments to give the relative emphasis they actually gave to a program irrelevant in many respects to the outcome of the political struggle in Western Europe (on which Moscow was staking everything) and only partially justified, as Moscow saw it, as a response to actual Soviet intentions.

This reaction on the Soviet side was probably fortified by the publicity which attended the negotiation of the pact in the Western countries and the arguments used to support it before the Western parliaments. To justify a treaty of alliance as a response to the Soviet threat, it was inexorably necessary to oversimplify and to some extent distort the na-

ture of this threat. To the Soviet mind this was a suspicious circum-
stance. The Kremlin leaders were attempting in every possible way to
weaken and destroy the structure of the non-Communist world. In the
course of this endeavor they were up to many things which gave
plenty of cause for complaint on the part of Western statesmen. They
would not have been surprised if these things had been made the touch-
stone of Western reaction. But why, they might ask, were they being
accused precisely of the one thing they had *not* done, which was to
plan, as yet, to conduct an overt and unprovoked invasion of Western
Europe? Why was the imputation to them of this intention being put
forward as the rationale for Western rearmament? Did this not imply
some ulterior purpose on the part of those mysterious and sinister
forces which, by Communist conviction, were at all times to be found
sitting like a spider in the center of the web of capitalist power, and
animating by their will all the impulses that might travel throughout its
far-flung structure?

As the military program worked out under the Atlantic Pact began
to take form, this sort of cosmic misunderstanding between the Kremlin and the Western powers was deepened by the general overrating of
the strength of the Soviet armed forces which attended the beginning
of remilitarization in the West. In part, the Soviet leaders were here the
victims of their own passion for secrecy and bluff; for they had really
succeeded, by one means or another, in presenting to foreign intelligence agencies a general picture of their capabilities that was to some
extent, certainly, an exaggeration of reality. But there were also natural
tendencies in the Western countries that contributed to the creation of
a somewhat inflated image of Soviet strength. The obligation of military planners to assume at all times the most pessimistic and unfavorable of hypotheses as the only prudent basis for planning, and the tendency to justify appeals for appropriations by references to the military
equation rather than by general politico-military considerations, both
contributed to the creation of such an image. And to the distortion of
the actual numerical and ordnance strength of the Soviet forces there
was gradually added a similar distortion of their state of readiness. The
unforeseen launching of hostilities by the North Koreans, in 1950, with
the ensuing tendency of uninformed people to blame the intelligence
services for their failure to foresee it, had precisely this effect; for it
compelled Western intelligence services thereafter to take the position,
for their own protection, that wherever they could not prove the contrary (and this meant practically everywhere) Soviet and Soviet-
controlled forces had to be considered as permanently in a state of

complete readiness for any conceivable type of operation, without need for any further preparations and without assurance of any warning whatsoever on the Western side. But this image, so out of accord precisely with Russian traditions and realities, was also unquestionably a distortion and an exaggeration.

In general, therefore, it can be said that in the implementation of the collective Western effort toward rearmament, involving as it did the understanding and consent of a multitude of people — officials, parliamentarians, journalists, leaders of public opinion — it proved impossible to retain the measure and subtlety of approach requisite to creating and holding before world opinion at all times an accurate image of the nature of the Soviet threat, and that in place of such an image there emerged in Western councils and in Western public opinion a somewhat oversimplified and inaccurate one, in which the real delimitations both of Soviet intentions and of Soviet strength became confused and distorted.

The result of all this was that the Soviet leaders, themselves in so many respects irrational in their approach to their external environment, found themselves confronted with a line of policy on the part of the Western powers for which they could discover no adequate rationale. Had they been people capable of examining attentively and dispassionately the nature of Western society, they would no doubt have understood the logic by virtue of which the surprised and indignant reaction of the Western public to their conduct of the "partial war" could not come otherwise than in the traditional form of a military alliance, designed to protect against overt aggression. They would also have understood why a collective Western effort at rearmament could not fail to be attended by considerable distortion of the intentions and strength of the main potential adversary.

But the Soviet leaders were not this sort of people, and not capable of such an analysis of their world environment. The belief that the capitalist world was a conspiracy, headed by a few powerful and clever schemers buried somewhere in the recesses of "Wall Street," was deeply ingrained in Soviet psychology. It occupied too prominent a part in the structure of their philosophy, and in the pattern of human behavior as they themselves knew it and practiced it, for them to dispense with it. Believing the Western world a conspiracy; finding themselves unable to discover a fully rational justification for the Atlantic Pact (in the form in which it was presented) as a move of their capitalist adversaries in the *political* war; noting that it was in fact in certain respects disruptive — rather than promotive — of firm political morale in the Western countries; observing, finally, that the pact was supported publicly by a portrayal of their own intentions and strength that they did not recognize as fully accurate — it was no wonder that the Soviet leaders found it easy to conclude that the Atlantic Pact project concealed intentions not revealed to the public, and that these intentions must add up to a determination on the part of the Western powers to bring to a head a military conflict with the Soviet Union as soon as the requisite strength had been created on the Western side.

It must be noted that such a conclusion was supported, to the suspicious Soviet mind, by such things as the sensational treatment of atomic capabilities in the American press, the publication of maps showing the accessibility of Soviet cities to the American strategic bombing weapon, public discussion as to whether the bomb should or should not be used as a means of political intimidation ("Come across, or we'll drop the bomb"), the somewhat fevered public attention in the United States to problems of civil defense, radar networks, etc. It was also supported, with a curious semblance of prophetic accuracy, by the ideological tenets of Marxism-Leninism, according to which the capitalists, once pressed into a corner by the advance of the revolution, would turn and attempt to destroy socialism in a last desperate convulsion of armed force. In 1918 Lenin had referred to the "monstrous and savage frenzy in the face of death" on the part of "that wild beast, capitalism." And in 1933, Stalin had said: "We must bear in mind that the growth of the power of the Soviet state will intensify the resistance of the last remnants of the dying classes. It is precisely because they are dying . . . that they will go on from one form of attack to other, sharper forms of attack." *

This sort of what might be called "misunderstanding between adversaries" was considerably heightened by the outbreak of the Korean war, for there is no evidence that in regard to this matter, either side understood very well the motives underlying the behavior of the other side.

The launching of the Korean venture was for Moscow primarily what might be called a "countervailing" move, the timing of which was probably occasioned mostly by the growing evidence of the intention of the United States to make a separate peace treaty with Japan and to retain armed forces in the Japanese Islands in the post-treaty period. There is no evidence that it was part of any global pattern of projected Soviet military moves, nor the product of any "new aggressiveness" on

---

* Both of these quotations are taken from Nathan Leites, *The Operational Code of the Politburo*, p. 59. New York: McGraw-Hill, 1951.

the part of the Soviet Union. It represented merely the unleashing of a military-political action (conceived as a move in the "partial war") which the Kremlin had obviously been preparing, with vigor and with little attempt at concealment, over the course of several years and which, if it were to serve the purpose for which it was designed, would obviously have to be launched at the moment of maximum military superiority of North Korean over South Korean forces and before a restored and rearmed Japan could be reinserted into the Korean picture. Furthermore, in point of form, the action in Korea was viewed by Moscow as a *civil* war in a third country, and thus something which could not be held to involve formally the responsibility of the Soviet government or its armed forces. Up to that time, at least, Moscow had considered the successful instigation of civil war in a third country as a perfectly fair and acceptable political expedient, which anyone was entitled to get away with if he had the skill and enterprise to do so. Moscow did not consider (and was quite sincere in its protests before the United Nations to this effect) that civil war constituted a proper subject for the invocation of international law or of United Nations action. In particular, it did not consider that it was any of the United Nations' business what political forces had inspired a given civil war.

In the United States, on the other hand, opinion rapidly coalesced to the effect that the North Korean attack was only the opening gambit in an elaborate program of Soviet armed aggression against the free world. The attack was subsequently freely cited in American official utterances as an example of new Soviet "aggressiveness." This came as a certain surprise to the Soviet mind, for the venture was thought of in Moscow only as an attempt to capitalize on a political advantage which the Communists had worked hard to establish and had considered quite within the rules of the game.

Let me stress that it was not the action of the United States in putting forces ashore in Korea that led to the type of misunderstanding I am referring to here. The fact of our entry came as a tactical surprise to the Kremlin, for the Soviet leaders had not thought it likely; but the rationale for it, under their concepts, was plain and unexceptional. It was rather our decision to treat a civil war as an act of international aggression and to invoke the authority of the United Nations on that basis, that seemed to the Soviets strange and disingenuous, and probably a mask for other intentions.

A similar reaction may well have been produced on the Soviet leaders by the failure of the Western powers, and particularly the United States, to seek what Moscow would have regarded as a realistic compromise over the disposal of Germany and Japan, and by the decision to proceed, instead, to the rearmament of Japan and Western Germany. The Soviet leaders would almost certainly have been prepared to acquiesce formally in a demilitarized and unoccupied Japan, and would probably not have attacked it by overt military action, so long as it succeeded in keeping its own Communist Party under control, and barring any drastic change in the world situation. Whether they could have been brought actually to accept a withdrawal of forces from Germany on the basis of a continued demilitarization of that country and genuine freedom for German political life is difficult to say — the probabilities were against it. But by the same token, they were probably puzzled by our failure to press for precisely this sort of a solution. Had the circumstances been reversed, and had their cause, instead of ours, had the unquestioned political support of by far the larger portion of Germany, they would surely have been howling boldly and incessantly for the withdrawal of troops, the removal of the division of Germany, and the immediate creation of a free German political life. That we, with what must have seemed to them our immense political advantage in Germany, failed to pursue this course and preferred to proceed instead to the rearmament and "integration" of Western Germany, must again have seemed to the Russian mind a policy going beyond what could be explained by mere timidity and caution, and presumably motivated by other and more sinister considerations.

We must not be misled by these reflections to the conclusion that *all* expressed Soviet suspicions of the United States are sincere, or that they all stem from such things as the conclusion of the Atlantic Pact, Korea, or Western policy toward Germany. One of the most confusing aspects of Soviet attitudes is that they are so often a mixture of the sincere and the disingenuous, the honest and the dishonest, the real and the feigned. An attitude of suspicion and cynicism about the motives of capitalist powers has been congenital to Soviet communism ever since its inception, and it is important to note that the fluctuations in the degree to which the Soviet Union has actually been threatened from the outside in the course of its history have never been matched by any corresponding fluctuations in the image of the foreign danger the regime has attempted to give to its own people. The attempt to portray the outside world as menacing, whether or not it actually was so at any given moment, has been part of the stock in trade of Soviet rule. But underneath that unvarying and cynical policy the Soviet leaders have naturally made their own calculations at every juncture as to the real degree of external danger, and the results of these calculations have varied widely at different times and in different situations. The evidence adduced above concerning Soviet reactions merely seems to me to indicate only that if one were able to strip away all the overgrowth of propagandistic distortion and maligning of foreign intentions which is the normal encumbrance of Soviet utterances and attitudes, one would find that there remained in recent years a certain hard core of genuine belief in the sinisterness of Western intentions and that this belief was in considerable part, though not entirely, the result of a misinterpretation on their part of Western policies in the years from 1948 to the present.

Accepting, then, the thesis that there is some degree of sincerity in the Soviet allegations of the aggressiveness of Western intentions, what have been the effects of this on Soviet policy and behavior? To what extent has it caused actual anxiety in the Kremlin? What displacement, if any, has it made in the threshold of Soviet tolerance to foreign threats or Western expansion?

These questions are extremely difficult to answer. The evidence bearing on them is so inconclusive, and in some instances so contradictory, that one wonders whether these questions have not been the subject of considerable differences and vacillations within the Soviet hierarchy itself. In attempting to form some idea as to the answers it is perhaps best first to isolate and note certain identifiable or calculable elements of the Soviet reaction. The following might be included in this category:

1. Unquestionably, as Western rearmament proceeded and as the emphasis on the military aspect of the problem was observed and absorbed in Moscow, there must have been a corresponding tendency in Soviet circles to put increasing emphasis on the military aspects of the East-West conflict at the expense of political ones. The development of Western policy must have led to a constantly higher rating in Moscow of the likelihood of an eventual third world war. This, in turn, must have affected to a considerable extent Soviet thinking and procedure.

The Soviet apparatus of power, while free of pressures of a parliamentary system and a free press, is nevertheless not wholly immune to the operation of that law of political affairs by which military preparations attain a momentum of their own and make more likely the very thing that they are supposed — by the invariable claim of all governments — to deter and prevent. For every government, the calculations of probabilities with respect to military conflict set up something in the nature of magnetic fields, which in turn affect behavior. To believe in the likelihood of war, whether rightly or wrongly, means in some degree to behave in a manner that will actually enhance that likelihood, insofar as it implies the neglect of alternative courses and some degree of commitment to the requirements of the course you would take if you knew definitely that war would come. Therefore, what was said about Soviet attitudes in 1945 and 1946 would no longer be fully applicable to Soviet attitudes in 1950 and 1951. By this time the Kremlin must have been seriously shaken in its original feeling that major warfare did not have to be reckoned with as something that might well occur in the near future. It must have been forced to gear its policy and plans more and more to the prospect that war might occur. Soviet policy, in other words, must also have been to some extent drawn into the magnetic field of belief in a relatively greater probability of war. And since what you do to be prepared for a war is very often the enemy of what you would do if you wished to avoid it, Soviet ability to pursue policies designed to avoid a future war must have suffered accordingly.

The great unanswered question is as to the *degree* to which Soviet policy may have been thus affected — the degree, in other words, to which the Soviet leaders themselves have come to regard a major military conflict as likely or inevitable within the next three or four years, and have committed their policy to this prospect. This is of greatest importance, for obviously belief in the inevitability of an *early* outbreak of war could even bring the Kremlin to decide to take advantage of the element of surprise and to bring on the conflict at its own time and in its own way.

There is, however, no evidence that Moscow has come to this point. My guess would be that Soviet minds are still relatively flexible and undecided on this subject. Soviet policy-makers have no doubt been materially aided in their task of analysis, as compared with ourselves, by the fact that their system of policy formulation does not require them to sit down and write papers on this subject. I believe they are much more conscious than we are of the interplay of action and reaction in international affairs, of the way in which events mesh into each other and reflect each other, of the number of variables that can enter into the determination of a situation some years removed; and that they would be less inclined, for this reason, to feel themselves under the obligation to arrive at any firm or final judgment at the present time about the likelihood of war in a more distant future. Within this limitation, my estimate would be that they would think it quite possible and perhaps likely that they would become involved in war with us, more probably through our initiative than through theirs, at some point in the next few years, though probably not in the immediate future; but that this would not affect their policy to the same degree as we might think, for the reason that they would be much more keenly aware of the importance of what might happen in the meantime and of the possibility that our actual ability to conduct a war against them might be appreciably modified during this intervening period by a course of events in the political war favorable to Soviet interests.

2. The Soviet leaders have of course been quick to sense the extent to which the overemphasis on the purely military danger in Western policy could be exploited to the detriment of confidence in the United States and unity in the Western camp. If one of the main facets of Soviet policy for the past three years has been the exploitation of the "peace" theme and the building up of a worldwide "peace" movement as a cloak for its own political warfare policies, this is because the issue, as they saw it, was presented to them ready-made by the Western powers. The fact that they were able to pursue their own military preparations with a complete absence of publicity and without the necessity of overcoming parliamentary pressure has placed them in an advantageous position to pose as the protagonists of peace vis-à-vis a Western world which could get military appropriations out of its parliamentary bodies only by a constant emphasis on military danger and the likelihood of war. The Soviet peace congresses of 1952 represent the price paid by the Western democracies for their inability to put the need for rearmament and military alliance to their peoples in less primitive and more accurate terms and for their consequent overemphasizing of the prospect of war.

3. Unquestionably, the Kremlin has increased its own levels of military preparedness to the best of its ability, in order to match what was occurring in the West. However it has done this without outward emphasis and without giving the impression it was departing materially from its peacetime developmental programs. It has contrived to give its people, and a portion of the world public, the impression that while others are arming to the teeth and talking of war, the Soviet Union is confidently going along the path of peaceful construction, building canals and hydroelectric projects, planting trees and irrigating land, increasing the fruitfulness of the earth and the possibilities of human productivity for peaceful purposes.

4. The Soviet leaders have maintained relatively strong forces at all possible points of military conflict with the Western powers and have shown themselves extremely sensitive and ruthlessly vigilant about the inviolability of their own frontiers. In this they have doubtless been animated by a desire to demonstrate that they are not intimidated by Western rearmament and not prepared to stand any trifling with their

territory or their armed forces. They are extremely conscious of the dynamics of evidences of strength or weakness, and particularly of the possibilities for blackmail that come into existence when anyone yields openly, or appears to yield, to superior strength without causing the adversary to expend that strength in the process. They will yield in many instances when confronted with superior force, but not unless by doing so they can reduce the pressure brought to bear against them and insure themselves against being asked to make further and repeated concessions in response to the same means of pressure. They will not, in other words, yield to pressure if they feel it starts them on a path to which they can see no ending. For these reasons, they will not tolerate trifling with any such thing as their territorial integrity, and will continue to be vigilant about the protection of their frontiers. This vigilance will not be apt to show any variation in accordance with alterations in the military equation.

5. In accordance with this reasoning, and in the growing consciousness of strong military force being arrayed against them, they have shown themselves particularly sensitive to their maritime border, which they are unable to protect by the usual device of a belt of puppet states. Their desire to have the Black and Baltic seas recognized as in effect Soviet internal waterways stems from the same cast of mind which seeks buffer states all around its land borders. The fact that they have not been able to achieve this goal makes them extremely nervous. It seems, in fact, to them, as a land-minded nation not accustomed to the problems of the sea, preposterous that foreign planes and naval vessels should be able to approach to within a few miles of their coastal installations with impunity. For these reasons they have shown and will continue to show an extreme, and almost pathological, degree of sensitivity about their maritime frontiers.

6. Despite these sharp edges and peculiar points of sensitivity, the Soviet leaders have thus far exhibited both in the Berlin blockade and in the Korean War, marked restraint and a clear disinclination to become involved at this juncture in a major military conflict with the Western powers.

7. In the real sense, the Soviet leaders have broken diplomatic relations with the Western world. The fact that they permit Western diplomatic missions to remain in Moscow, and maintain such missions themselves in Western capitals, does not alter this fact. The Western missions in Moscow have been isolated as completely and effectively as though they were on enemy territory in wartime. They are simply not considered or used by the Soviet government as vehicles for any real

exchange of views with the Western governments. This situation is not altered by the fact that communications of a demonstrative character, designed not to make any real impact on the thinking of the other party but only to embarrass him in the eyes of the world public, are exchanged through the technical facilities of these missions. The fact remains that during these past years diplomatic relations in the normal and traditional sense, which existed between the Soviet Union and the Western powers on a partial scale and in an imperfect form in the Twenties and Thirties as well as during World War II, ceased entirely to exist.

This has an important effect on the reaction both in the Soviet Union and in the Western countries to military events and impulses, insofar as it means that there is no longer the usual diplomatic cushion between impact and reaction. There is no opportunity, for example, for Western representatives in Moscow to explain in a normal way the meaning of individual Western military moves, or even to know when serious misunderstandings concerning such moves are arising in the Soviet mind. If these last should provoke counter-moves actually dangerous to peace, there is little the diplomat can do to prevent deterioration of the situation. Furthermore, since the exertion of normal diplomatic influence is excluded, the Western powers can easily be placed in a position where they cannot bring pressure to bear on the Soviet government by any means other than the demonstration of a readiness to go to war over a given issue.

This situation gives added and unique delicacy to all questions of military preparation in times of peace, particularly those involving use of the territory of third countries, for in the absence of any diplomatic language such moves, and the reactions to them, become in themselves a form of communication between the two camps, and one replete with opportunities for misunderstanding.

8. The Soviet propaganda apparatus has continued to encourage influential and responsible party circles in the Soviet and satellite area to believe that Western rearmament has not only *not* relieved the Western democracies of their fatal burden of weaknesses, divisions and diseases but has actually exacerbated these conditions and increased the momentum of what is referred to in Moscow as "the general crisis of capitalism." In these circumstances, we are probably safe in assuming that to a large degree this represents the belief of the highest Soviet authorities themselves.

If we were to base our analysis on these points, then the following might serve as a rough approximation of Soviet reaction to recent

Western policies, and above all to NATO activities (for the sake of vividness, I have put it in the sort of terms the Soviet leaders might themselves be expected to use):

"The Western leaders have decided to rearm and eventually to finish us, if they can, in a military encounter. This reflects their consciousness of their inferiority in the political war. It confirms the Marxist analysis of the illness of capitalism and the increasing sterility of its political capacities. It also confirms the Leninist analysis that the capitalists, when confronted with the hopelessness of their position and the inexorable nature of their own decline, would turn like a savage beast and attempt to strike a last desperate blow at the successful forces of socialism.

"We have always detested the capitalists and applied ourselves to the destruction of their power. For many years they were reluctant fully to recognize this, and it then proved expedient for us to profit by their semi-blindness, to put them off guard, and to tap their economic resources by a policy of diplomatic dealings with them. But today they, too, have become conscious of what divides us, and they have finally learned to see us as their enemies. We will continue, then, to place no real value on this sorry farce of participation in a traditional system of international relations; and we will treat the capitalist countries on the diplomatic level as though we were at war with them.

"As for the military danger, we must be wary and cautious; for the moment, there is no need for outward nervousness or abrupt actions. The Americans are not yet ready; their rearmament is still only in a beginning stage; they will not be apt to attack us deliberately at this juncture, provided we continue to show due vigilance and determination and do not offer them invitations to easy successes.

"Of course, they would like to be able at some point to attack and destroy us, but the question is: will they be able to? Will the time ever come when they will find it profitable and expedient to strike? War is obviously an extremely serious matter, nothing to be lightly considered. It could bring to us great dangers or great opportunities, depending on the context of circumstances in which it might occur, the mistakes our adversaries might or might not make, the nature of military operations, etc. But the prospect of it, while serious, is no occasion for any outward signs of nervousness. We are developing our own power fairly steadily, both in the industrial and military sense. The Americans are relying primarily on the atomic bomb and the possibilities for strategic bombardment; but we are developing our own atomic capability, and they will soon learn that the weapons of mass destruction cancel each other out when both sides have them in great force. Meanwhile, their own contradictions will continue to catch up with, and eventually lame, their will and their movements. Thus while *their* weapon, namely strategic air power, comes under the law of diminishing returns as our retaliatory power is developed, *our* weapon, namely political warfare, will grow in strength and effectiveness.

"The greatest danger, of course, is that war may develop prematurely and accidentally over some issue involving Korea or Germany. We will try not to encourage such a development, but we will not modify our policies in any important way to obviate it. If it must be, then let it be. It will be serious and full of dangers, but no more so than was the Hitlerite invasion. The Americans lack Hitler's land capabilities. Like him, they will make mistakes, and we shall profit from them. They can bomb us, perhaps, but the losses to themselves will be heavy, and the effect on our military capacity probably not fatal. If they concentrate their air attack on our cities rather than our points of maximum economic vulnerability, which they may do for their own peculiar reasons, then the injuries they inflict on our civilian population may actually improve, rather than worsen, civilian morale in our country. Meanwhile, our land forces will not be idle, nor the foreign Communist parties. We may have to take some bombing, but *they* may be forced to leave large parts of Europe.

"No major war at all would be preferable, from our standpoint, to a war of this sort; for if there is no such war we will perhaps eventually gain Europe anyway without suffering the damage to ourselves that a major war would involve. But if it must come, we can accept it. Meanwhile, the danger of it is not so great that we need give our population the impression we are embarked on a program of preparation or mobilization for war. By giving the opposite impression we will continue to pose as the champions of peace and to derive the political profit that flows therefrom in a world yearning for nothing more than for security and the absence of violence."

Actually, this résumé probably gives a somewhat too confident and decided image of the Soviet outlook. About certain elements of this, above all the likelihood of an early Western attack, the dangerousness of such an attack, and the advantages or disadvantages of attempting to promote Soviet interests by the resumption of something resembling genuine diplomatic dealings with the Western powers, there is probably considerable vacillation, doubt and conflict within the Soviet hierarchy, not only as between individuals or groups but also within individual minds. On these points, doubts, fears, hopes and spirits rise and

fall with the barometer of international happenings; and this barometer
is fairly sensitive to the utterances and conduct of the Western community itself. The image given above merely represents that which has
seemed to emerge from Soviet behavior and utterances in recent
months. But that is not to say that this cast of mind is not actually
under considerable strain at a number of points, especially the point of
interpretation of the trend of events in the Western world, and that it
could not be materially altered by the course of events and by the
decisions and actions of the Western powers.

Holding in mind the above, we face the final question as to the overall principles by which the NATO community might best be guided in
the conduct of its affairs with a view to avoiding the all-out conflict
with Soviet power on the military plane and winning it on the political
one (which words I suppose, could stand as a rough summary of Western policy). The following points seem to me to flow from the considerations put forth above by way of answer to this question:

1. The NATO powers, while clinging to their insistence on rapid and
vigorous rearmament, should make a deliberate and systematic effort to
avoid every sort of overemphasis of the military danger, saber-rattling
of all sorts, statements that appear to constitute threats of military action against the Soviet Union, words or acts that may be taken to indicate a belief in the inevitability or even the likelihood of war. A major
effort should be undertaken to make the peoples of the Western countries understand why rearmament and alliance are an important and
unavoidable part of the Western response to the type of political warfare conducted by the Soviet Union. This means that we must not seem
to assume in our statements, as we often do, that the Soviet Union is
probably planning to attack the West, although we must never wholly
exclude this possibility; and we must make people understand why rearmament is nevertheless required. At the same time we must be careful
to emphasize that it is *only* part of the answer, and can actually be
disruptive of the total pattern of Western resistance if it is not balanced
by many other factors, such as economic health and political confidence and the belief in, and hope for, a peaceful future. To the extent that
this can be done — to the extent, that is, that rearmament and alliance
can be portrayed simply as safeguards of something peaceful and constructive, for which we still confidently hope, rather than just as preparations for a war to which we have resigned ourselves hopelessly — the
"peace" card will be struck from the Soviet hand and Soviet success in
the political war will be reduced.

2. A given pattern of military preparations always appears to the

public as the reflection of a given pattern of calculations and intentions. It is important that the building of the NATO structure appear to reflect not the feverish preparations of people who regard war as inevitable and are working against a limit of time, but the calm and judicious measures of people simply building a fence, not in the belief that someone else is likely to try to knock it down, but rather in the normal and prudent desire to have clarity on all sides and to prevent any and all misunderstandings. Such a view must inevitably have certain disadvantages from the standpoint of the achievement at the earliest possible moment of the ideal military posture. But it must be accepted and remembered that there is an incurable conflict in certain respects between the goal of the ideal military posture and the goal of winning the political war — a war which is still in progress and which we have no choice but to continue to fight. The requirements of either of these approaches, the military or the political, would — if carried to extremes — be quite destructive of the requirements of the other. But neither could be successful if the other were fully destroyed. If problems were to be faced only from the political standpoint, the degree of actual military preparation that would ensue would be quite inadequate for purposes of a war, if one were actually to occur. On the other hand, if the professional military planner were to be given all that he desired from the standpoint of the preparation of an adequate military posture against Soviet power, the results would probably be quite disruptive of the political resistance of the Western peoples.

What we are faced with, therefore, is the need for a reasonable and sensible compromise between these two requirements; and it seems to me we would find it at approximately that point where Western rearmament would appear to the uninitiated public as the reflection of firm and reasonable precaution against misunderstandings or accident or ill will, but not as the reflection of a hopeless commitment to the dynamics of an arms race. What we must avoid is to appear to be fascinated and enmeshed by the relentless and deceptive logic of the military equation. What people need to be shown is that we are the masters, not the slaves, of the process of military and political tension.

3. The NATO community should bear in mind that the Soviet leaders are extremely curious people in whose minds there are areas of what we might call rationality but other areas that are quite irrational. They have shown restraint on several occasions and have exhibited no recent signs of an actual desire for an armed conflict. But they are secretive and often erratic in their reactions, and it is not easy to tell when you are going to touch one of the neuralgic and irrational points. They are

plainly sensitive about the frontiers of their power, and particularly such frontiers as can be approached by sea. They are also quite naturally sensitive about being surrounded by a ring of air bases plainly grouped with a view to penetration of their own territory.

Obviously, there is no clear line between the offensive and the defensive in military considerations. Many of our defensive measures must appear offensively motivated to the Russians. Equally obviously, we cannot let that be a reason for paralyzing our entire effort at an adequate Western defense posture. But here again *le mieux est l'ennemi du bien*. Surely as one moves one's bases and military facilities toward the Soviet frontiers there comes a point where they tend to create the very thing they were designed to avoid. It is not for us to assume that there are no limits to Soviet patience in the face of encirclement by American bases. Quite aside from political considerations, no great country, peaceful or aggressive, rational or irrational, could sit by and witness with indifference the progressive studding of its own frontiers with the military installations of a great-power competitor. Here again, a compromise must be struck, and one which will inevitably fall somewhat short of the military ideal. This compromise must be struck with a view to the peculiarities of Russian mentality and tradition. We must remember that almost the only language in which we can now communicate with the Soviet leaders is the language of overt military and political moves. If we still hope to have the ultimate decision confined to the political field and to win on that field, let us be sure the words we speak in this peculiar language do not operate to reduce the Soviet leaders to a state of mind in which for them, as for people everywhere who accept the belief in the inevitability of war, the only question is not "whether" but "when."

In conclusion, I would beg leave to say the following: The present situation has in it several of those tremendous dilemmas which in the past have been the makings of great wars, and there is as yet no visible prospect of a solution of these dilemmas by nonmilitary means. It is easy, in these circumstances, to argue for the inevitability of war and to sell one's soul to it. Unquestionably, the events of the past four or five years have brought war much further into the realm of possibility and have heightened the danger of its imminent outbreak, not so much as a result of any deliberate desire of either side that it should break out, but rather as a result of the inability of people in given possible contingencies to find any acceptable alternative solution. Yet an intensive scrutiny of the Moscow scene yields no reason to believe that war is yet inevitable, and provides no justification for those who would sell their souls to this assumption. We have, as an anchor of reassurance, the overwhelmingly important fact that there is no evidence that the Soviet leaders, obsessed as they are with hatred of the West and deaf as they are to the voice of reason, regard the turmoil and suffering of another world war as the preferred milieu in which to seek the satisfaction of their aspirations; and the contemporary development of weapons is hardly such as to impel them in that direction. For the moment, they seem content to continue to maintain the contest on their curious level of "partial war"; and I, for one, am reluctant to believe that they cannot be successfully coped with by us on this terrain. Whether, in the event the "partial war" should go badly for them, they would retain their preference for contest on the political level, or how long they would retain it, I cannot say. But I think we can say of them, as they now say of us, that if they were to be forced by political reverses to a point of great desperation, their military power would by that time have been appreciably deflated in its real capabilities, and their effort, in turn, would then be the sharp but unpromising struggle of the cornered animal.

For these reasons, I would plead for the continuation of a policy based on the requirements of the possibility that there may be no war as well as on the requirements of the possibility that there may be one. And if the skeptical voice of precedent and experience would seem to argue against this relative optimism, I would again submit that the peculiarities of our age are such that we have no greater right to accept the extreme pessimistic implications of past experience than to accept the extreme optimistic ones. Human history has recorded a great number of international situations, but none that would stand as a fully reliable precedent for the conflict between the Communist and non-Communist worlds in the year 1952.

GEORGE F. KENNAN
Ambassador

Index

ABOUT THE AUTHOR

George F. Kennan, a Pulitzer Prize and National Book Award winner, is the author of some eighteen books on Russia and the Soviet Union, the nuclear issue, and diplomatic history. He is one of the founders of the Kennan Institute for Advanced Russian Studies, and is an honorary chairman of the American Committee on U.S.-Soviet Relations. He is a member, and past president, of the American Academy and Institute of Arts and Letters. He is Professor Emeritus at the Institute for Advanced Study in Princeton, New Jersey.